TEACHING EACH OTHER

LINDA M. GOULET AND KEITH N. GOULET

TEACHING EACH OTHER

Nehinuw Concepts and Indigenous Pedagogies

UBCPress · Vancouver · Toronto

22 21 20 19 18 17 16 15 14   5 4 3 2 1

Printed in Canada on FSC-certified ancient-forest-free paper
(100% post-consumer recycled) that is processed chlorine- and acid-free.

978-0-7748-2757-7 (bound); 978-0-7748-2758-4 (pbk.);
978-0-7748-2759-1 (pdf); 978-0-7748-2760-7 (ePub)

Cataloging-in-publication for this book is available from Library and Archives Canada.

Canadä

UBC Press gratefully acknowledges the financial support for our publishing program of the Government of Canada (through the Canada Book Fund), the Canada Council for the Arts, and the British Columbia Arts Council.

This book has been published with the help of a grant from the Canadian Federation for the Humanities and Social Sciences, through the Awards to Scholarly Publications Program, using funds provided by the Social Sciences and Humanities Research Council of Canada.

Printed and bound in Canada by Friesens
Set in Minion, Calibri, and Kozuka Gothic by Artegraphica Design Co. Ltd.
Copy editor: Steph VanderMeulen
Proofreader: Helen Godolphin
Indexer: Dianne Tiefensee

UBC Press
The University of British Columbia
2029 West Mall
Vancouver, BC V6T 1Z2
www.ubcpress.ca

Contents

Acknowledgments / vii

1 Where We Are in Indigenous Education / 3

2 Where We've Been: Sociohistorical Realities / 27

3 What to Build Upon: Sociocultural Strengths / 47

4 How to Get There: Conceptualizing Effective Teaching / 77

5 *Weechihitowin*, Helping and Supporting Relationships:
   The Foundation / 98

6 *Weetutoskemitowin*, Working Together: Social Systems / 113

7 *Iseechigehina*, Planned Actions: Connection to the Process / 133

8 *Weechiseechigemitowin*, Strategic Alliances: Connection
   to the Content / 158

9 Breaking Trail: Stories Outside the (Classroom) Box / 176

10 *Ininee mamitoneneetumowin*, Indigenous Thinking: Emerging
   Theory of Indigenous Education / 197

Appendix 1: Cree orthographic chart / 218

Appendix 2: Model of effective teaching for Indigenous students
– Categories, subcategories, and attributes / 221

Notes / 224

References / 227

Index / 240

Contents

Acknowledgments

This book is the result of many people coming together to share their insights on Indigenous education. Although not directly involved in this book, Elders and their teachings, including those at First Nations University and the community of Cumberland House, have influenced the thinking of both authors. All too often in education, the voice of the teacher – the one who interacts with the students, parents, and community on a daily basis – is missing. This book would not have been possible without teachers: the named teachers who agreed to share their stories as case studies to illustrate the concepts in this book and the teachers who agreed to participate in the original research as confidential participants. We hope your knowledge and insights are respectfully represented in this book. A northern First Nation reserve opened its school to the initial school-based research, so we are thankful to the chief and council, the school staff, and the members of the First Nations school board. Those teachers who opened their classrooms to outside observers are especially appreciated. It was an honour to work and learn with you all.

To all those educators in our circles of friends and family, we value your conversations and feedback. Many colleagues at First Nations University and beyond contributed to our understanding of Indigenous and anti-racist education. We thank those at UBC Press, especially Darcy Cullen, Lesley Erickson, and Steph VanderMeulen, who patiently ensured that this book reached completion. Finally, to those blind peer reviewers who took the time to engage with the text, we are grateful for your insightful comments, which helped us clarify the ideas in the book and strengthen our presentation.

TEACHING EACH OTHER

Where We Are in Indigenous Education

We have cause to celebrate the significant gains that have been made in Indigenous education in recent years.[1] Those of us who were starting our teaching careers when "Indian control of Indian education" (National Indian Brotherhood 1972) was a call to action have seen positive changes in Indigenous education. The number of Indigenous students graduating from high school and postsecondary institutions over the last decades has increased. First Nations peoples now administer their own schools, and Indigenous administrators are moving into decision-making positions in various education systems. There is a large cadre of First Nations, Métis, and Inuit teachers and researchers working with Euro-Canadian allies involved in instruction and curriculum development in both First Nations and public schools.[2]

At the same time, Indigenous peoples continue to be under-represented at all levels of education. Changes to curricula continue to meet resistance, and schools continue to fail to ensure success for many Indigenous students. In 2009, when John Richards and Megan Scott (2009) conducted a comprehensive analysis of the statistics regarding Indigenous education in Canada, they identified key points to emphasize the need for all Canadians to attend to the education of Indigenous students. First, Indigenous populations have a higher proportion of youth and a faster-growing youth population compared to the Canadian population in general. Indigenous youth presently make up and will continue to constitute a significant proportion of the school population in Canada, especially in the western provinces and Ontario. As Indigenous peoples have migrated to urban areas, their numbers have increased in provincial schools.

In the past, high school achievement improved for Indigenous students, but the rate of increase in high school graduation for First Nations students has not been sustained. Thus, despite the educational successes of many Indigenous peoples, the gap between non-Indigenous and Indigenous student educational levels has widened, in part because of increased investment by non-Indigenous populations in education while First Nations schools continue to face chronic underfunding and in part because of the economic and social barriers facing many Indigenous peoples.

The social conditions challenging Indigenous peoples have been well documented and include "poverty, unemployment, family breakdown, physical and mental health problems, suicide, and incarceration" (FSIN 1997, 13). These social conditions and the growing number of Indigenous youth present the education system with its "greatest opportunity and challenge" (Tkach 2003, n.p.). In a study on schooling, workforce, and income status commissioned by the Federation of Saskatchewan Indian Nations (FSIN) in 2002, both the income levels and workforce participation of Indigenous people fall far short of those of non-Indigenous people (FSIN 2002b). The FSIN report asserted that workforce participation is directly related to school attainment, which remains low. For example, in Saskatchewan, the graduation rate for Aboriginal students is 32.5 percent (Pelletier, Cottrell, and Hardie 2013). One of the main conclusions of the FSIN (2002b, 23) report was that "the employment participation and unemployment rates of First Nations persons *cannot show any substantial improvement until there is a large increase in the number of [First Nations] youth who complete their grade 12*" (emphasis in original). According to this report, and a more recent analysis of the impact of education on lifetime earning for Aboriginal peoples in Saskatchewan (Howe 2011), improvements in educational success are the key to reducing the poverty facing Indigenous peoples.

Though these statistics can be disheartening, it must be noted that many schools have taken the initiative to make the changes needed to facilitate the success of Indigenous students. These successes have been documented in several publications (see, for example, Bell et al. 2004; Fullford 2007; Alberta Education 2007, 2008; and Pelletier, Cottrell, and Hardie 2013). More schools like these are needed: it is imperative that the rates of school completion and success of Indigenous students be improved. This will require a sustained effort and improvements by educational systems that have not been effective with Indigenous students (FSIN 1997; Sokoloff 2004). Enhancing teacher effectiveness has been cited as a key to improving educational systems and Indigenous student success (FSIN 2002a; Bishop 2012).

This book addresses effective instructional practice for teachers of Indigenous students in both theory and practice. Theoretically, one of the issues in Indigenous education is that educational theories are most often based on white, middle-class, Euro-centred views of teaching and learning. Many of these theories are useful, but they are limited and problematic when it comes to addressing Indigenous matters. In response to this issue, we present the Kaminstigominuhigoskak (Cumberland House) Nehinuw (Cree) theory of teaching and learning as an example of Indigenous educational thought.[3] We use stories of effective teachers of Indigenous students to illustrate the principles of Indigenous approaches to education. A conceptual framework based on these stories connects Indigenous thought to effective classroom practice. In this book, although the Nehinuw community of Cumberland House is located in Saskatchewan, Canada, and the stories are from teachers in Saskatchewan, the themes presented resonate with those emerging in the education research literature from around the globe on effective approaches to teaching of Indigenous students.

The teachers' stories of professional knowledge in this book demonstrate how Indigenous student success is related to success as defined by different Elders. For instance, the late Elder Ken Goodwill from the Standing Buffalo Dakota First Nation said that the purpose of education is to help students recognize who they are, to see their gifts, talents, and strengths and recognize the responsibility that accompanies these gifts, so they can survive, thrive, and contribute as they navigate through both the broader world and Indigenous cultures. Although effective educational practice for First Nations, Métis, and Inuit students is good education for all students, there are issues specific to Indigenous education because Indigenous people have unique histories and world views. As teachers, we have a responsibility to ensure that Indigenous students are successful in school while developing as Indigenous peoples. Students should not have to leave their Indigenous identities behind to be successful in school. It is incumbent upon teachers to find and incorporate Indigenous knowledge and understandings (epistemologies) and to use Indigenous practices and methods to support learning and fully develop students' potential.

Who Are We?

Before introducing ourselves, we would like to comment that the writing style of this book combines Nehinuw (Cree) cultural cognitive structures with Euro-Canadian narrative. Keith introduces a distinctive Nehinuw style in a modern academic context. Another Nehinuw researcher, Shawn Wilson from Opaskwayak Cree Nation in Manitoba, also combined academic writing with an Indigenous storytelling style in his book, *Research Is Ceremony: Indigenous Research Methods* (2008). Wilson's use of a storytelling voice reflects the Indigenous narrative approach that is similar to the voices of the teachers in this book as they share their stories of practice. The writing style also moves back and forth from research based primarily on Western methods to analysis based on Indigenous thinking. As the styles change, we ask the reader to think of this as moving among different cultures, negotiating the differences in styles of communication as one does when negotiating the move from the Indigenous world to the world of the dominant culture and back again.

Linda's Story

I am a Euro-Canadian educator who has spent my teaching career in Indigenous education. I grew up in rural and urban Saskatchewan and thus had occasional interactions with First Nations and Métis people. In the public schools I attended, I was not aware that the First Nations and Métis students I knew were, in fact, First Nations and Métis. That awareness only came as a teenager. Although my parents taught me directly and through practice to respect other cultural groups, my parents and I were immersed in the racist ideology regarding Indigenous peoples in Saskatchewan, so, as a young person, I had non-critical racialized notions of Indigenous peoples. At the same time, I had a family history of connection to the Indigenous peoples of this land. My maternal grandmother grew up in Pincher Creek, Alberta, where her peer group and playmates were Blackfoot (Siksika) children. She chose to maintain friendships with Indigenous peoples when she was an adult in Saskatchewan at a time when it was not acceptable practice in middle-class Regina, which was dominated by British colonial beliefs about First Nations and Métis peoples. As for my mother, in her early career as a teacher, she worked for a year as a child caregiver at a residential school. She didn't have much power in the hierarchy of the church-run school, but she did what she could to bring fun to the students' lives. I have pictures of my mother with her students playing in the snow and skating on the slough by the school. But my mother, even with her English beliefs in the authority of the teacher, told me that the priest at the school was mean, so she left to teach in the nearby provincial school, with its mix of Euro-Canadian, non-status First Nations, and Métis students. Even as I recall my family connection to Indigenous peoples, these stories in no way exculpate my family and my ancestors from

Linda with Black Lake Denesuline First Nation Teacher Education Students. *Front row:* Shirley Sandypoint, Linda Goulet, Carrie Toutsaint, Rita Bendoni. *Back row:* Maggie Robillard, Darcy Sandypoint, Tina Alphonse, Albertine Sayazie, Tracy Cook, Rose Bouvier, Jackie Echodh, Marilyn Mercredi, Margie Sayazie, Rhonda Sandypoint, Colleen Renie. *Photo by Val Toutsaint.*

their role and complicity in the colonial agenda. I recognize the privileges that my family and I had being Euro-Canadian in a settler state.

My own journey in Indigenous education began in Churchill, Manitoba, in 1971 with Cree, Dene, Inuit, and Euro-Canadian students. I have a warm place in my heart for those students, who taught me so much as they challenged me to think about my teaching practice. I searched for appropriate materials and tried different strategies to get them involved in learning. As I learned about them and the community, I strove to bring the curriculum closer to the reality of the students' lives in that small northern community. That experience introduced me to the challenges facing teachers in Indigenous education. I asked myself, "How can I as a teacher more effectively engage Indigenous students in ways that would better serve them and their communities?" Searching for answers to that question has been the challenge of my professional life since that first teaching experience.

Over the course of my career, I was fortunate to have many Indigenous and non-Indigenous colleagues and family members who were educators of

Indigenous students. Copious amounts of tea and coffee were consumed at kitchen tables and in restaurants as we talked about improving the education for Indigenous students and critiqued our own practice. As my work took me into Indigenous teacher education, I questioned what I was teaching in my classes, since much of the research was based on Western views of childhood and teaching and learning, with a vast majority of the research of effective practice based on teachers of white middle-class students. Although this situation has changed considerably in the last few years, I decided I needed to delve deeper into the personal and practical knowledge (Clandinin and Connelly 1995) of effective teachers of Indigenous students. I undertook research for which I interviewed a number of Cree, Métis, Dene, Saulteaux, and Euro-Canadian teachers who were known in their communities to be effective teachers. I also observed three classrooms in a Cree community over a three-month period. This book is based on the stories of those teachers and others. As I wrote about my research, I could see many of the concepts articulated by my Nehinuw husband evident in the teachers' stories. We decided to combine our knowledge and share it as a book.

Keith's Story

I was born and raised in the Nehinuw community of Kaminstigominuhig-oskak (Cumberland House), in northeastern Saskatchewan. The fishing, trapping, and hunting lifestyle was still a strong part our culture, so I was fortunate to have experienced life on a spring trapline for several years. We generally went to the trapline at the end of February and returned in the first or second week of May. I did domestic and commercial fishing with my dad, brother, uncles, and others. Except during mating season or other critical periods, we hunted all year round for big game like deer and moose. In the fall we focused on hunting grouse, ducks, geese, and swans. In my boyhood and youth during the winter, we snared rabbits and trapped squirrels and weasels.

Nehinuwehin is my first language; I learned English only after I started school.[4] Speaking the Cree language was the norm in our daily lives. We spoke English only in school and church. Most of the clerks in the stores were from the community, so they were Cree speakers. The services in the Roman Catholic church were carried out in Latin, while the prayers and songs were done in English, Latin, and Cree. Although I wanted to go to school at age six, I was not accepted until I was seven years old, because I was small for my age. My first teacher, Sister St. Joseph, was a good teacher. She taught us how to read using phonics and the Dick and Jane readers. Although the grouse I was

Family spring trapping on the Cumberland House Delta, circa 1950. Keith Goulet as a child *(far right)*. Photo by Jim Brady, courtesy of Glenbow Archives, PA-2218-441.

hunting on the way to school was not reflected in the curriculum, I do remember learning how to say "cock a doodle doo." We didn't know any English, and she didn't know any Cree, so communication was often difficult and frustrating. Sometimes we laughed together, and other times she laughed alone. I also saw her wiping her eyes as she was looking out the window. Sometimes, the learning was exciting, but I do also recall the frustration, boredom, and the disciplinary practice of corporal punishment.

After attending school in Cumberland House from Grades 1 to 10, I took Grades 11 and 12 in Prince Albert. From there I attended university, then went to Ontario for my teacher education. My first year teaching was Grades 2–4 in an Anishinaabe community called Aroland in 1967–68. In addition to my experience-based approaches for curriculum materials development, my only other meaningful sources for materials were the fish and wildlife charts from the Lands and Forests government department. In 1969–71, I taught Grade 6 in Moose Factory in James Bay Cree country, where we integrated Indigenous knowledge in social studies, science, math, and language arts. In 1972–73, while taking classes at the University of Saskatchewan, I developed and taught a non-credit Cree-language course. In the following year, I taught a first-year university accredited Cree-language course that was designated as an anthropology class. I graduated with a BEd in 1974.

From September 1974 to February 1976, I was a Cree-language consultant doing developmental work on Cree writing systems, curriculum, and instruction as well as curriculum materials development. In summer of 1975, I taught a Cree course to language instructors, teachers, and civil servants in La Ronge. It was the first university accredited course taught in northern Saskatchewan. In February 1976, I was hired as the Northern Teachers Education Program (NORTEP) developer. I arranged and taught the first NORTEP class in September 1976 and remained there as faculty until 1979. I then became the principal of the La Ronge Region Community College, which had an array of programs, including trapper training, bush pilot training, diamond drilling, and truck driver training. In 1984–85, I became the executive director of the Gabriel Dumont Institute, a provincial Métis-controlled research and program institution. I completed my MEd from the University of Regina in 1986.

Beginning in 1986, I served seventeen years as a member of the Legislative Assembly in the Saskatchewan provincial legislature. I was a cabinet minister from 1992 to 2001. Although it was supported by all major political parties in Canada and the provinces, I voted against the Meech Lake Accord in 1987. In 1992, as a member of the Cabinet and as the provincial secretary, I chaired the Charlottetown Accord. I was also involved in Treaty Land Entitlement, the Métis Act, the Northern Development Board, the no-fault insurance plan, sewer and water for northern communities, and the Cumberland House Bridge. Presently, I am working on my PhD dissertation on the Cumberland Nehinuw concept of land.

Overview of Indigenous Education

Now that we have given you a glimpse of who we are and some of where we've been, let's take a look at "the lay of the land" of Indigenous education. Getting a lay of the land is something Keith does every time he goes to a new city. He stops to look around and orient himself to the four directions as well as to the rise and fall of the land. With this orientation, no matter where he goes in the new city, he knows roughly where he is situated in this new place. Similarly, we invite you to explore a brief history and overview of the emerging discipline of Indigenous education as it relates to classroom-based instruction.

Indigenous education is a broad term with different meanings to different people. Wikipedia defines it as "teaching indigenous knowledge, models, methods, and content within formal or non-formal educational systems."[5] In this book, the term is used to refer to the education of Indigenous students, usually to quality education for Indigenous learners in formal education settings. Because the term is used so broadly, it is multifaceted, and thus can include Indigenous pedagogies, Indigenous school systems, curriculum, staffing, and relationships. In contrast, Indigenous pedagogies view education from an Indigenous perspective and "are embedded in complex systems of knowing, inclusive of their own suppositions about knowledge and being" (Friedel 2010, 6). For example, in her discussion of Anishinaabe pedagogy, Rebecca Chartrand (2012, 152, 157) sees it as having a humanistic focus that explores the interrelationships among all things, "taking into account feelings, attitudes, and values that can add affective components to conventional subject matter curriculum" while specifically being defined "in living our [Anishinaabe] language, culture, and relationship to the land, space and being." Also closely related to the term *Indigenous education* is *decolonizing education*. Decolonizing education places more emphasis on the power relationships within education and serves to deconstruct past colonial systems of education and recreate new ones, usually based on equity and Indigenous principles. On the other hand, *indigenizing education* usually refers to the integration of Indigenous content, understandings, and processes into the formal education system.

Since the National Indian Brotherhood's call for "Indian control of Indian education" in 1972, there have been various initiatives to improve education for Indigenous students. Prior to the late 1960s and early 1970s, the high failure rate of Indigenous children was discussed in the educational literature but was often based on ethnocentric views that Indigenous peoples were racially inferior or culturally deprived (Swisher and Deyhle 1989). Because this research had an ethnocentric bias, it was not useful in improving education for Indigenous children. Since 1972, research has shifted from blaming Indigenous children, their families, and their communities for the lack of school success to an exploration and examination of effective educational practices for Indigenous students as well as an articulation of Indigenous pedagogies.

Early Initiatives

Forty years ago, it was clear that education was failing Indigenous children (National Indian Brotherhood 1972). Researchers entered classrooms to find out why schools were not meeting the needs of Indigenous students and what could be done to improve instruction. The focus of the early research has relevance to this day in that the issues identified in the 1970s remain pertinent today.

Judith Kleinfeld (1975, 318) has examined characteristics of effective teachers of Indigenous students and states in her research that effective teachers are those who combine personal warmth with the "demand for a high quality of academic work." These teachers show genuine caring for students and expect them do well at school. On the other hand, in examining why English-speaking Warm Springs Indian students were not doing well, Susan Philips ([1972] 1983) found that the communication structures of the teacher's English were different from those of the students. Differences in communication style included non-verbal signals and the grammatical structure of English usage, so even though they all spoke English, the Warm Springs Indian students often did not understand the teacher's instruction. Other studies have established that some teachers had negative beliefs or stereotypical views about Indigenous children (Rampaul, Singh, and Didyk 1984; Taylor 1995; Wax, Wax, and Dumont 1972), and in some communities, parents were reluctant to approach school personnel (Wax, Wax, and Dumont 1972). There was a gulf between students and teachers, and between schools and communities.

Differences between Indigenous students and their teachers have been examined in research on learning styles: the learning styles of Indigenous children have been compared to those of non-Indigenous children, and to the instructional styles used by teachers (Erickson and Mohatt 1982; More 1987; Swisher and Deyhle 1989). The premise of the learning and communication styles theories of this research is that cultural differences between the Euro-centred basis of school culture and the Indigenous culture of the home and community cause the lack of school success. Various authors have thus proposed that teachers improve instruction by integrating Indigenous languages and culture into the curriculum (Gilliland 1988; Reyhner 1988).

Curriculum Development

Curriculum change was a main thrust of Indigenous education in the late 1980s and 1990s and has continued into the new century with many international initiatives. In the 1980s, educators believed that if content relevant to Indigenous children was used in the various subject areas in the classroom, the students would be more responsive to learning in school (Gilliland 1988; Goulet 1987; Reyhner 1988). The goal then was to ensure that teachers used culturally accurate material to replace the biased, stereotypical information prevalent in curricula of the day (Hirschfelder 1982; Manitoba Indian Brotherhood 1977; Preiswerk 1981). Projects were undertaken to produce material that would identify the positive aspects of and reflect more accurately Indigenous history and culture (see, for example, Bopp et al. 1984; Mokakit 1992; Saskatchewan Education 1985; Saskatchewan Indian Cultural Centre n.d.). As culturally relevant curricula were developed, Tarajean Yazzie (1999) critiqued the often-used approach in which curricula are developed by those outside the community, often in isolation from those who are expected to implement cultural programs. In their review of Indigenous education in Canada, Jean Barman, Yvonne Hébert, and Don McCaskill (1987, 4) found that using culturally appropriate materials was more difficult than initially expected: "The need to incorporate a traditional cultural perspective into the contemporary context has been easier to assert in principle than in practice." Indigenous cultures have often been viewed as static or vibrant only in some distant time in the past. At times, the decontextualized "craft" approach to teaching culture has led to a trivialization of cultural knowledge (Stairs 1996). Superficial cultural programming has also been critiqued by Sheila Watt-Cloutier (2000), who decried the watering down of programming for Inuit children. In her research, she states that the purpose of any education is to prepare people for the opportunities and challenges facing them in their lifetime and argues that education must above all be empowering, thus preparing Indigenous students for "responsible self-direction" (122). Tarajean Yazzie (1999) states that successful curriculum projects are those that include historical and traditional knowledge as well as current tribal issues and concerns. In developing a curriculum for Indigenous adults studying early childhood education, Jessica Ball and Alan Pence (2006, 40) documented a method of curriculum development (the Generative Curriculum Model) that included both Western knowledge and local Indigenous knowledge. University personnel identified the program topics and consulted collaboratively with local knowledge keepers to identify important Indigenous concepts and understandings. The process demanded that participants be open to unpredictability and different ways of educating: "In the Generative Curriculum Model, the curriculum is dominated neither by the university's nor the community's contributions but is suspended in the space between – a space where disparate ideas can meet, combine, and transmogrify, with unforeseeable results." Similarly, in addressing issues in Indigenous science education, Herman Michell (2007) has identified the importance of linking curriculum development to the students' lives, community, culture, and language. He states that place, including the land and environment of the community, and local Indigenous knowledge and knowledge keepers, including Elders, are needed to indigenize science education. Summarizing the research on Indigenous science curriculum development, Herman Michell, Yvonne Vizina, Camie Augustus, and Jason Sawyer (2008, 47) conclude that "community-based, participatory, and action research projects with adequate funding are needed to support teachers and university researchers in the development of localized curriculum and alternate performance assessment indicators."

One of the problems of curriculum development at the local level is that it often places the burden for curriculum innovation on the individual teachers and can disappear from the school when the teacher leaves. In addition, funding for curriculum development projects has not been forthcoming. Jo-ann Archibald (2008) reports that it took a year to secure funding from eight different sources for their curriculum development initiative regarding First Nations views of justice. In addition to issues of funding, Glen Aikenhead (2006) asserts that locally developed curricula material may be difficult to transfer to other locations. He maintains that curriculum change needs to take place across educational systems, so that the entrenched beliefs about science education can be renegotiated. To have long-term impact, curriculum development needs to be addressed both systemically and locally. Educational authorities and governments responsible for curriculum need to provide the resources, including funding, to ensure that curriculum change takes place both globally and locally, because curriculum adaptation is a necessary first step but, as more recent research has shown, is insufficient by itself to make the gains needed in Indigenous education (Bishop 2003; Dion 2009; Tupper 2011).

Program Initiatives

There are and have been countless schools that have taken initiatives to improve education for Indigenous students. The characteristics common to these schools were summarized at a national conference called "Promising Practices in Aboriginal Education," and include strong leadership and governance structures, high expectations for students, focus on academic achievement and long-term student success, secure and welcoming climates for children and families, respect for Aboriginal culture and traditions to make learning relevant, provision of a wide range of programs and supports for learning, exceptional language and cultural programs, a high percentage of Aboriginal staff and quality staff development, linking assessment to instructional and planning decisions, and vigorous community partnerships and beneficial external alliances (Phillips and Raham 2008, 10).

Joanne Tompkins (1998) and Jerry Lipka (1998) were involved in school initiatives to create change in northern Inuit and Yup'ik communities, respectively. These educators found that the creation of an environment for Indigenous student success was multidimensional, and that the model of cultural inclusion alone was insufficient. Tompkins and her staff implemented program planning based on both traditional and contemporary themes that balanced student interest with culture and the demands of the mandated school curriculum. Theme planning supported Inuktitut-language program development that, over time, resulted in immersion programming up to Grade 4. Elders became a part of school programs, and learning activities that occurred out on the land increased. The structure of programming changed to emphasize hands-on activities and small-group work to address the wide range of student ability in each class.

Other program initiatives have drawn from Indigenous language concepts in program design. Language with its embedded cultural concepts (Ah Nee-Benham 2000) was key to the Māori initiatives in New Zealand as they implemented their language nests or preschool Māori immersion programs (Te Kōhanga Reo). The early Te Kōhanga Reo were followed by primary schools (Kura Kaupapa Māori), secondary schools (Whare Kura), and postsecondary sites (Whare Wānanga). As the programming began, the movement was driven by the political will of the parents and community members. All these initiatives were based on Kaupapa Māori, or the use of traditional and contemporary notions of *whānau* (extended family) values, practices, and structures, as a theory and practice of transformation (Smith 2000). Extending the Kaupapa Māori principles to mainstream institutions, Russell Bishop (2003) found that Māori students were able to achieve success when deficit beliefs of their abilities were replaced by an emphasis on empowerment, co-construction of knowledge, cultural recognition, and the use of Māori concepts, values, and beliefs to guide program development.

Similar to the Māori initiatives, traditional cultural values, or key Indigenous language concepts, "bundle words" (Wheeler 2000, quoted in Absolon 2011, 155) are being used to guide innovations in Indigenous programming at sites globally and across institutions. For example, in Hawaii, traditional Hawaiian chanting is being used to achieve the educational concept of *Ho'olakalaka,* or, "calming the mind to make it ready to learn" (Alo, Hodges, and Taniguchi 2012). In Canada, Lorna Williams (2012; also see Williams and Tanaka 2007) uses many Lil'wat concepts as foundational in her program initiatives. Concepts such as *cwelelep* (being in a place of dissonance and uncertainty in anticipation of new learning) and *celhcelh* (each person is responsible for their own learning and self-care, finding answers, knowing how to fit into the community, self-knowledge) are but two examples Williams uses to teach from and within an Indigenous perspective. The use of these key Indigenous concepts creates new forms of teaching and learning environments – forms that are more culturally relevant particularly for Indigenous students.

Culturally Relevant Teaching

In her research on effective teachers of Black students, Gloria Ladson-Billings (1990, 24) introduces the concept of culturally relevant teaching, which has been applied in Indigenous education. Culturally relevant teaching uses the student's culture to help her or him achieve success. Ladson-Billings explains that the main difference between "mainstream" effective instruction and culturally relevant pedagogy is context: research on effective instruction has identified generic teaching skills that are decontextualized, while with culturally relevant teaching, effective teaching is tied directly to the context in which the instruction is taking place.

Indigenous authors Faith Maina (1997) and Cornel Pewewardy (1999) describe culturally relevant pedagogy as it applies to Indigenous peoples. In culturally relevant pedagogy, teachers use students' prior cultural knowledge and compatible classroom and community language patterns and social norms, reflect diversity in assessment, view students as assets, and help students function in multicultural, multilingual situations without the loss of their original culture. Maina argues that although Indigenous children can learn about other cultural ways in school, it is alienating to assume that the dominant culture's way of being is the only one.

Barry Osborne (1996), Linda Miller Cleary and Thomas Peacock (1998), and Jeff Orr, John Jerome Paul, and Sharon Paul (2002) have found similar classroom interaction patterns in their examination of effective teachers. Orr, Paul, and Paul (2002, 350) describe good teachers as "political agents, choosing to teach from a perspective that embodies cultural practical knowledge in relation to their students' lives in the present, remembering their collective ancestral past, and imagining a different cultural future." Miller Cleary and Peacock (1998) state that successful teachers of Indigenous students do not need to come from the same ethnic background as the child so long as they develop trust and respect and have close personal relationships with students. Successful management strategies are culturally sensitive and guide children indirectly rather than confrontationally. Effective programming includes culturally relevant curriculum, uses the students' first language, and involves parents and families.

Language is important in culturally responsive teaching. Cora Weber-Pillwax (2001) explains that it is both the Indigenous language and how the language is used that conveys knowledge, ways of being, and relating to the world. When Philemon Chigeza and Hilary Whitehouse (2011) examined how Torres Strait Island middle-year students developed their understandings of scientific concepts, they found that students who were more fluent in Creole than English had difficulty labelling drawings to show their conceptual understanding, yet were able to apply the concepts using direct actions and dramatizations when speaking in Creole. The students knew the concepts; how their knowledge was being measured was problematic.

The importance of Indigenous language to academic success is also evident in immersion programming. Russell Bishop, Mere Berryman, and Cath Richardson (2002, 49) report that in their research, immersion teachers used personal skills that were "culturally located." Teachers treated the children with respect but also extended the integration of respect into the children's interaction with others – that is, their peers, adults, extended family, and Elders. Students learned in ways that developed and reinforced their identity as Māori. Thus, "teaching and learning relationships are such that children are able to bring who they are and how they make sense and meaning of the world to the learning interactions" (58). In their observations, Bishop, Berryman, and Richardson state that Māori humour was valued and always present. The firmness of the teacher was contextualized in Māori intergenerational relationships that typically identify distinct roles and responsibilities for Elders, adults, youth, and children. Starr Sock and Sherise Paul-Gould (2012) conducted a follow-up study of a Mi'kmaq kindergarten to Grade 3 immersion program in their community. When the immersion program graduates were in Grade 7, their reading assessment levels were compared to those students who had not been in the immersion program. The immersion students had overall higher test scores. Teachers reported that immersion graduates had more focus and confidence in academic learning while being open to sharing and supporting other students' learning in the class. It would appear from these results that students are learning much more than language in the Mi'kmaq immersion program.

Indigenous languages are often present in the classroom when Elders are involved. Elders use their Indigenous language when they bring prayers, ceremony, and ritual to the classroom to "signal a time for caring and connection to the spiritual, to each other and to oneself" (Archibald 2008, 51). They are the holders of important Indigenous knowledge (Battiste and Youngblood Henderson 2009), especially that which relates to language concepts that hold important cultural values, as well as land-based scientific, biological, geographical, and historical knowledge, world views, and philosophies. Elders are seen as storytellers and historians who educate communities, sustain cultures, and "help each person to know who we are as Indigenous peoples" (Iseke-Barnes 2009, 69). This connection to the culture and contributions of one's peoples is especially important for those Indigenous students who are struggling with issues of identity (Fayant et al. 2010).

In addition to developing language skills, stories teach moral lessons, convey values, and promote emotional wellness. Orality, in both skill development and meaning making on the part of the teller and the listener, is an important aspect of traditional storytelling (Weber-Pillwax 2001). Stó:lō storytellers say we have "'three ears to listen with, two on the sides of our head and one in our heart' ... Listening requires the concomitant involvement of the auditory and visual senses, the emotions, the mind, and patience" (Archibald 2008, 76). Traditionally, meaning making was primarily the responsibility of the listener; the teller paid attention to the context and needs of the child to know which story to tell and when and how to tell it. For example, Keith's mother often told scary stories in the bush while berry picking, to entertain the children and keep them close.

For teachers, the art of telling traditional stories can be very complex. Jo-ann Archibald suggests that teachers who are unfamiliar with the form of traditional storytelling seek a mentor or Elder to guide them in their development, or invite a community Elder to tell the stories and thus ensure they are shared in a way that is respectful of both the story and its context, including protocol. When shared respectfully, stories have the energy and power to engage students, causing them to respond positively to activities associated with the story. For example, Grade 5 Nisga'a students in British Columbia reported that they liked hearing "the stories being told, writing about the stories, drawing characters, crests and petroglyphs associated with the story but they didn't like the vocabulary exercises and dictionary work" (Archibald 2008, 132).

Stories are often about places, tied to the land, water, plants, and animals of a particular location. Many Indigenous educators have successfully implemented land-based teaching, primarily because learning on the land is holistic, and students are able to make many connections with what they learn (Elliott, Guilar, and Swallow 2009; Goulet and McLeod 2002; Greenwood and de Leeuw 2007; Lee 2007). For example, Kainai children in Alberta have their Blackfoot-language immersion program on the land with Elders and ceremonies that teach students their relationship to the human and non-human world. Similar to Starr Sock and Sherise Paul-Gould's (2012) findings, Alvine Mountain Horse (2012) reports that students in their land-based Blackfoot immersion program score higher on academic achievement tests. Lee (2007) has conducted research on a program that partnered with community members to focus on land-based issues facing the surrounding Pueblo communities in the southern United States. Reading student journal entries, she found that the students identified important academic and professional skills they wanted to learn and made connections between their learnings and the broader concerns of the community. The fieldwork actively engaged students, who did hands-on work. The embodied nature of this experience meant that learning was holistic and meaningful.

Challenges for Euro-Canadian Teachers

Euro-Canadians continue to make up the majority of teachers in all areas of Canada (Ryan, Pollack, and Antonelli 2009). Recently, questions regarding settler Canadian teachers of Indigenous students have received more attention in the literature.

John Taylor (1995), a Euro-Canadian educator, has reflected on the actions of non-Indigenous teachers in various First Nations schools in western Canada in which he taught for several years. In his observations he notes that many non-Indigenous teachers were not prepared for the cultural differences they encountered in Indigenous communities and thus experienced culture shock. While some teachers were able to overcome this shock and find suitable points of entry into the community, others isolated themselves to protect themselves from the mental and emotional strain of interacting within a culture different from their own. Taylor states that although these teachers were hard-working, well prepared, and well intentioned, students often viewed the teacher's isolation from the community as rejection of the students' community and, by extension, as dislike of the students themselves. Some settler Canadian teachers were unable or unwilling to deal with cultural differences in a positive way and instead complained about actions in the community that reflected values different from their own, while others found safety in feelings of superiority.

Yatta Kanu (2005) has examined the integration of Aboriginal knowledge and perspectives into the curriculum by urban high school teachers teaching diverse students. Using James Banks's (1989) typology of the inclusion of multicultural perspectives, Kanu found the Aboriginal teacher used the transformative approach, while Euro-Canadian teachers tended to use the contributions and additive approach. Challenges to integration identified by teachers were lack of knowledge and confidence regarding the subject matter, lack of resources, and racism. Susan Dion's (2009) study of settler teachers integrating Indigenous content and teaching non-Indigenous students shows similar findings. In her research, Dion reports that teachers tended to present Aboriginal content as factual personal stories of characters with whom students could empathize, but failed to engage students in broader, systemic issues. Dion theorizes that it was the teachers' "systems of reasoning" (80) that constrained their teaching approach. Even though students appeared ready for "disruptive" discussions, teachers led students away from controversy, bound by their beliefs and pedagogy of mastery and control when dealing with systemic issues that could lead to controversy, the disruption of Euro-Canadian beliefs about history and identity, and negative feelings on the part of their settler Canadian students. Teachers feared that this kind of controversy might lead to a backlash from parents and administration.

On the other hand, in their research of effective teachers of Inuit students, Robert Renaud, Brina Lewthwaite, and Barbara McMillan (2012) report that when teachers are prepared to change their teaching to respond to their students and legitimize the local culture and community in school learning, students become more engaged in learning. The teachers developed a profile of teaching practices they used to create positive learning environments for Inuit students. Similarly, Russell Bishop et al. (2006, 1) report achievement gains for Māori students when mainstream teachers are supported in professional development using principles of the Effective Teaching Profile based on the experiences of Māori students, their *whānau* (extended relationships), principals, and teachers. Effective teachers reject deficit beliefs about Māori students; instead, they "care for the students as culturally located individuals; have high expectations of the learning for students; manage their classrooms to promote learning; engage in a range of discursive learning interactions with students or facilitate students to engage with others in these ways; implement a range of strategies that can facilitate learning interactions; promote, monitor and reflect upon learning outcomes that in turn lead to improvements in Māori student achievement and share this knowledge with the students."

Beverly Klug and Patricia Whitfield (2003), both non-Native educators, believe that non-Native teachers of American Indian children need to become bicultural. Bicultural understanding has been achieved through a process that includes interrogation of one's own prejudices; continuous reflection of one's teaching; incorporation of accurate, contemporary information regarding students' cultural groups; engagement with community members and attendance at appropriate social events; and communication with community members to solve educational problems. Bicultural teachers prepare students for successful functioning in both their home community and the larger society. These teachers understand students' resistance to learning as protection against distancing themselves from their own culture when they consciously or unconsciously interpret education as a tool of assimilation. According to Klug and Whitfield, education for American Indian students needs to move beyond content and method and address issues of social justice.

Sociological Issues

Beginning in the 1990s, many authors identified the need to examine sociological issues of colonization, racism, and oppression in classroom practice (Goulet 2001; Klug and Whitfield 2003; Lipka 1998; Miller Cleary and Peacock 1998). Educators asserted that in addition to culture, issues of racism (Friedel 2010; St. Denis and Hampton 2002; Osborne 1996; Wilson 1991) and the legacy of colonization (Goulet 2001; Orr, Paul, and Paul 2002; St. Denis 2002; Tompkins 1998) had an impact on the education of Indigenous students. These educators called for attention to social issues in the examination of educational practice.

Social Attitudes and Structures

Social attitudes influence perceptions of what constitutes effective teaching. In her work in Australia, Merridy Malin (1994) found that judgments of good teaching for Indigenous children were culturally based. For her research, Malin had three panels of Aborigine parents, Aborigine teachers, and Anglo university teacher educators from the university respond to videotapes of a Yup'ik Eskimo teacher, an Anglo Australian teacher, and an Aborigine teacher. Each group identified most with their own cultural background, and the results thus revealed the cultural differences that existed in the perceptions of the characteristics of good teachers and good teaching. Those in power positions in education, the Anglo teacher educators, felt that the "Aborigine teacher's discipline, preparation, and teaching strategies were wanting" (Malin 1994, 100), whereas both Aborigine panels preferred the Aborigine teacher's warmth and understanding to the Anglo teacher's efficiency and task orientation. The Aborigine participants were more concerned about human relations in the classroom. They maintained that regardless of the strategy or how well prepared the teacher was, if a child was not comfortable in the classroom, he or she would not learn.

Besides social attitudes, social structures – such as the use of power and racial stratification of our society and our economy – influence minority students' success. Sociological theorists such as John Ogbu (1991) argue that cultural differences between the home and school alone are not enough to explain minority students' failure; one must consider the historical and structural context in which those differences are embedded.

Power Relations, Racism, and Colonization

Social issues are evident in the research regarding classroom practice. In their review of Indigenous education, Donna Deyhle and Karen Swisher (1997, 147) state, "We believe that what teachers *do* to students – how power relations are negotiated in the classroom – is critical in understanding American Indian student performance in school." Similarly, Beverly Klug and Patricia Whitfield (2003, 155) advocate the development of a pedagogy that uses the knowledge of subordinated groups to address the issue of "knowledge production" and to "challenge racist assumptions" that inform social identity and power relations.

Recently, Indigenous educators have begun to use anti-racism theory in the analysis of Indigenous education (Friedel 2010; St. Denis 2002, 2010; St. Denis and Hampton 2002). When improvements in Indigenous education focus primarily on cultural programming, taught within the framework of current schooling practices, the initiatives do not expose or challenge power relationships within our society. Verna St. Denis (2002) argues that the theory of cultural difference that dominates the discourse of Indigenous education does not provide sufficient explanation for the failure of Indigenous students in schools. In her view, cultural programming alone ignores the reality of social and economic issues in the lives of students. In doing so, it fails to prepare students to deal with the rapid economic and social changes that have and are taking place in Indigenous communities. St. Denis asserts that cultural programming designed to support positive Indigenous identity development often privileges one form of cultural expression. Culture is frequently presented as existing in some past that has been lost and must again be found. The complex variations of cultural identities of Indigenous peoples are simplified, and only one form of cultural expression is seen as authentic. To St. Denis, when culture is identified as the problem, it can cause confusion rather than assist Indigenous students in sorting out the complexity of multiple identities and multicultural competencies. St. Denis asserts that an anti-racism analysis can address current issues to ensure the inequalities perpetrated in the past are not continued in the present. Anti-racism can also examine the unequal power relations in our society that affect a person's opportunities and choices. Ruth Paradise (1994) argues that the power relations of society are reflected in the everyday reality that is co-constructed between children and their teachers who live within historical, social, and political contexts. In specific instances, the teacher and students can construct or reconstruct their particular arrangement to make it more equitable.

However, it is not helpful to frame the issue of Indigenous education in a restrictive view or reduce practice to only sociological problems of inequality and racism. Culture and language revitalization complements the inclusion of decolonizing, anti-racism education. The history of racism is not only the rejection of peoples from a biological or sociological basis; it is also a cultural and linguistic rejection. In her study, Ruth Paradise (1994, 69) observed Indigenous and non-Indigenous teachers who taught in a way that allowed students to challenge the authority of the material used in schooling while the teachers implicitly practised "respect and appreciation of [Indigenous] values related to individual autonomy, respect for the person, and group solidarity." These educators used culturally congruent interactional and social organizational strategies that allowed children to choose to follow their leadership. Similarly, in her observation of a Cree teacher in an urban setting, Angela Ward (2001) notes that the teacher established more equitable relations through her use of cooperative learning techniques and a talking circle (an object was passed around a circle so that each person in the class was given the opportunity to participate).[6] Russell Bishop et al. (2006) used the phrase "culturally responsive pedagogy of relations" to describe effective teachers creating learning contexts in their classrooms such that power was shared, culture counted, learning interactive, and teachers and students shared a common vision of educational excellence.

Power relationships are also enacted in the students' sense of belonging or authority in the classroom. Eber Hampton (1995) states that since Indian peoples are and are seen to be a minority in their own land, a sense of land, territory, or place is crucial in Indigenous education. To Hampton, Indigenous peoples need a sense of belonging, a place where they can be themselves. The importance of land was a prevalent theme among Indigenous educators in Maenette K.P. Ah Nee-Benham's (2000) work, and, as in Hampton's research, this concept was also used to emphasize the importance of a safe place where culture could be nurtured, learned, and practised in educational settings without being under attack from a colonial system.

Social relations of power are also evident in school-community relationships. In his work with Yup'ik educators, Jerry Lipka (1998) found that the leadership of Elders and community members in curriculum development produced relevant curriculum change and created a forum for the production of Indigenous knowledge, thus changing power relationships in knowledge production in the school. Community members came to believe in their ca-pability to take leadership in the process of formal schooling – capabilities that had been denied to them through past colonial practices. Through community involvement in curriculum production, Lipka and the Yup'ik educators with whom he worked changed the "what" (curriculum), the "how" (classroom interaction), and the structure of power distribution in the education system.

Poverty and Social Issues

Very few classroom-based studies have addressed the effects of poverty brought about by colonization as an aspect of Indigenous education. Rita Bouvier (2001) discusses the impact of poverty on educational programming for children who attend inner-city schools. She emphasizes the importance of additional funding received by community schools in impoverished areas: a necessary initiative if social justice is to be achieved.

At the classroom level, Linda Goulet (2001), Jeff Orr, John Jerome Paul, and Sharon Paul (2002), and Joanne Tompkins (1998) have found that effect-ive teachers of Indigenous students deal with issues of poverty. Tompkins (1998, 49) states that positive results were achieved by implementing two interconnected streams of school change in a northern Inuit school: changes dealing with Indigenous language and culture and those dealing with "poverty and despair." In urban schools, LaVina Gillespie and Agnes Grant (2001) and Celia Haig-Brown et al. (1997) found that attendance was an ongoing issue because of social problems such as poverty and addictions, which played a significant role in students' lives. In their field of study, Haig-Brown et al. (1997) found that school staff were constantly trying to find the balance be-tween teaching for healthy lifestyles and teaching academics. Mi'kmaw teach-ers in Jeff Orr, John Jerome Paul, and Sharon Paul's (2002, 348) study addressed personal problems faced by students by sharing stories from their lives and encouraging students to engage in conversations "supportive of their own struggles and concerns." They used curriculum content to teach about social issues, such as alcohol and drug abuse, that were affecting their community.

The Complexity of Indigenous Education

The modern era of Indigenous education began with an emphasis on curricu-lum adaptation and adjustment in methods of teaching. Cultural programming needed to include contemporary Indigenous issues as well as traditional practices and history. More recent research has included the examination of socio-historical factors, illuminating the complexity of teaching Indigenous students effectively.

Successful Indigenous teachers use the Indigenous language and their cultural knowledge to build classroom relationships that encourage children to express themselves in culturally responsive ways. Successful non-Indigenous teachers bring culture into the classroom in a way that shows respect and encourages children to value the current culture and learn about past traditions. Both view Indigenous cultures as rich, vibrant, and diverse.

Effective teachers also deal with the results of colonization in their classroom. They attend to issues of poverty, address personal problems, and incorporate social issues into the curriculum. Historical, colonial, and authoritarian relationships are replaced with more equitable relationships in the classroom, in school decision making, and in the community. Community and context are integral to effectively teaching Indigenous students. Effective teachers view students, their families, and community members as contributing members of a learning community, not as outsiders.

Language, culture, social conditions, power relationships, the child, and the teacher, as well as the history of schooling, all interact and influence actions in the classroom. The education of Indigenous children, and indeed all children, requires a more comprehensive view of life in its totality. Culture, education, social development, and economic self-determination have to be combined with practices that challenge racism and colonialism in all its forms.

The above review is based primarily on research into school programs and classroom practice. Other research is recognizing the value of indigeneity at all levels of education. Many Indigenous scholars (see, for example, Battiste 2002, 2013; Smith 1999; Swisher and Tippeconnic 1999) have critiqued Western knowledge systems and are exploring concepts of Indigenous research that articulate principles of Indigenous epistemology that have the potential to support educational developments in the classroom. In addition, teachers can draw ideas from authors such as Kathleen Absolon (2011), Margaret Kovach (2009), and Shawn Wilson (2008) who have gathered stories of Indigenous researchers' methods to articulate principles of Indigenous knowledge systems and ways of coming to know.

As this chapter illustrates, teachers can make changes in their practice to improve education for Indigenous students. In this book, we begin our narrative by situating Indigenous education in the history of colonization, which continues to impact the realities of schooling. We combine Linda's research on effective teachers with Keith's educational experience and Nehinuw knowledge and understanding to help us think about how we can improve teaching and learning. We use various teacher narratives to illustrate this Indigenous understanding in practice. The path forward in Indigenous education is coming into focus. We hope this book can contribute to our growing understanding of Indigenous pedagogies in the reality of classroom practice.

Where We've Been: Sociohistorical Realities

The history of Canada situates Indigenous people in a unique context compared to the rest of the population. As teachers, if we do not know something of our colonial past, it is difficult for us to understand the issues facing Indigenous peoples and students in our classrooms. The cultural strengths of Indigenous students are too often ignored or problematized in education; students, parents, leaders, or the general community are blamed for the poor success rate of Indigenous students in schools, when, in fact, it is these very people who are struggling to resist and deal with the legacy of colonization. The social problems facing First Nations, Métis, and Inuit peoples in this country are embedded in our history, our decisions, and the unequal distribution of resources. These complex issues require thoughtful, innovative, collaborative solutions.

On the Ground

As teachers, we need to deal to the best of our ability with the effects of colonization as they present themselves in ourselves, our classrooms, and our students. Classrooms are microcosms of the broader community and society. Children and teachers bring their histories and lives outside school with them into the classroom. Indigenous students bring a wide variety of cultural strengths since there is great diversity in Indigenous communities. Some Indigenous students have the family, community, and cultural resources to support them as they encounter life's problems. Unfortunately, because of colonization and ongoing racism and sexism, the poverty endured by many Indigenous families and communities means that many students do not have access to adequate support and resources. Thus, teachers need to be prepared to assist students who may be struggling with social problems in their lives.

Throughout this book, we illustrate the topic of each chapter with a case study that presents the subject from a teacher's point of view. Each of these case studies represents the teacher's experience in his or her particular teaching context. As they admit in their stories, these teachers, like all humans, are not perfect. We may not agree with all of the approaches, but they do provide us with a picture of what is possible, on the ground, in the classroom, and in our work with Indigenous students.

In the following case study, Anne Dorion describes her work with students who are facing tremendous challenges in their lives.

Good Kids with Bad Problems

Anne Dorion

Anne is Cree, fluent in the language. In her long teaching career spanning most grade levels, she has often been given the most "difficult" students and classes. She has worked in alternative high school programs and is currently teaching middle years. When asked what to say about her, she commented, "Focus on the students. The less said about me, the better."

In teacher training, we were taught to teach the curriculum to children. Instead, I found it more effective to teach children about themselves and their place in the world by using the curriculum, with some methods not exactly found there.

In the second year of my teacher training, I volunteered at a school to field test a reading program in a Grade 5 class. While I was there, I set up student-teacher "conferences." I taped a schedule to the classroom door and invited students to sign up. I explained that we would just sit in a private spot and talk, and I would mostly listen. I tried to arrange a private space, but the only place that was offered was the resource room, and the teacher had students in during the time I had available. After the first week, the schedule was still blank. The following Monday, I encouraged the students to fill in a spot, reassuring them that our talks would be strictly confidential. The next day, Mary's name was on the schedule [all

Anne Dorion and Jaycee Misponas, Grade 7, Churchill High School, LaRonge.
Photo by Linda Goulet.

student names used in this book are pseudonyms]. At the appointed time,
I invited her to meet me on the second floor stairwell.

Mary was a quiet, overweight girl, uncertain about our meeting. I
promised her that everything she said would be confidential. She said that
she was worried about her weight and that the other students were starting
to make fun of her. I practised the suggested techniques of listening to
make sure she knew she was heard. I offered no advice. I just let her talk.
After about five minutes, she started to talk about her home and the family
problems she was experiencing. Fifteen minutes went by too quickly. I
thanked her for sharing her thoughts and experiences, because this would
help me become a better teacher. I praised her for her courage, and suggested she set up another meeting if she wanted. The next day, my
schedule for the week was completely full, and remained so until my
reading program was done.

About ten years later, I met Mary, who was now a young woman, in
the change room of a water slide park. She came over and asked shyly,
"Do you remember me?" I said, "Yes, of course. How can I possibly forget
you? You were the bravest student I ever met." She then asked if I had ever
told anyone about the things we had talked about. I said no, because I had

promised her I would never disclose anything. She said, "You can now," and she hugged me. She taught me the power of trust.

For my internship, I made it a priority to get to know the students in the junior high school where I was doing my practicum. I found the best opportunity was during recess supervision. I learned the students' names, the names of their siblings, parents, and other relatives. They were eager to talk about anything as long as someone older was listening and not judging. After a couple of weeks, I always had several students walking around with me in the school yard during recess and lunch supervision.

A boy in Grade 8 started walking with me during recess. One day I asked him if there was something he wanted to talk about. He said that he was being bullied because he was so small. I told him he could help me supervise anytime I was outside or in the hallway. I also told him a big whopping lie. I said that one day he would spurt up and be taller than any of the kids who were harassing him, to just be patient, and not to try to get even. I felt like I had to be a merchant of hope.

For the next few days I agonized over this lie. It was a big one. His parents were both short; his father was shorter than me. His mother was even tinier. This is the first time I remember praying as an adult, invoking God to help me out, to find the long-lost tall genes in his family, to not make a liar out of me.

I saw this boy again when he was eighteen. When I stood up to shake his hand, my forehead was at his chest. He told his friends that I used to be his teacher. In fact, I had not taught him one single class.

I did not tell another lie like that until a decade later, to Brian, an obese, Grade 5 bully. I made a home visit to follow up on a disciplinary matter. When I knocked on the door, his mother was screaming obscenities and threats at him. When she opened the door, her manner changed instantly. In the kitchen, several people were sitting around eating pizza and drinking beer. I was invited in, introduced as Brian's teacher, and offered a beer. I told her that I didn't drink but I would accept a piece of pizza. I stayed and visited for about half an hour, and left after checking on Brian.

The next day I took him aside and let him talk freely. He said he hated being fat and all the kids were making fun of him all the time. I told him that he would need all that extra padding because soon he would start getting taller and he would lose it all when he started playing volleyball and basketball. He didn't stop bullying right away, but by the end of the school year he had friends and was doing well in his grades. I still see him around. He is tall, thin, and athletic. He has many friends, a cheerful disposition, and has graduated from Grade 12.

From these two students I learned the power of belief.

I do not recommend this method. It's very tricky. It's awfully stressful. And it is seen to be unprofessional …

Almost immediately upon becoming a teacher, I encountered two serious problems: fetal alcohol spectrum and substance exposure disorders, and the impact of abuse and neglect. It broke my heart. I was so unprepared. I was superbly trained to teach the curriculum, but my exceptional education classes had merely scratched the surface of these issues.

Kathy would fly into destructive rages, intentionally injuring herself and others. The first few times she raged, I pinned her down in the classroom, then removed her to the hallway. In my desperation I would just hold her, controlling my breath and staying as calm as I could. Then I would tell her I loved her and cared about her, and ask her to breathe with me. Eventually she would settle down, and I would invite her to come back into class when she was ready. She has grown up now. She came to see me when she was expecting her first baby, and told me that she neither smoked nor drank because she wanted her baby to be healthy. She taught me that I needed to learn to love my students unconditionally.

Another student taught me that there are limits to what I can do as a teacher. Rosie was twelve. She was very angry with me for getting her into protective care before the school year was over. She said, "I thought you were my friend!" I told her, "I am not your friend. I am much more than that. I am your teacher. That is why I do what I do."

She informed me when school started again that she was returning to her family, but that she'd had a good summer despite my having had her put into a foster home, "like a jail." I arranged for her to be placed back into care for Friday after school, then I left town for the weekend, having been promised that she would be picked up from school. Instead, she went and stayed with a friend for the weekend. On Monday morning, the school social worker met me at the front door, and told me, "Anne, you did everything you could do. Sometimes these things are outside of your control." Rosie had burned to death in a house fire on Saturday.

I cried and raged against the child welfare system and the family at first. I was horrible. And for a few days, everyone stayed out of my way. It was hard to see the wisdom in my colleague's words, but I eventually realized that I could not raise my students safely to adulthood, although there were times when I tried.

These two problems are ones I struggled with for a long time. I searched for different ways to help children with severe learning and behaviour difficulties. I read the literature, took professional development courses, and tried various classroom and teaching strategies, arranged for professionals to test my students, and used school and outside resources whenever I could. I didn't do this all in my first year. It took me two decades to adequately prepare myself, and I'm still learning.

At mid-career I became overwhelmed by the demands of teaching and the constant roadblocks in helping students deal with their challenges. I had been offered and was contemplating a lucrative contract: an offer of twice my teaching salary and no students. Then I came across a Sufi teaching story and decided to take a teaching mission retreat. I left my first teacher meditation retreat with a written mission statement and an understanding that establishing a personal relationship (reaching the heart) is what allows real learning (teaching the mind) to take place. There were many times I seriously considered leaving the teaching profession. Then I would reread the year's mission statement taped to the top of my desk. And I would stay.

My most profound insight into the critical need for teacher relation-ships with students and their families came after my first year of teaching. One of my brightest and most delightful students committed suicide. I was one of the first people her mother called, so that I wouldn't have to hear it on the news. She thanked me for having taught her daughter, and told me that she knew her daughter had loved being in my class. She told me not to blame myself for not seeing the signs, because her family hadn't seen them either. This released me from soul-searching my decision to become a teacher.

It also gave me permission to try anything to reach the children and to help them cope with their problems: hugging (despite policy), inviting myself into their homes, dropping off food packages, feeding them in class, taking them on a variety of wild excursions (like the garbage dump and the symphony), buying clothes or shoes and gifts when I could afford it, [doing] breathing and relaxation exercises, meditation, skiing and hiking, being in nature, using ridiculous humour, trying all kinds of science experiments from any grade level, volunteering and service to others, treating cuts and sprains, swinging and sliding with them in the school yard, showing up at weddings, wakes, and funerals. [I apologized] to a student in front of the whole class when I made a mistake or when I had been annoyed and harried, showing them that their teacher was human.

Over the years, students have told me the things they remembered of me as their teacher. I listened, I helped them in some way, I made school fun even though they had to work hard, and they felt safe with me. Always, usually on the first day of school, a student will ask me, "Do you drink?" or "Do you do drugs?" My answer is NO. And the rest of the students then visibly relax because they know our classroom will be a safe place.

Extracurricular activities cost money, [things] like learning to use chopsticks in a Vietnamese restaurant, having a bowling and pizza afternoon for hard work and results, or baking birthday cakes for each student. At first this money came out of my own pocket. Then I discovered the art of asking. I found that most everyone was happy to donate or give a big discount for activities for children and youth. Most parents could afford a little bit for classroom parties or tickets. The students also learned to fundraise for a purpose, not just for themselves, but for community events and tragedies. They also learned to cook and bake for other children who were hungry.

When students were misbehaving or not attending, I found that besides calling to let families know about their children's successes, the most powerful tool in my teaching arsenal was the dreaded home visit. Initially, it was very time-consuming to establish these connections, but once I made positive contact, the payoff was immediate and long term. I still have these contacts, and am regarded as a family friend who is a teacher. I also know who to call if I need information on anything going on in the community. Parents have called me to find out where their kids are, or to ask me for advice on parenting issues, or just to have someone who will listen to their problems.

I still do what I decided was important to do at the beginning of my life as a teacher – getting to know my students and their families, seeing past their behaviours to the pain and suffering they have experienced, the neglect and abuse, the broken promises, their desire for material things in the midst of their poverty, but most importantly, validating their spiritual yearnings and searching for the meaning to their struggles. Listening, mostly; encouraging, often; reassuring, continuously; and constantly experimenting with different strategies to reach them. Because with what most children are facing, what do I have to lose?

At the start of my teaching career, a veteran teacher shared this with me: *Deal with your own issues before you try to help students with theirs.*

I took these words into my heart and proceeded on a long journey of trying to become a good human being. I pray and meditate to find the calm within myself so I can share it with those around me. As I enter the end of my teaching life, I still sing the Gayatri mantra on my way to work: *Goddess, help me be a righteous human being today.* She is, after all, the Goddess of Education.

I very rarely have classroom management problems – usually only at the beginning of the school year. I ritually ask my students why they are so good, and they consistently answer "because you love us." Students can teach humility to the teacher within.

If anyone cared to ask me the important things I have learned about working with good kids with bad problems, [I would tell them] this:

1. Make your classroom and your school a safe place.
2. Show your students that they are lovable and loved and valued.
3. Get an understanding of the world in which they live.
4. Help them meet their physical, social, spiritual, and emotional needs in whatever way you have open to you.
5. Help them believe that they have within themselves the power to rise above their present existence.
6. Be prepared to make mistakes, learn from them, and never, ever give up.
7. Grow big ears.
8. Then you can teach.

Certainly, I have made a lot of mistakes. And I am not always a pleasant person to be around. I get frustrated and discouraged. I still regularly fall foul of the school rules and policies. Sometimes my job has been in jeopardy. But I know that I am a good teacher, that I've done the best I could, and held to what I believe is in the best interest of my students.

The greatest truth I have found as a classroom teacher is that [of] the more than 6 billion people on earth, I have only to make a difference in the life of one. Otherwise, why are all these other people here? Hopefully, this thought may help liberate us from our society's and our own expectations that WE have to fix all the problems.

Anne's is a story of heartbreak, hope, and triumph – the realities of a teacher's life. Her story reminds us that teaching is a human act and a holistic endeavour that encompasses the social, spiritual, and emotional aspects of us and our surroundings, in addition to the intellectual and physical. Anne emphasizes the importance of compassion and caring in teaching. As a teacher, she is aware of and responds to the physical, social, and emotional stressors caused by the colonial history and ongoing oppression of Indigenous peoples. *Kitimagesihin* is a Nehinuw generic word that approximates the English concept of poverty. While the English word *poverty* tends to focus more on the physical and material conditions, *kitimagisihin* places more emphasis on the socio-emotional aspects. *Kitimagenimew* is used when one expresses compassion for others. It is the empathetic and sympathetic acknowledgment and response to the emotional or physical stress of another, and includes the physical, emotional, social, cultural, and psychological realms of a person. A person may have stress due to socio-psychological or emotional abuse, or they may be crippled in some way, or lack sufficient food, clothing, or shelter. Being compassionate and giving special care and attention to others who are under stress is an important Nehinuw value.

In addition to compassion, Anne's story reminds us of the importance of *ńdootumowin,* or, listening in teaching, especially listening without judgment. She describes her work in a way that presents the reality faced by some of her students, but her approach of "the heart is the way to the head" leaves us with a sense of hope and belief in the enduring nature of the human spirit.

As teachers, we have a role to play in supporting students as they deal with life's problems. To create solutions, we need to know something of our history so that we can overcome societal stereotypes of Indigenous peoples. When we see children suffering or acting out in our classes, it can become too easy to blame the victim – the student, the families, the community, the leadership, the culture – when, in fact, it is those very people who are struggling to resist and deal with the legacy of colonization. What follows is a brief introduction to some of the structural conditions that thwart simple or easy resolutions to social issues in Indigenous communities.

The History of Canadian Indigenous-White Relations

From an Indigenous perspective, the history of Canada has too often been marked by conquest, mortality, displacement, and oppression. It wasn't always so. The Royal Commission on Aboriginal Peoples (RCAP) (1996) identifies four different stages of European-Indigenous history, the first being the separate development of distinct peoples in Europe and North America. The second stage began when Europeans came to Canada and were reliant on Indigenous peoples for survival. For a long time, the relationship between the Indigenous peoples and newcomers was marked by trade, exchange, and alliances, and was of mutual benefit to both peoples. Many European men chose to leave their communities to live with and become a part of Indigenous communities (Saul 2008). Indigenous trappers, fishers, and hunters were pivotal participants in the fur industry that laid the economic foundation of Canada. Indigenous women contributed their labour (Iseke-Barnes 2009), especially their knowledge and skills of food preparation and clothing production to make survival possible for those involved in the fur trade (Farrell-Racette 2005). Unfortunately for our country, this time of cooperation was followed by a period of displacement, assimilation, and decimation of Indigenous peoples in the global context of European powers building imperialist empires. The Indigenous peoples in many parts of the world were subject to the process of colonization with its inherent ideology of Eurocentrism, patriarchy, and racism, and acts of conquest and oppression. In eastern Canada, partnerships deteriorated after the wars with the United States, when agreements among the British and their Indigenous allies were broken. In the West, the harshest colonial practices were implemented following the Indigenous resistance movements in 1869 and in 1885, when leaders who were fighting for the survival of their peoples were jailed and killed. In Manitoba, Elzear Goulet was stoned to death, and in Saskatchewan Métis leader Louis Riel was hanged, along with Cree and Nakota warriors Kahpaypamahchukways (Wandering Spirit), Manchoose (Bad Arrow), Nahpase (Iron Body), Apischakoos (Little Bear), Kitahwahken (Miserable Man), Pahpahmekeesik (Walking the Sky), Itka (Crooked Leg), and Waywahnitch (Man without Blood) in the largest mass hanging in Canadian history (Chaput 2005; Saskatchewan Indian 1972). Today, as we have historically, Indigenous peoples continue to resist oppression and deal with the legacy of past colonial practices while looking towards the fourth stage of Indigenous and settler relationships in Canada: that of restructuring relationships through negotiation and renewal (RCAP 1996).

Colonization

Linda Tuhiwai Smith (1999), a Māori scholar, identifies colonization as the process that facilitated the economic, political, and cultural expansion of European power and control by subjugating Indigenous populations. Historians who have presented Canadian history in terms of colonial expansion from an Indigenous perspective include authors such as Howard Adams (1989), a Métis from Saskatchewan, and Daniel Paul (1993), a Mi'kmaw from Nova Scotia. These authors have described the devastation and documented the complex system of European colonization in Canada that used, among other things, trade and military power combined with Eurocentrism and racism to secure the resources of the Indigenous peoples of Canada. The process of colonization continued with the enactment of colonial policies and practices by the federal and provincial governments (Episkenew 2009). The resistance of Indigenous peoples to colonization took many forms, including armed struggle, political movements for self-determination (Adams 1989; Paul 1993), court challenges (Smith 1999), and narratives that asserted their identity and their own peoples' histories (Episkenew 2009; LaRocque 2010; Said 1993).

The Ideology of Colonization

Colonization was and still is based on the ideologies of Eurocentrism and racism. In practice, the two ideologies are intertwined: Eurocentrism advocates and reinforces superiority by postulating that European language, knowledge systems, and culture are superior, scientific, and civilized (Smith 2000), while racism propagates inferiority. This binary relationship of Eurocentrism with the notion of "Other" (Said 1978) constructs other peoples as different and separate from Europeans and thus not subject to the same treatment and laws. In the past, Europeans stereotyped the Indigenous peoples of the Americas as "wild, promiscuous, propertyless, and lawless" or as "the noble savage who lived with natural law but without government, husbandry, and much else" (Youngblood Henderson 2000, 68). James [Sákéj] Youngblood Henderson states that European thinkers ignored empirical evidence that did not reinforce their constructed stereotype of Indigenous peoples. For example, Europeans were seen as the most civilized, with the most highly developed forms of law and governance, and the fact that Indigenous peoples also had highly developed forms of democratic governance, such as the Mi'kmaw or Iroquoian confederacy, was ignored or trivialized (Paul 1993). On the other hand, the Indigenous peoples were appalled by the extent of the poverty in European society, where people did not look after one another, especially those who were suffering.

Racism, the other aspect of the ideology of colonization, is defined by Louise Derman-Sparks and Carol Brunson Phillips (1997, 2) as a "system of economic, political, social, and cultural relations that ensures that one racial group has and maintains power and privilege over all others in all aspects of life"; it is a "system of beliefs, attitudes, and symbols constructed and legitimized by those with political and cultural power." In her work, Roxanna Ng (1993, 51) emphasizes the intersection of race, class, and gender in systemic oppression and defines racism and sexism as "systems of domination and subordination that have developed over time as taken-for-granted societal features." She states that racist and sexist attitudes and practices develop as

> systems of oppression and inequality based on the ideology of the superiority of one race and/or gender over another ... Systems of ideas and practices have been developed over time to justify and support the notion of superiority. These ideas become the premise on which societal norms and values are based, and the practices become the "normal" way of doing things. (52)

Racism as an ideology is enacted in the practices of our society that create opportunities and privileges for one group of people and oppress and deny freedoms and opportunities for other groups.

Both the discourse of superiority and inferiority and the material reality of military might and exploitive practices created a history of colonization throughout the world. The material conditions of poverty haunt the world to this day, and the ideology and structure of superiority based on racial or cultural difference continues to inform relationships among groups of people.

The Effects of Colonization on Indigenous Peoples

Colonization affected, and continues to affect, Indigenous people economically, politically, socially, emotionally, and spiritually. The loss of territory and land, and the depletion of resources such as buffalo and fish, wiped out the economic base of Indigenous societies, causing death and poverty (Adams 1989; Daschuk 2013; Paul 1993). Many Indigenous authors, such as Janice Acoose (1995), Howard Adams (1989), Maria Campbell (1973), Jo-Ann Episkenew (2009), Emma LaRocque (2010), and Linda Otway (2002), have documented the effects of historical and continuing societal, institutional, and personal racism on Indigenous peoples and community well-being (Canadian Council on Learning 2009). Indigenous peoples always have been active participants in the resistance against colonization and its inherent racist ideology (Adams 1989; Battiste 2000; Episkenew 2009; Graveline 1998; LaRocque 2010; McLeod 2002; Paul 1993; Stonechild 2002). Indigenous communities have begun to rebuild an economic base, with many examples of success across Canada, but the challenge of poverty remains a major issue.

During colonization, the governing and decision-making processes of the Indigenous peoples were suppressed, often by military force (Adams 1989), then replaced with a European model of governance (Paul 1993) where most decision making took place outside the community and authority was externally imposed. Colonial relationships were (and continue to be) marked by the abuse of power, with one side imposing its history, beliefs, and way of doing things and denigrating others' ways of being, thinking, and doing. Paternalistic views of Eurocentrism were evident where day-to-day decisions were made by Indian agents, conservation officers, priests, police officers, or other government agencies who believed they knew what was best for Indigenous peoples. Practices, beliefs, and the actions of Indigenous peoples were viewed through a Eurocentric lens, measured and judged using European values and norms. For example, by the 1950s, traditional herbalists and medicine people who healed the sick in Cumberland House were systematically displaced and disparaged by health practitioners, priests, police, and others in authority. People involved in traditional potlatches in British Columbia were identified, prosecuted, and jailed, with some of their most treasured spiritual artifacts ending up in the possession of the same judge who jailed them (Shein and Wheeler 1975). Through resistance and the perseverance of Indigenous peoples, traditional practices of spirituality and healing were carried on, hidden from the authorities, but much knowledge and self-reliance was lost through colonization. Restrictive government laws, policies, and actions took place in all realms of Indigenous life (Episkenew 2009) resulting in the loss of populations, land, economy, governance, intergenerational connections, knowledge, and language. Today, Indigenous people struggle to regain their democratic rights through the development of self-determination, but it is a slow process because in so many communities, capacities were decimated.

It is a testament to the strength of Indigenous peoples that they survived the onslaught of colonization, but survival was not without its toll. While racism is a social construct existing in societal and institutional structures, it is also an internalized condition (Miller Cleary and Peacock 1998). Racism affects individuals' belief systems. It can influence perceptions of personal and cultural worth and the view of a person's capabilities and those of their peoples (Acoose 1995; Adams 1989; Goulet, Episkenew, et al. 2009). The turmoil caused by colonization is enacted in personal and social problems of the community and can be handed down from one generation to the next (Silver et al. 2002).

Ongoing Racism

Because racism is a system embedded in our society, it occurs in different forms that coexist, interact, and reinforce one another (Derman-Sparks and Brunson Phillips 1997). For purposes of analysis, it is useful to differentiate how the forms of racism are enacted at societal, institutional, and personal levels.

Societal forms of racism occur at the level of the whole society – for example, when laws are passed that deny rights to or restrict the freedom of one particular group of people. The past Indian Act in Canada is one example of a racist law: it denied Indian status to women who married men who were not designated as Indians under the Act, and granted Indian status to women (including settler women) who married Indians. Societal racism is also inherent in widely held belief systems that promote the superiority of one group over another. Although writings of racial superiority are not as common today as they were in the past, authors like Thomas Flanagan (2000) continue to use Eurocentric value systems, beliefs, and arguments to analyze the issues of Indigenous peoples.

Personal racism occurs in interpersonal contacts when one's culture, language, or appearance is denigrated. Although all racist slurs are harmful to any individual when directed towards a group of people, individual acts of racism carry more weight when they are embedded in a history and ideology of racism (Derman-Sparks and Brunson Phillips 1997). For example, when an Indigenous student is called a "dirty Indian" in high school (St. Denis and Hampton 2002; Silver et al. 2002), it is damaging because it calls to mind both the different power relations among Indigenous and non-Indigenous students and denigrating stereotypes of Indian peoples. "Dirty whiteman," though also offensive, does not have the same weight or history reinforcing it.

Today, one of the most pervasive types of racism is that which occurs in our institutions (Derman-Sparks and Brunson Phillips 1997). Institutions organize people so that through collective action, services are delivered to people in our society. When these services are delivered in ways that exclude or do not meet the needs of racially labelled groups, the institution, in effect, becomes racist. Although racism in institutions can be overt, such as blatant racist attitudes of those who hold power, more often it is covert, as when actions of those in power in effect discriminate against Indigenous peoples. Examples of the extremes of institutional racism abound in the judicial system in Canada from the *Donald Marshall* case in Nova Scotia, where an innocent man was jailed based on the prejudicial attitudes of the police (Harris 1990), to the *Betty Osborne* case in The Pas, where although people had information regarding the perpetrators of her murder, they remained silent with no prosecution for over fifteen years (Priest 1989), to the freezing death of Neil Stonechild in Saskatoon after he was last seen in a police car (Wright 2004), to the lack of sentencing for three white males in their twenties who sexually assaulted a fourteen-year-old Saulteaux girl (McNinch 2009). Too often laws and policies are implemented that are not intended to discriminate against a particular group, but when carried out in practice, in effect do result in discrimination. The lack of attention in the past of police forces to the murdered and missing Indigenous women in Canada is one example. The following describes how institutional racism takes place in schools.

Institutional Racism in Schooling

The failure of the school system to meet the needs of Indigenous students is a form of institutional racism. There are many factors that lead to this failure, such as the chronic, systemic underfunding of First Nations schools (Bell et al. 2004; Carr-Stewart 2010), teacher beliefs and expectations (Sterzuk 2009), and discriminatory practices (Silver et al. 2002); however, only staffing, including teacher beliefs, curriculum materials, and learning processes, are addressed here.

The teaching staffs in Canadian public schools remain predominantly white and middle-class. Colonization affects both the colonizer and the colonized. Eurocentric beliefs and general beliefs of superiority infuse our society and our institutions so that Euro-Canadian teachers are often blind to their own unearned opportunities that come from being white in our society (MacIntosh 1998). Many Euro-Canadian teachers are not prepared to examine their white racial identity and the privilege that confirms their position of power in our society, or acknowledge the effects of our colonial history on Indigenous peoples (Schick and St. Denis 2003). White teachers often have a deep resistance to discussing racialization in education, because it challenges positive constructions of their own identities as good people who will help others (Dion 2009). Carol Schick and Verna St. Denis (2003, 306) state, "The effects of racialization are considered beyond discussion, and conversations about it are therefore silenced, or at the very least not considered for polite company." Without acknowledging our colonial past and the ongoing racism that infuses our beliefs and practices in education, it remains all too easy to fault Indigenous students or their families rather than critically examining our classroom and school practices that contribute to the lack of Indigenous student success (Bishop et al. 2006).

Racism is sometimes expressed overtly in staff room comments of denigration or even hatred (Hesch 1995). More covertly, some teachers' practice reflects a belief that the culture of Indigenous children is inferior (Miller Cleary and Peacock 1998; Silver et al. 2002; Sterzuk 2009). Others are simply unaware of differences in cultural ways of being and of the need to adjust their teaching patterns. For example, some Indigenous children require more time to think about what they will say before responding to the teacher's question (Huff 1997; Fayant et al. 2010). School practices are also influenced by teacher attitudes when white administrators see interracial student conflicts from a non-Indigenous perspective and ignore the possibility of the role of racism in the incident, resulting in an imbalance in discipline, or suspensions for the Indigenous students (Farrell-Racette et al. 1996; Silver et al. 2002).

Curricula remain problematic in teaching Indigenous students. Mainstream academic knowledge, used as a basis for the development of curriculum materials for schools, seldom recognizes or identifies the inherent bias, assumptions, perspectives, and points of view that have victimized people of colour while normalizing identities of whiteness. James Banks (1996) sees curriculum as representing the national identity with its selective memory loss of the racist history of North America, privileging one perspective of knowledge and trivializing or excluding others. Decisions regarding curricula are made by those in power positions that reflect their perspective. Western modes of thought remain dominant in the curriculum (Sammel 2009), with little recognition for diverse systems of knowledge (Battiste 2005). The structure and learning of content privileges certain forms of knowledge, as when rationalism is elevated above other ways of knowing (Graveline 1998). Programs of learning are often linear and sequentially based (Hesch 1995), ignoring the possibility that there may be other ways of learning (e.g., circular or holistic) (Absolon 2011; Graveline 1998; Wilson 2008).

The Effects of Colonization and Ongoing Racism in Education

In considering Indigenous education, one cannot ignore the impact of past colonial practices on Indigenous peoples. Schooling had serious impacts on Indigenous peoples because it disrupted intergenerational connections (Binda 2001; Kirkness 1992; Milloy 1999) needed for cultural retention and renewal. Residential and industrial schools, with their isolation and imposition of a foreign language, culture, and ideology, were especially damaging. Children were taken from their parents, families, and communities and separated by gender from their siblings. In cultures that emphasize a relational view of the world, the fracturing of social, emotional, physical, intellectual, and spiritual connections are devastating. Children were removed from the social network that taught them how to relate to one another, from the stories that taught values, the language with its embedded world view, the cultural activities on the land that shaped character, the Indigenous knowledge of their peoples, and the belief systems and ceremonies that give a child faith in the future. The residential schools were harsh examples of "cognitive imperialism" (Battiste 2000): only Western knowledge and ways of learning were deemed worthy. Students were taught that the cultural and spiritual practices and beliefs of their families and people were not only wrong but "pagan," which meant that all of them would be "going to hell" – scary thoughts for little children (Bea Lavallee in Elders' Roundtable 2002, 111). The forced isolation and imposition of a foreign language, culture, and ideology often left individuals without a sense of who they were in the world.

The schools for Indigenous students were hierarchical in their structure, with curriculum-making agencies far removed the students they served. Communities, families, and parents did not have any authority over what or how their children were taught. Parents were seldom allowed to visit their children in residential schools. In the classroom, teaching was an authoritarian, one-way process. These schools had a history of demanding submission to authority that brought about learned irresponsibility among the children in their care. Cree educator Verna Kirkness (1992) states that the legacy of the residential schools was one of cultural conflict, alienation, poor self-concept, and a lack of preparedness for independence, jobs, and life in general. Many Métis students also attended residential schools. Others attended provincial schools, where they faced the denigration of their peoples, history, heroes, language, and themselves. One of our older Métis friends who spoke only Cree as a child now cannot speak the language due to the mental block she has, instilled by the severe punishment she received for speaking Cree and humiliation she felt from students and teachers alike at the town school she attended.

Indigenous resistance to colonial practices was vigorous as Indigenous leaders and community members petitioned governments for change and formed new political organizations to challenge colonial practices (McLeod 2002; Stonechild 2002). The struggle for a quality education is also evident in the oral stories of individual and political acts of resistance. A Cree Métis father whose son attended a school operated by the church was worried because his young son was not home when he got in from work one night. He found his son at school, locked in a room, crying because he was being punished for speaking Cree (Bev Cheechoo, personal communication with author). After admonishing the nun responsible, the father began a letter-writing campaign to the provincial government regarding the need for parental authority over education. In southern Saskatchewan, a group of Saulteaux women, including the wife of the chief, handcuffed themselves together to blockade the highway on which the Minister of Indian Affairs was travelling, to protest the lack of funding for education on their reserve (Elder Clara Pasqua, personal communication with author).

The hierarchical structure of education continues to the present with the norms of unequal power relations and competitive individualism that can result in inequities. Although curricula decisions continue to be made by centralized agencies, there is now some input by Indigenous peoples. But as teachers graduate from education programs that emphasize their role as decision makers, many continue to determine the "what" and "how" of teaching with very little thought of how power could or should be distributed or shared with students in the class.

Current racism in schooling has a serious impact on the identity of Indigenous and white students alike. Many white students do not see themselves as having a culture because it is the norm in their daily lives, outside and in school. Carol Schick and Verna St. Denis (2005, 300) state:

> Whiteness operates so that white teachers and students benefit simultaneously from two seemingly contradictory processes. First, dominant cultural practices are always "on," always the standard or fallback position for "the way things are done." This gives enormous privilege to those whose histories, ethnic backgrounds, social class, family assumptions, and personal knowledge are in line with these dominant practices. Second, the fact that these practices are not the norm for everyone and that one's achievements may be at the expense of others is often an invisible reality for privileged groups.

The overall higher levels of achievement of white students on standardized tests scores, designed by white educators, serve to reinforce beliefs of superiority in white students. Because institutional racism in schools is structural and the norm, it is invisible to students, so white students come to believe that their success is due to their own efforts and abilities.

Indigenous students who experience success at school sometimes do so at a price. Robert Bennett (1997) tells of his experiences in the school system, where he felt that he had to suppress his Indigenous identity in order to succeed. Even his grandmother realized this contradiction, which is evidence of the intergenerational effects of past schooling practices. When asked why she did not teach him Lakota, she responded that English was important in school and she did not want the other kids to make fun of him, as they did of her.

When Indigenous students do experience racism in schools, some resist the oppression. In a study conducted in inner-city schools in Winnipeg, Jim Silver et al. (2002) found that some students refused to accept the racism in school, and thus rejected the educational process and didn't succeed in their studies. Those who fought racial slurs were labelled troublemakers. They were subject to disciplinary measures, often suspension from school. Other students, unprepared to pay the price of the humiliation and cultural denigration they felt in school, simply dropped out. Indigenous resistance to racism in schools continues to be countered by a lack of appropriate response on the part of school staffs. A recent incident in an urban high school illustrates this. An Indigenous teenage girl was being teased by her white male peers. The teasing was vicious, sexually explicit, racially charged, and ongoing. The girl became so distraught by the constant attack on her identity and fear of escalating violence towards her that she considered suicide. Her parents found out and met with the school staff, who were made aware of the serious nature of the boys' actions. The school assured the parents that the behaviour would not be tolerated. Yet when the incidents continued, even in the presence of a classroom teacher, they were ignored by the school. The parents, both professionals, removed their daughter from the school to homeschool her. Unlike many others without access to resources, these Indigenous parents were fortunate enough to have other professionals help them deal with the school and support their daughter, yet the school remained a barrier to the completion of their daughter's education and to her success as a young person.

Decolonization

Progress has been made since the call for Indian control of Indian education, not just in education but in society as a whole. The process of decolonization is gradually taking hold. Indigenous peoples are re-establishing their own authority from the local to the national level. There are now Indigenous peoples involved in decision making, even as cabinet ministers at the federal and provincial level. Changes are slowly being made to redress some of the injustices of the Indian Act while the Métis have achieved recognition in the Canadian constitution and won victories in court cases. Some land claims have been settled. There is a renaissance of Indigenous culture and traditional spiritual ceremonies in both reserve and urban communities. The Idle No More movement is serving as a grassroots call to action, particularly for young Indigenous peoples. Indigenous academics are challenging colonizing practices of knowledge construction in the academy (see, for example, Absolon 2011; Kovach 2009; Weenie 2009; Williams and Tanaka 2007; Wilson 2008). Educators are creating culturally based curriculum, changing institutionalized racial practices, and indigenizing education.

The process of decolonization has been slow and arduous. It is far from becoming the norm in Canadian society. However, as the late Elder Ken Goodwill said, "I have faith that we will prevail. We're Indians, we've always had to struggle" (personal communication with author). Gains have been made in Indigenous education but, at the same time, issues of dropout, poor attendance, and poor academic achievement indicate that further changes are needed in schools to provide quality education for Indigenous students. Verna St. Denis, Rita Bouvier, and Marie Battiste (1998, 75) report that policy initiatives in Indigenous education in Saskatchewan "have been impressive and sometimes bold," influencing change in all aspects of education from early childhood to university, including curriculum framework and policy development, funding support for program initiatives, and the establishment of partnerships; however, the "change envisioned by these initiatives has been slow and sometimes meets with resistance." The improvement of instruction at the classroom level remains an issue because, in spite of the glacial pace of decolonization, Indigenous students are achieving success with teachers who can and do make a difference. In a school achieving success with Indigenous students, one teacher stated, "[The teachers in this school] believe students *can* and *will* achieve what they need to do and what they set out to do. That optimism is a defining factor in this region *(Teacher at Chief Jimmy Bruneau School)*" (Fullford 2007, 308; emphasis in original).

3

What to Build Upon: Sociocultural Strengths

Culture is important in Indigenous education. Language and other cultural signs and symbols organize children's thought processes and establish how they view and interpret the world (Vygotsky 1986). Children learn in interaction with others and their environment. They interpret these interactions through a cultural lens because the social, physical, and individual past and current reality of each person and his or her environment are inherent in every interaction.

Recent research has documented how much language and culture influence the development of our brain and our thinking processes (Boroditsky 2011; Li 2009). Our thinking is directed, shaped, and supported by sources in our culture. Cognitive mediators are the tools used to assist and extend thinking, to make sense of the world, and to support memory.[1] They allow a person to have an understanding of the world that sense alone cannot provide, because mediators facilitate the "intermingling of 'direct, natural, phylogenetic' and 'indirect, cultural' aspects of experience" (Cole 1996, 119). A person can learn about fishing by doing it (using tools developed by previous generations), by reading about it (using a cultural sign system), or by talking to a fisher (using a person as a cognitive mediator). Sport fishing differs from fishing for sustenance or as way of making a living. The cultural practice of fishing shapes a person's concept of fishing, as does the source of learning – for example, studying fishing in a biology text or learning by doing it on the water with a more experienced person.

Some cultural forms tend to persist through time while other forms are created and recreated by new generations and different individuals. The particular culture of the Indigenous child is shaped by current and historical cultural norms and the practices of his or her family, by the community in which he or she lives, by the particular Indigenous nation to which he or she belongs, and by Indigenous people in general, the Canadian nation, and global cultural developments. Just as Canadian culture is continuously transforming, so too are Indigenous cultures. For example, fishing in northern Saskatchewan has changed culturally and historically from traditional spear fishing, to hook and scoop net fishing for sustenance and trade, to angling and other modes of domestic and commercial fishing, to catch-and-release sports fishing programs, and, finally, to an explosion of fish derbies for cars, cash, and other prizes. There are similar cultural influences among all Canadians, but differences do exist between how they affect settler Canadian and Indigenous peoples.

In this chapter, we present key concepts that illustrate the complexity of differences between English and Nehinuw thought. We begin with a story that both foreshadows themes in the book and showcases Nehinuw ways of being and doing. Lily McKay-Carriere describes a project that brought local Nehinuw culture and language to a school through a collaborative curriculum project among Elders, teachers, school staff, and community members.[2] Lily's story emphasizes the importance of the incorporation of Indigenous language and cultural practice in teaching. Underlying her description of the unique storytelling abilities of different Elders is the importance of the oral narrative and different Cree narrative structures to the Nehinuw. The story illustrates Indigenous ways of being and doing by introducing key Nehinuw concepts of social relationships, particularly *weechiseechigemitowin* (alliances for collaborative action), that involve interactive learning with each other. With colonization, Elders have often been ignored, but in Lily's story the knowledge of Elders is recognized and valued. We see shared leadership in action as those with expertise in the particular aspect of the task lead others. The direction and flow of the project changes as leadership shifts among participants.

In this type of shared leadership, we see the important concepts of self-determination and collectivity in action. Community members choose materials and make decisions regarding the curriculum. They do so by drawing on the expertise of those involved: the traditional knowledge of the Elders, the academic training of the language teachers, and the artistic skills of community members. Lily's story illustrates how teachers can work together with others *(weetutoskemitowin)* and draw on aspects of modern culture and technology to create culturally meaningful curricula, curricula that are in the language of the community and reflective of its history, world view, and thinking.

Decolonizing "Cree-atively" through Elders' Stories

Lily McKay-Carriere

Lily is Cree and a fluent speaker. She is the principal of the provincial school in her home community, where they implemented a bilingual Cree-English program for kindergarten to Grade 3. Since 1999, Lily has been part of a team of educators who have worked on Cree language preservation.

The inclusion of community Elders in curriculum brings education full circle to the students. Students need language and cultural links to help them understand where they come from in order to know where they are going. In partnership with the community, schools play a pivotal role in helping students meet success in language retention and in general.

Some of the Cree-ative collaborators with authors. *Front row:* Helen Sayies (teacher, developer), Leonard McKenzie (Elder, musician), Bertha McKay (teacher, developer, editor). *Back row:* Linda Goulet, Clifford Carriere (Elder, storyteller), Lily McKay-Carriere (researcher, coordinator), Sharise Rosteski (artist, illustrator), Keith Goulet. *Photo by Koonu Goulet.*

As the forces of modern culture and technology diminish the use of Indigenous languages, with many languages already becoming extinct, language rejuvenation and retention are critical issues for most Indigenous communities in Canada.

In her article "Canada's Aboriginal Languages," Mary Jane Norris (1998, 1) states: "During the past 100 years or more, nearly ten once flourishing [Aboriginal] languages have become extinct [in Canada]; at least a dozen are on the brink of extinction. When these languages vanish; they take with them unique ways of looking at the world, explaining the unknown and making sense of life." Long after their departure to the spirit world, we remember Elders for their stories. Through oral tradition, they have shared powerful messages that value our language and culture. From generation to generation, their stories continue to be passed on in our semi-remote community. Jackson was one of the best storytellers in our community: *e gee neeta achimot* (he was a remarkable story teller). He was the village favourite for telling nighttime stories. His tales about Weesagechak were particularly effective in putting children to sleep. His stories stirred the imagination with the underlying message of the need to respect others. Cheechigun had a remarkable memory for detail. He passed on history, survival knowledge, and genealogy, being adept at retelling what had been passed on to him: *e gee neeta tapachimot* (he was very good at retelling stories). Exactness was a necessity in his storytelling because the information he shared was of extreme importance. Soominis told stories that linked the Creator to day-to-day events. Her words created an understanding of interconnectedness to a spiritual source. Skew shared humorous stories that were mostly about the antics of her husband. Her stories were extremely entertaining, *e gee tapachimot* (retold many times). Laughter was easy in her home! By transmitting their knowledge to us, these Elders helped shape our identity through language and culture.

In my community, language loss is one of the many negative legacies of the demeaning process of colonization. Unless ongoing action is taken to reclaim Aboriginal languages in our communities and schools, hope for language revival in the next generation may disappear. Reversing language loss is a form of decolonization whereby Indigenous people bring back traditional cultural knowledge into the new society. It is an enormous task in terms of time, human capacity building, resource creation, and financial support.

Aboriginal languages are at the interface of cultural connectivity and Indigenous ways of knowing. Recently, I coordinated a research project of teachers, support staff, community Elders, and resource people, including local musicians and artists.[3] By tapping into the Indigenous ways of knowing in our community and harnessing that knowledge into teachable units, the Elders helped us expand our understanding of education. The Elders' gathering was reminiscent of storytellers from the past who taught through oral tradition while we listened. Our Elders embody Aboriginal knowledge with their rich life experiences, fluent Cree, and remembrances of stories, legends, traditions, and life on the land. The gathering proved to be the cornerstone for the project as the Elders' stories captivated the participants, who laughed and cried with them, and thanked them. The gathering of Elders created awareness of the impact of colonization and helped us as teachers understand that further action can lead to change. Said one school-based collaborator (March 2008), "I do realize how much we have lost our language and culture and how we need to give every effort to bring it back to our people." Since identity is integrally linked to culture and knowledge, it is necessary to reclaim Indigenous ways of knowing and secure knowledge that is endangered.

The stories of the local Elders were made into teacher/student-friendly units that Bilash (2004) calls "sequences." As part of a second-language acquisition method, the sequences incorporate activities that appeal to Howard Gardner's Multiple Intelligences (1993). The method uses a structured spiral curriculum of daily review and recycling of vocabulary in familiar and new contexts for five to fifteen minutes per day over an eight-to-ten-day span. For each Sequence, seven words are selected that are then generated into visuals, flash cards, games, songs, and activities in the Cree language. These resources are used not only to introduce the new content but also to practice, review, and use the vocabulary in fun ways. Various forms of carefully selected teacher-guided student engagement are required in the initial days. The students are then slowly weaned off the teacher guidance and are expected to create projects in pairs and as individuals as proof of learning.

Through their gift of story, the Elders helped us create classroom material while developing the intergenerational connection between Elder and child and passing on the gift of language and culture to students. One Elder told me, "When there is no language, the culture fails to be transmitted – the feeling, the language, the advice." Regarding the

Cree language, she also said, "*Kawina cheska pugicheek*" (Louisa Buck, February 2008), a quiet command for all of us not to give up. Encouragement from the Elder and many others gives us hope.

The collaboration with the Elders demonstrates the profound impact of culturally relevant curriculum on our students. Teachers are enabled to pass on traditional knowledge to a new generation. One example serves to illustrate this point. A moose was an easy association for these students and was linked to the moose hide in the beadwork Sequence. Yet, one teacher had to go into detail to explain the moose hide visual. Many of the students hadn't seen a moose hide stretched out on a frame (to scrape it in preparation for tanning) and some thought it was a trampoline! The teacher looked for a video clip on making moose hide. She also made a request for moose hide preparation to be done during Cultural Week, an annual event in our school to showcase Cree language and culture and to provide an opportunity for hands-on experiences. Simply put, moose hide tanning, once commonplace, is now a rare occurrence in our community. Fortunately, the preservation of that knowledge will be passed on through Sequence teachings. This traditional knowledge is now embedded in the curriculum.

By working with Elders, we created a rightful place for diversity. Linking the community and the school in decolonizing the curriculum is helping develop our cultural and language identity and build capacity within our community. We found local artists, singers, musicians, writers, coordinators, speakers, recorders, technicians, and editors to help us create our story sequences.

The sharing circle was utilized as a technique to share ideas or brainstorm solutions. On some days, it felt like we were operating at a Hollywood pace in a northern village. The incorporation of video, audio, and print was an enormous production, and the school-based collaborators were all at different learning places. In terms of training others, the experienced classroom teachers took a leadership role in the production. In several daily entries, the school-based collaborators reflected on the learning atmosphere. One teacher, who had been taught about the second-language instructional method of sequencing, in turn taught another team member. It was the true practice of our traditional Cree values whereby those with mastery helped others. For the school-based participants, collaborating with Elders was a new experience. Capturing the essence of stories meant careful attention to detail and listening to Elders at another level. Upon collaborating with an Elder, a school-based participant (2008) reflected:

> I did the first interview [to review the story sequence] with the Elder. She appreciates the effort we the teachers are doing in trying to save our language. I think she was a little surprised to see how much work can be done with one story. She only wished that work such as this was done a long time ago. I made the sequence with a lot of thought put into it. I wanted the vocabulary, pictures (visuals) and song to portray the life on a trapline as lived by a young girl. I wanted to make sure that I did justice to her story.

When local Elders agreed to collaborate with our school, their stories ultimately became classroom resources that we collectively call our own. By giving voice to our language and our people in the curriculum, we experienced a sense of balanced ownership for the school, community, and researchers. They are resources made for, by, and with the Cree people of our community.

The creation of the teaching material had to meet the expectations of the Elders and teachers. So, changes to sequences were made in response to Elder input at any given stage. Interaction between the researcher, Elders, and school-based Cree-ative Collaborators was central to the research method throughout the three-week summer project. A big challenge in our project was in finding or illustrating visuals for the sequences. Many of the visuals about the lived experiences are not common-place. Image searches for many of the *Ininee-muskeegiya* (Indigenous medicine) items were not found on the Internet. Visuals for the *wuneehige-apucheehitahina* (trapline tools) sequence were also hard to locate. Therefore, the role of the Elders as supervisors and inspectors of the artwork for accuracy was of paramount importance.

The sheer appreciation demonstrated by every Elder who saw the development of sequences instilled positive reinforcement in the team. An atmosphere of growing ownership continued. In six instances, sequence development brought immediate family members together in their roles as Elders and developers. It was an indicator that inclusive practice establishes family connections between the school and the com-munity, much closer than we anticipated. Home visits were made where necessary. In one instance, the Elder's family was part of the collaboration and amusement. When reviewing the *Nigiskisin* (I Remember) sequence, the teacher told us the following:

> The Elder was very humbled and so proud of the pictures that came out of his story. The pictures capture how it was long ago and how they lived to get food on their table; how they got together for entertainment such as jigging, square dancing, and storytelling. He was encouraged about our work keeping the language alive and helping children learn it. He said, "Kimumeecihinawau ooma ka itootumek e-weechiyayegok awasisuk igaheega kita wunigiskisichik" (You have made me so proud of the work you have done to help children so that they will never forget).

In the twenty-first century, there is an increased and almost panicked interest in gathering up information from Elders so that their stories can be written down and passed on to future generations. The panic is understood because for every Elder who dies, a slogan reminds us that an entire library burns down. Storybooks that build identity and increase Cree literacy are needed. Children who encounter print in their homes and make a smooth transition to reading in school have read and remembered almost two hundred books before they enter kindergarten (Bilash 2004). In contrast, there are not even two hundred stories written for children in any Cree dialect. The inclusive approach to education in the production of our booklets gives promise to booklets serving a dual purpose.

The research helped me understand how Elders "can be tremendous human catalysts in the pursuit of culturally relevant and dynamic programs which are created in concert with the communities they serve. They can provide a voice that will enable schools to become more aware and responsive" (Monica Goulet quoted in Saskatchewan Learning 2001, 10). When I asked how I could support teachers in the Cree Immersion and bilingual programs, I discovered the power of including Elders in my own practice. On previous occasions, we had invited them into our school to serve as resource people to showcase culture, to be guest speakers in classes, or to help as Cree-language speakers in the classrooms. However, I had never engaged with Elders in inclusive curriculum practice within a school setting until I started this project. It helped me reflect on Elders as an important part of culturally relevant pedagogy in my practice. Elder teachings had stemmed from my own childhood and I was closely connected to the knowledge. The research helped me realize that the familiarity with the local knowledge had made it hard for me to recognize that I could "do things differently" with it in my practice. What started as inquiry into stories of lived experiences of Elders ended as inquiry into my own lived experience as a northern Cree person and practitioner. For many of us, the stories evoke childhood memories and, by doing so, tell our story, too. We as teachers feel connected to the curriculum.

Lily's story demonstrates the multifaceted benefits of locally developed, collaboratively created curricula. First, the project produces books in Cree for children to read. The story sequences are being used in Cree-language teaching to ensure that the language remains alive in the community. Because the stories are not translations from English to Cree, they have embedded within them the thought structure, values, and world views of the Nehinuw. The students are connected to the knowledge of the people of their community, and so too are teachers. This connection facilitates learning, as the students work with what is familiar to them while learning about the lived experiences and histories of their families and their community. This cultural connection is not just important for the development of language and self-esteem, it is also the key to effective learning.

Indigenous Language, Knowledge, and Understanding

In the past twenty years there has been a gradual validation of Indigenous knowledge, which has also been called local knowledge, traditional knowledge, or traditional ecological knowledge. In 1987, in the scientific community, the authors of the World Commission on Environment and Development (1987, 114–15) (also known as the Brundtland Commission) stated, "These communities are the repositories of vast accumulations of traditional knowledge ... the larger society ... could learn a great deal from their traditional skills in sustainably managing very complex ecological systems." A gradual shift in education towards the recognition of Indigenous knowledge in Canada occurred in the 1960s. By the 1990s, strong statements were being made by many authors, including Marie Battiste, James [Sákéj] Youngblood Henderson, Eileen Antoine, Graham Smith, Linda Tuhiwai Smith, Cecil King, and Lorna Williams, to name a few. Educational practitioners have introduced Indigenous knowledge as part of establishing relevant and meaningful curriculum change. With the complementary addition of various methods to curriculum content, other issues, including those of philosophy or world view, have been undertaken. A significant part of the discussion has included the topic of Indigenous languages.

The deliberate and qualitative inclusion of Indigenous languages can play a central role in achieving greater understanding in research, curriculum development, teaching, and learning for Indigenous students. For example, in Cree we have a concept expressed in the language and its structure that Keith translates as the "life force system." The word *pimachihowin* is usually translated as "life" or "survival," but it also signifies the intentional action or activities of life force beings. It is a difficult concept to translate because it includes the life forces of the universe such as the sun, people, ice, animals, spirits, plants, rocks, and so on. The life force system encapsulates the centrality of life, action, and intentionality for living beings. To the Nehinuw, as people, we are life force beings that carry out the self-determined actions for living and survival. The concept is further complicated because, in addition to living beings, it includes life force entities such as toboggans, spears, cars, record players, and so on. These latter entities are considered forms of life, not inanimate objects or things. Also, life is not only about living beings and entities; the universe, nature, culture, and the inanimate tools we create and use also become an essential part of the overall life force system. Within this life force system, people take an integrated view of life that encompasses not only life force beings and entities but also what in English would be considered life's non-living aspects – for instance, natural and cultural processes and the use of all senses, artifacts, instruments, and tools. To the Nehinuw, it is difficult to examine pedagogy and epistemology without including non-living aspects. Knowledge is gained through interactive processes between and among living and non-living beings and things. For example, thinking and speaking and all the five senses are considered inanimate processes. The access to knowledge, pedagogy, and methodology would be difficult without the latter inanimate realm that is included in the life force system.

The educational potential of Indigenous language inclusion has yet to be fully realized. The rich, dynamic complexities of Indigenous languages need revitalization and full integration with linguistics, language teaching, education, neuroscience, and other disciplines. Language is not a simple reflective mirror or medium of experience; it is part of the complex cognitive neuroscientific framework that governs our thinking and actions. Even in the context of language loss, it is important to recognize that the cultural historical thought patterns that are expressed in the English language by Indigenous peoples often continue to reflect the cultural and cognitive linguistic structures of the Indigenous languages. Language is also interconnected with the biological, sociobiological, and biocultural and cultural realms of human experience.

Nehinuw Knowledge and Understanding

The following section provides a brief introduction to selected concepts of Nehinuw thought, concepts reflective of the philosophy and epistemology of the Cumberland House Nehinuw. We ask the reader to remember that, although it is not always a "perfect fit" because of the unique challenges to translation, the underlying structure of Nehinuw thought and experience can indeed be conveyed and articulated through the integration of the meaning of key Nehinuw words and concepts. Some of the Nehinuw concepts presented in this chapter include the life force system, self-determination, and the dimensions of social interaction. Other Nehinuw and Nehinuwehin dialects will have similar concepts with unique variations and interpretations, while other Indigenous peoples will have different key concepts based on their culture, linguistic heritage, and environments. These ideas are presented to give the reader examples of key concepts of one particular Indigenous group to inform the reading of the case studies and the analysis of effective teaching of Indigenous students. Some concepts may not be so evident in the classroom realities, while others will echo throughout the chapters.

Stories of (Mis)understanding and Language

KEITH: In school we were taught by Roman Catholic nuns. On one occasion I was trying to solve a math problem, when the teacher came over to help. After she gave her instructions, she said in Cree, *"Kinistooten neena?"* I was pleasantly surprised and understood what she was saying, except that how she was expressing herself was grammatically incorrect. The form she used was based on the English grammatical structure of "Do you understand me?" In Cree, the inclusion of "me" *(neena)* in conjunction with the specific verb form *kinistooten* (Do you understand?) is redundant and therefore not used. In Nehinuw thinking, given the classroom context, the focus of understanding is on the student rather than on the speaker; therefore, the use of "me" is not linguistically logical. In Cree, as it is in English, "Do you understand?" *(kinistooten)* would have been sufficient. To a Nehinuw speaker, when one focuses on the understandability of a speaker, "Do you understand me?" is *"Kinistootuhin?"*

This example shows the importance of language and language structure in the teaching-learning situation. There were many things happening at this brief moment. Here we have a teacher who was sensitive to the cultural-linguistic situation and had taken the time to learn some key phrases in the language of the student. I remembered feeling a certain sense of respect for people who took the time to learn our language. But it is also interesting that I remembered the mistake made by the teacher. I understand now that it was not a "mistake" per se. She was merely following the cognitive and grammatical linguistic patterns that she regularly used in English. She was transporting English-language structures into her Cree. A similar situation occurred when we were learning English as Cree speakers. In the process of learning to speak English, Crees use their language and cognitive structures, transferring the Nehinuw way of thinking into the new language structural demands of English. This example shows that a greater degree of emphasis must be placed on the centrality of Indigenous languages and the cultural-linguistic context in Indigenous education.

My second example deals with a situation that occurred when I was a cabinet minister. One of my staff, a young person from the southern Cree and Anishinaabe (Saulteaux) area, expressed an interest in the Cree language. In order to illustrate some of the comparative differences between English and Cree, I explained one aspect of the third-person structure. In English, we differentiate between male and female gender by using "he" and "she." In Cree, there is no gender differentiation between male and female. Instead, Cree speakers differentiate between animate and inanimate.[4] Nehinuw speakers therefore have a difficult time switching to the gendered form of English. In learning English, Crees will often interchange "he" and "she." Even after attaining fluency in English, the structure of the Cree language still affects the thinking and speech patterns in English. Maria Campbell (2010) refers to this language use or interference in her introduction to "Stories of the Road Allowance People."

After I gave this explanation, the staff member who'd asked me about the Cree language was quite excited because it triggered a memory about her grandfather, who was always interchanging "he" and "she" in English. It gave her a great sense of relief: "Here I always thought that there was something wrong with my grandpa's thinking but now I understand."

Translation of Words versus Translation of Ideas

Presenting Nehinuw concepts of philosophy and epistemology in the English language is challenging. Even the word *epistemology* is problematic to a Nehinuw speaker, since Cree has two major concepts of knowledge and understanding that include the embedded aspects of action and interaction. The Nehinuw word for knowledge is *kiskeneetumowin*. The meaning of the root stem, *kisken-*, is "to know." However, in Cree, it is understanding that is emphasized. The Nehinuw word *nisitootumowin* encapsulates both the English concepts of meaning and understanding and is a central concept in learning. In the Nehinuw view, knowledge acquisition is not enough. Knowledge needs to be complemented with understanding. This Nehinuw concept of *nisitootumowin* (understanding and meaning) is interwoven with interaction, practice, and action by doing. Action and interaction in the Cree language are designated by the word stems *-ito*, *-otu*, and *-ato*. These word stems are used extensively in Cree, and when they are part of words, they connote interactivity. The use of these word stems demonstrates the importance of the interactive dimension, of action between the self and one's social and physical surroundings. For example, *weetumatowin* is the interactive sharing of information among people on a daily basis. In addition to the aforementioned medial stems, interactivity is inherent in many other structures in the Cree language. The interactional view of the world is the link between the self and others that includes the totality of life, the environment, and the universe. To the Nehinuw, development in life takes place through dynamic interaction. *Itootu* is "do" or "act," so the stem *-itootum* in *nisitootumowin* (understanding and meaning) relates to a person's activities or doings. The action combined with the inherent interaction in *nisitootumowin* gives a conjoint sense that learning by interactive doing is dynamically interconnected with understanding. Hence, the English concept of epistemology in Nehinuw thought includes actions and interactions, knowledge, meaning, and understanding.

The Life Force System

One of the central concepts in Nehinuw thought is that of life, or lifehood, and that which is created by the forces of life, including belief in spirit beings. The philosophy and thought of the Nehinuw is reflected in our terms for life. *Pimatsiwin* translates as "life" or "the state of aliveness," while *pimachihowin* is the lifehood act.[5] It must be remembered that in presenting these concepts, there is often no word or idea in English that accurately captures the Cree meaning. Such is the case with *pimachihisowin*, which is the prevailing form and most commonly used word when referring to life in Cree. *Pimachihisowin* is the self-determined action of individuals, groups, and nations in the quest for life, livelihood, and survival. The main stem, *pim-*, indicates action as demonstrated in words that start with *pim-*, such as *pimoote* (walk), *pimpahta* (run), *pimiska* (paddle), *pimeena* (fly), and *pimosinew* (throw). In each of these examples, the action orientation of life is exemplified. A philosophy of action is therefore a significant part of Nehinuw thought and practice.

There is also a strong element of intentional action embedded in the concept of *pimachihisowin*: life is seen as "conscious" action. The middle stem, *-ihiso*, signifies the self-determined intentionality of an individual or self-group. "Conscious" is in quotation marks here because the concept of action and life (life force) is not restricted to people, but rather includes all forms of action by entities and living beings. As the previous examples of the sun and stars show, it is not restricted to biological beings. The Nehinuw life force system is an interactive, dynamic process of causal forces that are the source and foundation of life and all non-living creations and emanations. This life force dynamic exists in beings and entities such as people, animals, plants, the sun, spirit beings such as the thunderbird, and also in the creations and processes of entities and beings, whether cultural or natural. The life force is the spark and energy source that gives people and other entities and beings the creative and imaginative impulse for action, as well as the generation of the various multidimensional systems of continuous change in the universe. Aspects of the life force system can be represented in different ways. For example, there is a direct morphological connection between children, the stars, and the sun. The etymological root stem *waso*,[6] which means "he/she/it shines" in the Nehinuw word *awasis* (child), has its origins in the light given off from the radiant power of the sun and stars. *Awasis* literally means "the little being that shines." In traditional Nehinuw culture, it is children who epitomize the light, sparkle, and vibrancy of life.

Self-Determined Action and Collective Thought

One of the many ways the strong collectivism in Nehinuw philosophy is featured in the Nehinuw language is through the social organizational and interactive positioning of key concepts such as *weechi*, which means "help" or "support." However, because of the emphasis in the literature on Indigenous collectivist thought (Bryde 1971), there has been a tendency to downplay or exclude important forms of individuality. It needs to be emphasized that the individual and the collective are both important in Nehinuw thought. For example, when referring to self, the designation can refer to the self as an individual or the self as a group (a self-group on their own) in the plural form.

The idea of individuality within an interactive concept such as the helping relationship is exemplified by *weechihisowin* (helping oneself/themselves). *Weechi* can be used by itself as a command, but when it is combined with the medial stem -*iso*, as in *weechihisowin*, it becomes a generic term that includes both the individual (helping oneself) and the self-group who help themselves. Other examples that include the frontal stem *weechi-*, such as *weechiyauguneetowin* (partnerships) and *weechiseechigemitowin* (alliances), will be dealt with in the upcoming section "Nehinuw Social Relations." At a more specific level, the medial stem -*iso* includes the singular form *weechiso*, meaning "one helps oneself," and *weechisowuk*, which means that a particular group or self-group helps themselves or simply "they help themselves." When one talks about people or a person, the above illustrates the idea that self-determination is not only a group or national phenomena but also an individual act. Self-determined support systems therefore include both the individual and the collective in its many forms.

The ideas of interaction, collaboration, cooperation, reciprocity, and sharing are also very important aspects of Cree Nehinuw thought. Within the specific domain of the helping or supporting relationship, this interactive dimension is captured in the word *weechihitowin*. When a word includes the medial stem -*ito*, interactivity becomes its dynamic component and, as such, *weechihitowin* translates as "helping or supporting each other." Whereas the focus of *weechihisowin* is on the self or self-group support, in the case of *weechihitowin*, the focus is on interactive collaboration and cooperation within the context of a supportive relationship.

The idea of interactivity is not limited to actual physical or cognitive activity; it is also given expression through language, communication, and discourse. For example, in the case of *weetumatowin* (sharing news) the frontal stem, *weetu-*, means sharing or disclosing information and is an ancient form of newsgathering. For greater emphasis, the semantic morphological structure and meaning of the medial stem -*ato* denotes this interactivity. *Weetumatowin* is therefore the dialogic sharing of information or the everyday news among individuals, people, and various self-groups or groups. Depending on the phonetic context, the idea of interactivity in -*ato* is also represented by -*ito*, as in the word *weetutoskemitowin*. When *weetu-* (sharing) is combined with *utoske* (work) and -*ito* (interactivity), as in *weetutoskemitowin*, the meaning becomes the shared collaborative work among individuals, self-groups, and people, or simply the idea of working together.

The Nehinuw have a unique way of differentiating collective interaction at the level of the self-group and the larger collectivity. The preceding example of *weetutoskemitowin* focuses on the interactivity of the group while the concept of *mamuwiatoskehin* (working together) focuses on the working together of the whole, usually larger group, or the totality of all groups and individuals.

Mamuhi- or *mamuwi-* refers to the joint pulling together of all where the focus is on collective action of the whole. *Mamuwi-atoskehin* is a strong part of Cree tradition and is still commonly used today.

Action in Cree thought is reflected in changes to the structure of language in use. In Nehinuw knowledge and understanding, the importance of the concept of interactivity is presented as designated by *-ito* and *-ato*. In Cree, the verb and noun structures change to designate who is initiating the action and to whom the action is directed. *-Iso* or *-aso* is action by or towards the self or self-group, while *-ito* or *-ato* is interaction between the self or self-group and others. The Nehinuw concept of collectivity, and particularly the self-group, is important and difficult to use in English, but it reflects the significance of interactivity and the balance between individual and collectivist thought. For example, *weechihiso* means "one helps oneself," *weechihisowuk* means "they help themselves," and *weechitowuk* means "they help each other." In addition, *mamuhi weechitowuk* means "they all help each other." *Weechihitowin* is the generic concept that applies to all contexts. The importance of the ideas and practice of individuality and collectivity for Nehinuw people is embedded in most verbs. For example, Crees will state (in the singular form) *pimachihiso* when a child grows into a young adult and learns to live on his or her own, independently, apart from parents. The plural form, *pimachisowuk,* refers to a collective or self-group living on its own. In addition to *pimachihisowin,* other important Nehinuw concepts related to the development of independence, responsibility, autonomy, and authority over oneself include *mamitoneneetumasowin* (thinking for oneself), *atoskestumasowin* (working for oneself), and *neepuhistumasowin* (standing up for oneself). These words can be used in the plural forms and for the self-group. At the same time, there is a negative concept of going to the extreme or going too far with anything that you do, including the focus on the self. *Pehegenimisowin,* which literally translates as "number one thinking," signifies a form of excessive individualism, that someone is self-centred, with the negative connotation that one will not share with others. In this way, a balanced approach is advocated between self and other. Self-determined action (by the individual and the self-group) that includes independence, responsibility, autonomy, and authority over oneself is integral to Nehinuw thought.

Oral Narratives

Oral history and oral tradition are the oldest forms of history in all cultures in the world. The long-term history of people and the sometimes spectacular changes that have taken place on our planet are reflected in the cultural linguistic traditions of all peoples. With the Nehinuw emphasis on the oral tradition and oral history, people with *saseepigiskisihin* (prodigious and accurate long-term memory) are valued in the community. The social history of people and the environment is carried through story, memory, cognitive devices and structures, cultural creations, the land, and the universe. Indigenous people have been attacked for oral tradition and oral history by certain academics who see memory as only useful for that which is experienced directly and is thus only good for one generation, but this is not so. Stories, practices, and ceremonies carry knowledge through multiple and countless generations. Indigenous oral history documents the past events of people and the environment going back thousands of years (Coutu and Hoffman-Mercredi 2002; Masse et al. 2007). As Masse et al. (2007, 10) state in a researched volume of the geological sciences, the rich detail of natural events are contained in myths from long ago, and these are confirmed by physical evidence in the field. The fact that most scientists continue to "presume [myths] do not represent factual historical events is a disquieting conundrum that tells us more about the biases of western science than the nature of myth." Masse et al. (2007, 25) maintain that "myth presents us with the surprising opportunity to extract from the historical cultural record of many regions an unprecedented view of the impact of geological and solar system process and events during the past several thousand years."

This idea of the embeddedness of history in ancient oral traditions is exemplified in one of the cornerstones of Nehinuw Cree philosophy regarding the earth, sky, and the four directions, and more particularly about the direction of the North, or *keewetin*. The word *keewe* means "to go home." In historical terms, who went home? Was it the ancient peoples, Kuyasi-Inniyuk? Was it the ancient Cree, Kuyasi-Nehinuwuk; the ancient Dene, Kuyasi-Cheepuhauneeyuk; or others? In a story told to Elder Danny Muskwa by his paternal Cree grandmother, Harriet Muskwa (née Key), originally from the Cree community of Shoal River, Manitoba, the answer is that *Muskumee,* the ice or glacier, went home.[7] The north wind is the ice or glacier's wind. For the Cree in the territory where this story originates, this event occurred between ten and eleven thousand years ago. In addition to its exposition in mythical terms and its use in ceremonies, this naming of a great natural historical phenomenon presumes that the Nehinuw Cree also knew that the glacier had come down south and was now going back home to the North.

Other than ethnographic information, much of the early literature on Indigenous narratives tended to focus on myths and legends *(achunoogehina);*

thus, very little work has been done on the other Nehinuw narrative structures. In addition to many Cree discursive forms and quasi-narrative structures, the Nehinuw pass on their stories through three major structures: *achunoogehina* (legends), *achimohina* (stories of people, living beings, and entities), and *ahtotumohina* (stories of events and happenings). In the Cree categorical perspective, there is an animate-inanimate connection between *achimohina* and *ahtotumohina*. *Achimohina* are stories of animate beings and their experiences, so the focus is on the people or animate beings or entities, whereas *ahtotumohina* tells of inanimate processes and focuses more on the happening or event. For example, *achimowin* would be a story about a person who caught a large number of fish, whereas *ahtotumowin* would be a story about the time when spearing sturgeon was an important part of life.

Certain story forms such as legends and historical narratives demand a greater level of formality, accuracy, and truth. Other story forms have a greater degree of flexibility and creativity, such as the creation of narratives to share experiences and events of self and others told by adults and children in daily interactions. For example, the interactive forms of *achimohina*, where people, including the young, are telling stories to each other, are called *achimostatowina*.

Most of the existing writing regarding Indigenous narrative has tended to focus on *achunoogunuk*, the legendary beings and their actions. Even modern-day Canadian historians exhibit this conflation of Nehinuw narrative to legends *(achunoogehina)* in their university history textbooks (Francis, Jones, and Smith 2004) without recognizing other major Nehinuw narrative forms. Although *achimohina* and *ahtotumohina* and other quasi-narratives and discourse forms for use in schools are becoming more available (see, for example, Burton and Patton 2011; Campbell 2010; Enzoe and Willett 2010; Highway 2001; Jordan-Fenton and Pokiak-Fenton 2010; Mishenene and Toulouse 2011; Pelletier 1992; Sanderson 2010), they are still underrepresented in the curriculum.

Each of the three main Nehinuw narrative forms has over fifteen substructures, including empathetic stories, mysterious stories, fearful stories, powerful stories, and wordplay/fun stories (Goulet forthcoming). For example, *minauchimowin* and *minautotumowin* refer to positive stories of people and their actions and stories of positive events, respectively. In contrast, there is another subcategory in which people tell stories about their enemies, opponents, or competitors. Stories of exaggeration (*osamachimohina* or *osama htotumohina*), or lying stories (*kinaskahtotumowin* or *kinaskachimowin*), are similar to what we call "fish" stories in colloquial English. These are popular stories because they are often entertaining and so are told at cultural events such as trappers' meetings or in "lying" competitions then repeated with much laughter around campfires and kitchen tables over tea.

As teachers, we need to be careful not to trivialize oral history or present oral stories in an undifferentiated manner. Some narratives presented as legends contain historical information (Coutu and Hoffman-Mercredi 2002). Because the history is oral, it is given a certain narrative structure to assist in the memory of that oral history (Barber and Barber 2004). From a teaching perspective, it is important to include all forms of oral narrative in the classroom because they use and develop a cognitive structure familiar to many Indigenous students (Grant 1988). *Achunoogehina* (legends) teach important character traits, values, and life lessons, while *achimohina* (stories of people) and *ahtotumohina* (stories of events and happenings) provide Indigenous and other students with Indigenous heroes, as well as teach history and literature from an Indigenous perspective. Indigenous oral history includes the history of the land and people of the country that we now call Canada (Campbell 2010; Coutu and Hoffman-Mercredi 2002; Goulet forthcoming) and is not usually included in the Euro-Canadian documentation of knowledge. Educators therefore need to seek out oral history both in the community and from other sources that are slowly beginning to document these other narrative and discursive forms. Gathering oral narrative forms of Indigenous knowledge from the community is important not only to access the different stories that can be incorporated into the curriculum (McKay-Carriere 2009) but also to learn the protocols for storytelling in the different communities.

Nehinuw Concepts of Teaching and Learning

In Cree, there are three main forms of education, or the teaching-learning process: *kiskinaumagehin* (teaching another), *kiskinaumasowin* (teaching oneself), and *kiskinaumatowin* (teaching each other). The Nehinuw word for education, teaching, and instruction is *kiskinaumagehin*. The frontal stem *kiskin-* means to know, show, demonstrate, indicate, or expose, while *kiskinaum-* is to teach or instruct, and *-age-* indicates a processual act. Rather than centring on the learner, *kiskinaumagehin* is a focus on teacher-directed knowledge or teacher-directed action. This word is used when referring to both formal and informal education.

Kiskinaumasowin (teaching oneself) is the Nehinuw concept of the self-determined act of learning – the effort to learn is on the part of the learner. *Kiskinaumasowin* occurs when learners are placed in a situation of autonomous

Teaching another – Anne Dorion and Janelle D'Amour. *Photo by Linda Goulet.*

learning. The connotation is that one takes responsibility for his/her/their learning. Again, as in our examples of *weechi* (support and help), this can mean a single individual or self-directing group.

As introduced in the previous section on Nehinuw philosophy, self-determined action is a key concept. We see this concept of action by or towards the self (*-aso* or *-iso*) embedded in the term *kiskinaumasowin* (teaching oneself). The medial stem *-aso-* refers to action that is self-directed by an individual *(kiskinaumaso)* or the self-group (an independent group without an expert or an outsider doing the teaching) when plural *(kiskinaumasowuk)*. From a Nehinuw viewpoint, an important component in the development of responsibility is generated by self-directed activity or self-teaching. The autonomy of decision making is recognized when youth are growing up and learning how to take care of themselves and make decisions for themselves. For

Teaching oneself –
Janelle D'Amour. *Photo
by Linda Goulet.*

example, the Nehinuw will say "*Eti tipenemisot*," which literally means "one is starting to have a measured authority over oneself." The *eti* that precedes the word designates a transitional beginning, while *tipen-* is a form of ownership, control, or authority.

Hunting, gathering, harvesting, trapping, or playing alone provides an opportunity for independent action and trying something new on your own. For example, as a young person, I (Keith) watched older people make a bow and arrow, then went ahead and made one for myself. Another example would be in setting up your own camp. You do it on your own after observing how others have set up camp, but it needs to be done differently in different locations so one learns on their own to make adjustments. Making fires when camping without adults, one learns which wood gives off which kind of heat and the rate at which different wood burns, so you learn what wood to burn for different situations such as a hot fire for boiling water and a slow fire for overnight. An example in the plural form, *kiskinaumasowuk,* was used when we as young boys went camping and hunting in the bush on our own, away from adults and the community – we were teaching ourselves to do all those things for managing the camp and providing for our survival. *Kiskinaumasowin* emphasizes self-determined learning by doing, which leads to a better understanding of why things are done a certain way by others, reconfirming certain cultural practices. At the same time, an individual will bring to the learning situation his or her own unique way of doing things, which is recognized as a unique characteristic of that person. People will comment on these

Teaching each other – Braelyn Herman and Janelle D'Amour. *Photo by Linda Goulet.*

unique styles and ways of doing in the unique forms of, for example, animal calling, paddling, or modern dancing, jigging, or powwow dancing.

The interactive dimension of Nehinuw philosophy (-*ito* or -*ato*) is evident in the concepts for teaching and learning. The idea of interactional practice or dialogic and social construction of knowledge is similar to the Nehinuw concept of *kiskinaumatowin,* or teaching each other. As in earlier examples, the stem -*ato*- denotes interaction, so the emphasis is on the interactive dimension of learning. There are two aspects to *kiskinaumatowin*: one of interaction and the other of equality of learners. In the aspect of equality, no one is superior to or has authority over another. All knowledge is shared on equal terms no matter who is in the teaching-learning situation, whether it is adults and youth or males and females. One example of this type of learning is when people sit together to do beadwork so they can observe each other's techniques and designs to improve their own beadwork.

To summarize, *kiskinaumagehin* is the act of teaching by someone who tends to have more knowledge or expertise and generally more authority over the learners and the learning process. *Kiskinaumasowin* is the self or independent learning of an individual or group under his/her/their own authority or responsibility and thus is self-directed activity. *Kiskinaumatowin* is learning from each other in such a way that learning is interactive and interdependent, based on the equality of those involved. All learners have an equal opportunity to contribute in the learning situation.

Nehinuw Social Relations

Nehinuw philosophy emphasizes the dynamic, interactive nature of the world. The Nehinuw have several different important concepts to define their social relationships with one another: *wagootowin* (relatives), *weechihitowin* (supporting and helping each other), *weechiyauguneetowin* (partnerships), *otootemitowin* (openness to others), and *weechiseechigemitowin* (alliances for common action).

Of all the different forms of social relationships, the emphasis in the literature has been on the concept of *wagootowin* (Cardinal and Hildebrandt 2000; Macdougall 2010; Office of the Treaty Commissioner 2007; Settee 2011), which refers to a person's relatives and relations through marriage, including the extended family as well as custom adoption. *Wagootowin* also refers to the Nehinuw relations of the kinship system with the connotation of social closeness. Although there are similarities, there are important differences between the European and Nehinuw kinship systems. For example, English differentiates between great-aunts and -uncles and grandparents, whereas in Cree they are all addressed as Nimosoom (my grandfather) and Noogom (my grandmother).[8] In English, you traditionally have only two sets of grandparents, whereas in Cree, in addition to your parents' parents, all of their brothers and sisters as well as their marital partners are designated as your grandparents. In the case of other relatives, Crees differentiate based on gender. The relatives of the mother are differentiated from those of the father. Terms for aunts, uncles, nieces and nephews, cousins, and sons- or daughters-in-law are different based on whether the relative is maternal or paternal. Relational terms may also be used for non-relatives in the case of adoption or close friendships.

In addition to *wagootowin,* right from an early stage in a person's life, there are two other important relational concepts in Cree – *weechihitowin* (supporting and helping each other) and *weechiyauguneetowin* (partnership, to go along with). Partnerships are one of the key social relationships of the Nehinuw. As in the earlier examples, the stem *weechi-* is to help and support with the connotation of accompaniment. These terms are important aspects of Nehinuw social relations due to the emphasis in the Nehinuw world view on interactivity. As explained earlier, the concept of interaction (*-ito-* and *–ato-*) is used extensively in Nehinuw word structures. *Weechihitowin* (interactive support) is central to the well-being of people who depend on others to support them in the reality of life in northern and central Canada. This support is extended to others even though they may not be related. Whether on the trapline or in hunting, fishing, or gathering, one depends on partnerships *(weechiyaugunee-towin)* to sustain life. This relational support is especially critical in challenging situations or in times of physical or emotional hardship. In answer to a specific question I (Keith) had asked about social relationships, Kagiwmosoo-miyan (my late grandfather), Moise Dussion, stated that *weechiyauguneetowin,* or partnership, was even more important than *wagootowin* (relatives) because partnerships were more open and inclusive. In the context of the Cumberland Cree, survival in the past depended on partnerships in the bush or on the water, so your system of interdependence was important. In *weechiyaugunee-towin,* your reliance on others is expanded when you can include both relatives and non-relatives in your economic and social activities.

Two other important Nehinuw social relational concepts for teachers to understand are *otootemitowin* (respectful openness and acceptance of others) and *weechiseechigemitowin* (alliances for common action). In *otootemitowin,* the stem *-tootem* relates to open friendship. The closest English translation for *nitootem* is "my friend." In Cree, this term is a broader concept, relating to someone who makes others feel welcome and accepted. When I was growing up, in addition to *niwagomaguntik* (my relatives), the term *nitootemitik* (those with whom I am open) was used in speeches. When Nehinuw adults made speeches, they would address their audiences as "*Nitootemitik, niwagomagun-tik*" (those to whom I am open, relatives). The openness was to everyone, including people from outside the community. Thus, the term *nitootemitik* is also used in nation-to-nation meetings.

Weechiseechigemitowin is people coming together and creating alliances to participate in common action. The middle stem *-iseechige-* means to actively make or create, while again the latter stem *-ito* denotes that this creative, common action is interactive and done together. *Weechiseechigemitowin* (alliances) differ from *weechiyauguneetowin* (partnerships) in that the word *weechisee-chigemitowin* tends to be used for adults and thus has the connotation of higher levels of organization, which emphasizes the creation of something, or impacted common actions, whereas *weechiyauguneetowin* can be used for children, so the focus is more on the supportive relationship. The word *weechiseechigemitowin* is used in a broad sense for alliances made when an important project needs to be done, such as the Cree-language curriculum project used to introduce this chapter. With *weechiseechigemitowin,* people who may have different perspectives or positions come together when a united position is required to change and accomplish something. The term is also used in larger scale circumstances such as political alliances – for example, between Indigenous peoples and Europeans during the fur trade. Nowadays, it can also be used to describe group work in the classroom. In modern use, *weechiseechigemitowin* has the connotation of democratic, distributed leadership as opposed to authoritative leadership. In the social relation of *weechiseechigemitowin,* people come together in a group without giving up their authority over themselves and enter into an interactive situation wherein they share and draw upon each other's knowledge and resources. Leadership is not designated by external authority – for example, by a designated role or title – but by consent or agreement between the participants, whether implicit or explicit. From a comparative, analytical view of Nehinuw teaching and learning, *weechiseechigemitowin* lies in a similar sphere to *kiskinaumatowin* (teaching each other), wherein one does not relinquish one's authority in that social situation.

The Determination Framework

The concept of authority is important for the teaching and learning process as well as for larger systems of governance or decision making in our society, including educational institutions. In this section, we present three forms of authority – societal or public determination, self-determination, and co-determination – as a framework for moving beyond colonial relationships:

DETERMINATION FRAMEWORK*

The nation-to-nation relationships between Indigenous peoples and Europeans have evolved into three different but sometimes overlapping forms. Although usually referred to as government-to-government relationships, these relationships operate at various levels of our society, including corporations, institutions, organizations, groups, and individuals.

Societal or Public Determination
Past relationships were marked by an assimilationist view. Within colonial structures, decision making was dominated by settler peoples, and Indigenous peoples had only weak decision-making powers. As control of resources and policies were taken over by external agencies and governments during colonization, the ability of Indigenous governments to be independent weakened.

Indigenous people had little or no representation in public governments, corporations, or institutions in the societal form and therefore had little influence on policy making, implementation, or enforcement.

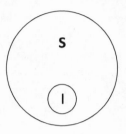

Self-Determination

Despite the impact of colonization, self-determination remains important to Indigenous people. Strong self-determination for Indigenous peoples combined with an independent view of the governance of settlers in Canada constitutes the second type of relationship, which is often represented by the two-row wampum belt. In this relationship, the Indigenous and settler peoples move forward on their own with little or no cooperation or interconnection with the other, each "paddling his or her own canoe."

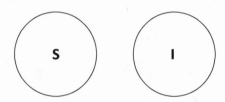

Co-determination and the Determination Framework

In addition to strong self-determination, Indigenous people want significant and decisive roles in partnerships and in society at large. They want to replace the colonial model of relationships, in which Indigenous people have only token representation, with the strong, meaningful, strategic input of Indigenous peoples. Rather than the "either-or" approaches of societal or self-determination, the determination framework allows for three forms of relationships to be used as warranted in different situations. It proposes a strengthened position for Indigenous peoples in both self- and societal determination and adds a third option for dynamic interaction among all participants – that of co-determination. It builds upon the strong self-determination of the two-row wampum belt and creates a co-determined link or interconnection between self-determination and societal determination. Co-determination takes a partnership approach based on equity and autonomy for both but with a structure for shared decision making. Self-determination may refer to one or more Indigenous peoples, and societal determination may refer to one or several settler and/or international peoples.

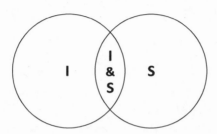

* The determination framework was developed and presented by Keith Goulet at the Symposium on International Cooperation in Aboriginal/Minority Education hosted by First Nations University of Canada, in Saskatoon, Saskatchewan, August 18, 2003.

In this framework, self-determination is strengthened. As we have seen in the discussion of Nehinuw philosophy and linguistics, self-determining action is a key concept. Nehinuw see self-determination as the ability to exercise authority over oneself as a person, group, community, nation, or as peoples. The Māori people have a similar concept, as Bishop (2011, 32) explains: "Self-determination ... [is] the right to determine one's own destiny, to define what that destiny will be and to define and pursue means of attaining that destiny. However, there is also a clear understanding among Māori people that such autonomy is relative, not absolute, that it is self-determination *in relation to others.*"

The concept of self-determination is in contrast to the colonial concepts of domination, assimilation, or "integration" and thus is widely used to refer to the goal of self-government for Indigenous peoples. Today, we see self-determination enacted in education systems in the creation and development of Indigenous-controlled schools and institutions such as the First Nations University of Canada, Gabriel Dumont Institute, or the Saskatchewan Indian

Cultural Centre. Self-determination is a process that has developed historically, from the initial internal forms of authority to the colonized forms of externalized authority and back to a more internalized authority. But in the transition to the latter, during a period of rising expectations with regard to national and provincial standards, many Indigenous schools and institutions are jeopardized and placed under great stress as a result of the unequal and severe underfunding on a per capita basis when compared to provincial schools and institutions (see Carr-Stewart 2010). The situation continues to deteriorate as provincial per capita funding increases each year while federal per capita funding remains the same. To move forward in education, self-determination needs to be adequately funded and supported with initiatives that meet the unique needs of Indigenous students, needs such as language and cultural programming, adequate materials development and distribution, and in-service for teachers, including anti-racism and cultural programming for those teachers new to teaching Indigenous students.

In the determination framework, the term *societal determination* (or *public determination*) is used in reference to the system or society at large. It includes public governments at the federal, provincial, and municipal levels; institutions such as the justice system, schools, and churches; and corporations such as banks, mining companies, and publicly owned Crown corporations. Historically, Indigenous peoples have been excluded from any role in law and policy development and implementation other than as clients or "wards" of these systems. Today, we see a growing number of Indigenous people working in this sphere, in government departments, institutions, and private corporations; thus, the level of impact of Indigenous peoples on decision making in Canada is gradually increasing. To ensure this trend continues and expands, a strong policy of inclusion of Indigenous peoples is required by governments, institutions, and private corporations at all levels, including training, hiring, and management, as well as meaningful representation in governance and board structures. Inclusion through weak or medium involvement is not enough, as it produces tokenism. A robust policy of positive and qualitative inclusion of Indigenous peoples in the societal sphere will have a significant long-term impact on the forward movement of Indigenous peoples.

In addition to self- and societal determination, another important structural change comes with co-determination. Co-determination is an English concept reflective of the Nehinuw concept of *weechiseechigemitowin* (alliances for common action) and of *weechiyauguneetowin* (partnerships). When I (Keith) was involved in the Canadian constitutional debates at Meech Lake, and when I chaired the Saskatchewan hearings on the Charlottetown Accord, it was often stated that a strong Canada requires strong provinces. I would add that a strong Canada also requires strong Métis, Inuit, and First Nations governments and institutions. Weak to mediocre neocolonial and assimilationist models of governance and management have to be replaced by strong and inclusive initiatives of equitable interaction. The Māori have articulated a similar co-determined approach to moving forward. Russell Bishop (2011, 32) states:

> [Kaupapa Māori (theory of discourse and practice)] is a call for all those involved in education in New Zealand to reposition themselves in relation to these emerging aspirations of Māori people for an autonomous voice ... [and] seeks to operationalise Māori people's aspirations to restructure power relationships to the point where partners can be autonomous and interact from this position rather than from one of subordination or dominance.

As presented earlier, interactivity is an important concept in Nehinuw thought. This idea of inclusion is a key part of the "Determination Framework." In addition to the importance of self-determination and societal determination, there has to be room for strong partnerships, cooperation, and collaboration in a new framework that reflects co-determination. Co-determination requires well-developed, strong, self-determining Indigenous governments, institutions, organizations, and peoples in order to move beyond token involvement and unequal partnerships. Co-determination is the formation of strong alliances and partnerships in which parties recognize the unique resources of the other. With *weechiseechigemitowin* (alliances) and *weechiyauguneetowin* (partnerships), each partner has something of value to offer and thus participates in decision making and implementation without surrendering authority. Results and benefits, including the development of capacity, knowledge, and skills, accrue to all parties involved.

As previously shown, these concepts can also be applied in a micro setting, in pairs or small groups. Effective education for Indigenous students includes development in all forms of authority, whether it is in the context of self-determination, co-determination, or the public/private sphere of societal determination.

Strong independent, bilateral, and multilateral systems of determination at *all* levels, from the classroom, administration, and management, school board, ministry, and government levels, have a greater chance of creating success in the education of Indigenous peoples.

Concluding Comments

This chapter offers a brief, basic introduction to the complexity of Nehinuw thought and practice. It must be emphasized that Indigenous languages are an important aspect of the development of Indigenous education and knowledge. An examination of educational concepts in Indigenous languages provides insights into the deeper meanings of Indigenous thought. All the Nehinuw concepts presented here support the importance of the inclusion and use of Indigenous languages in education. We introduced one of the central concepts in Nehinuw thought, *pimachihowin* (the life force of intentional action), to introduce the epistemology. Action, self-determined action of the individual and the self-group, and interactivity are key concepts embedded in Nehinuw thought. Historically, oral narratives combined with action have been the main pedagogical form for sharing knowledge. We introduced three major types of Nehinuw narrative to highlight the complexity of sharing knowledge and passing it from one generation to the next. Nehinuw pedagogy is encapsulated in three common terms for learning and teaching: *kiskinaumagehin,* teaching another; *kiskinaumatowin,* teaching each other; and *kiskinaumasowin,* teaching oneself. These forms of teaching and learning flow from Nehinuw social relationships: helping and supporting each other *(weechihitowin)*, relatives *(wagootowin)*, partnerships *(weechiyauguneetowin)*, and alliances *(weechiseechigemitowin)*. Running throughout even this brief introduction is the Nehinuw emphasis on responsible authority over oneself as an individual or group, or self-determination while interacting, supporting, and helping others.

In changing our schools and society to overcome the economic, political, and social barriers faced by Indigenous peoples and others in this country, we need to draw on the knowledge and abilities of Indigenous peoples. If we are to have strong self-determining Indigenous communities, then schools need to develop self-determining individuals who can work independently and with others in the community or in the societal sphere of businesses and public institutions and governments. Equally, our society needs to support the development of strong, self-determining Indigenous individuals, groups, institutions, and communities who can partner with others in a co-determined manner to draw upon the strengths of both Indigenous communities and the organizations of the society at large.

How to Get There: Conceptualizing
Effective Teaching

Our conceptual framework or model for effective teaching summarizes actions that engage Indigenous students in learning. The model compiles the actions of individual teachers into a representational configuration of effective teaching practice. It was developed based on interviews, observations, and stories shared by Indigenous and non-Indigenous teachers. The model reflects the relational nature of teaching and the interactive philosophy of the Nehinuw. Teachers emphasized that relationships were the key to effective teaching – that is, relationships between the teacher and students, among the students and class, with the learning environment (the how, or the process, of learning), and to the construction of knowledge (the what, or content) in the classroom. This chapter provides an overview of the model. Subsequent chapters provide the details of teacher actions in each of the four categories, with illustrative case studies for each category.

Developing the Model

LINDA: As a Euro-Canadian living with Indigenous peoples and working in Indigenous education, I have tried to understand Indigenous ways of being so I can incorporate that philosophy into my life and teaching. My understanding of Indigenous philosophy has grown as I've worked with many Elders and interacted with various Indigenous peoples over the years. For example, as mentioned earlier, the late Elder Ken Goodwill from the Dakota First Nation of Standing Buffalo saw human (and spiritual) development as learning about your place in this world – finding out who you are, including who you are in relation to the world, discovering the gifts you have, developing those gifts to make your contribution in this world, and assuming the responsibility for the use of those gifts. This view of life speaks to the purpose of learning for all children. If a young person grows up not knowing who they are, how will they know what knowledge to seek, what talents to develop, and the responsibilities of those talents? How will they come to understand that their talents and strengths carry with them an obligation to use them to make a positive contribution to the society in which they live? Is this not what education should be about?

The principles of effective teaching for Indigenous students apply to all students, but Indigenous education has unique features based on the history, culture, and philosophies of First Nations, Inuit, and Métis peoples, who tend to view the world in a more holistic way than the European framework that is the basis of our education system in Canada. As mentioned earlier, effective teaching for Indigenous students is about relationships and connections – that is, relationships between the teacher and student, among students in the class, and connections to the content and process of learning. In talking about spirituality and human development, Ken Goodwill was describing the essence of good teaching. If we as teachers, in our classroom actions and interactions, can open ourselves and make positive connections with and for our students, we create a place where we all, students and teachers, learn about ourselves. We learn how to be in the world, how to interact with others and through reflection, come to have the knowledge of who we are as a person and as a people.

The model presented in this chapter was developed based on interviews and in-school observations, using grounded theory methods first articulated by Glaser and Strauss (1967) that have since been expanded upon (Corbin and Strauss 2008; Glaser 1978, 1992, 1998; Strauss and Corbin 1990, 1994). Interviews were conducted with effective teachers of Indigenous students (as identified by the researcher through observation, by their communities, or by administrators) from a variety of teaching contexts in mid-Canada. Face-to-face interviews ranged from one to two hours in length and were transcribed and returned to teachers for verification. Some of the teachers participated in more than one interview. Although fifteen teachers were initially interviewed, due to saturation of the categories, the model and quotes are based on the data from eleven teachers. Seven were Indigenous teachers who self-identified as

Cree, Dene, Métis, and Saulteaux, while four were Euro-Canadian. Although the initial focus was on elementary teaching, four teachers had high school experience. In addition to the interviews, observations were conducted in three elementary classrooms at one First Nations school over a period of three months to compare interview data to teachers' actual behaviour. Field data included the researcher's descriptive notes, photographs, and audio- and video-taped activities.

Data was analyzed using the "constant comparative method" (Glaser and Strauss 1967) in which data analysis accompanies data collection. As data was collected, it was coded for similarities and differences. Categories were developed as patterns became evident and connections among the different categories were made (Glaser 1992). The model emerged from the process of conceptualization using several grounded theory techniques such as memoing (taking reflective notes of what appears to be important features in the data) and different forms of coding (see Goulet 2005) as well as comparison to other field-based research on effective teachers of Indigenous students. Initial analysis of the categories was presented for feedback to the school board and all the teachers in the school where the observation took place. After the model was developed, stories or the case studies were gathered from additional teachers whose experiences clearly illustrated the categories of the model.

Observing a great teacher at work is like watching a beautifully choreographed dancer or athlete perform. It looks easy until you try it yourself. Teaching is further complicated because what works in one context with one group of students may not work in another context. Also, it may be impossible for me to achieve the same results as a teacher whose gifts differ from mine. This chapter examines the different aspects of effective teaching to identify the beliefs and actions of effective teachers of Indigenous students and how those beliefs and actions interact with each other to create positive learning environments for Indigenous students.

Contextualizing the Model

The model of effective teaching flows as it does because of the context of Indigenous education. There are general and particular aspects to the context that influence the actions of the teachers. The general aspects are the socio-historical context of colonization and the ethnocultural context of Indigenous cultures. The particular aspects include the local community, school, classroom, and student conditions.

In Canadian schools, when Indigenous students enter a classroom, they face the possibility of discrimination from the teacher, their fellow students, or the curriculum (RCAP 1996; Schissel and Wotherspoon 2003; St. Denis and Hampton 2002). Their attitudes are shaped by their own past schooling experiences, as well as those of their parents and siblings. Many are justifiably wary and do not trust that the learning process will benefit them. The denigration of Indigenous peoples in Canadian society (St. Denis and Hampton 2002) can be internalized by Indigenous students and reproduced in their behaviour in the classroom, which can cause some students to lose belief in themselves and their own abilities (Brendtro, Brokenleg, and Van Bockern 1990; Mussell 2008). Lack of self-esteem and confidence can affect how students approach learning. Learning is a risk-taking endeavour because in order to learn, one has to function on the "edge of one's competence or on the border of incompetence" (Rogoff 1990, 202). In the Canadian experience, rather than "nurturing the individual, the schooling experience typically erodes identity and self-worth [of Indigenous students] who regularly encounter racism, racism expressed not only in interpersonal exchanges but also through the denial of Indigenous values, perspectives and cultures in the curriculum and the life of the institution" (RCAP 1996, 434).

Racism plays itself out in schools in myriad ways, but primarily, "oppression is a situation or dynamic in which certain ways of being (e.g., having certain identities) are privileged ... while others are marginalized" (Kumashiro 2000, 25). Given this situation, the teacher needs to demonstrate to Indigenous students that she cares about and respects them, their culture, and ways of being, that she doesn't blame them for their colonized situation, and that the students and their culture will not be marginalized by her or other students in the life of the classroom and curriculum.[1] In the model of effective teaching, teachers address issues of colonization while reinforcing Indigenous beliefs, values, and practices to create culturally meaningful learning environments for Indigenous students.

Teacher Characteristics

The teachers whom we interviewed and observed had diverse personal, social, and cultural characteristics. Despite this diversity, there were common features in their beliefs about teaching Indigenous students. These teachers recognized the uniqueness of Indigenous students in terms of culture and colonization. They were committed to teaching. They believed in themselves and stood up for their students and their beliefs.

Angie Caron and Hailey Whitehead. *Photo by Keith Goulet.*

These teachers believed Indigenous children had unique needs that required adaptation in instruction. Most were aware of the historical aspect of colonization, either through involvement in an Indigenous-teacher training program or through self-education. Some of the non-Indigenous teachers had taken Indian Studies courses because they felt they did not know enough about the Indigenous perspective of history. Indigenous teachers sought, through oral history or archival records and journals, to learn more about community history so they would be more knowledgeable in their teaching.

All the teachers expressed a strong commitment to the profession of teaching, to the children they were teaching, and to the communities in which they worked. Many put in long hours of preparation, finding activities and materials to which students would respond. They recognized the importance of taking responsibility for student attendance and student learning. Genuine appreciation of students was evident, as many teachers expressed the love they had for their students. All the teachers were involved in community events and/or extracurricular activities for their students.

These teachers trusted their ability to do their best for students. Val talked about "having high expectations of yourself and just going – taking the kids above and beyond."[2] Sometimes they faced situations in which they had to trust their own instincts, especially when working through emotional or social issues with their students or in dealing with parents. Often, changes they made were not easily accepted by others in the school or community, so inner strength was needed to stand firm when their instructional adaptation engendered student learning. All the teachers talked about passion – finding your passion, gift, or strength as a teacher, so you could "make the curriculum come alive" (Fran) or engender that sense of mature pride and responsibility in the lives of their students.

Effective teachers were aware that the cultures of their Indigenous students were unique. They recognized that students who live in communities where English is spoken as an additional language or dialect may have limited experience with school English. These teachers compensated for the effects of poverty of Indigenous communities and the racialization of Indigenous students. Although not stated explicitly by all the teachers, they recognized their students' lived experience of racism. Yvonne, a Cree Métis teacher, talked about this reality of racism in her life:

> [When I was at university] we were asked by one of our professors how many of us, as Métis people, had been made to feel embarrassed about or to deny our Indian ancestry. Practically everyone in the class raised their hands. The stories spilled out ... as we began the process of healing, reclaiming and celebrating our identities, especially our Indianness. We recognized our common experience was not a mistake. Rather it was a direct consequence of our lived experience with racism in and out of the classroom.

As Yvonne indicates, Indigenous peoples share common racializing experiences. In Cree, racism can be expressed in a variety of ways. *E muchenimeet* means one is looked upon negatively, as incapable of a good or excellent performance. *E peewehenimeet* is another demeaning word; it literally means that one is looked upon as tiny, minuscule fragmented pieces, with the underlying thought of irrelevancy and not worthy of attention. There is also *e tupatenimeet,* meaning one is looked upon as being low to the ground. The flip side of the latter statement is captured by *e ispahugenimisot,* which means that one is exhibiting the aura of elitist superiority.

Teachers also talked about the unique characteristics of the different communities, school systems, and schools. Each had different resources available to them. The varying styles of administration at both the system and the school levels influenced the teachers' actions. Doris reported that the principal made a difference in her willingness to take risks in her teaching. If the principal was supportive, she could push herself and really follow the lead of the children and herself. If the principal was not supportive of innovation, a teacher needed to be more cautious. Val said she experienced pressure from past principals to cover aspects of the curriculum in a certain way.

The teachers also taught differently from year to year depending on the grade level they were teaching, the group of students they had, and the characteristics of their students. The process of engaging students in learning also differed from one teacher to another depending on her or his individual strengths as a teacher. Teachers reported that what works for one teacher or one group of students will not necessarily work for another. For example, teachers used the talking or sharing circle in various ways. Val found the talking circle extremely effective for young children, but it did not work well with her middle-year students. On the other hand, when Yvonne, a middle-years teacher, had students evaluate her teaching at the end of the year, they told her the talking circle was the most effective strategy she used. Teachers who had been teaching for many years also stated that their strategies and materials had changed over the years.

The passion of these teachers carried over into their actions within the school as an institution. Many of the teachers described situations when they took a stand against racist policies or practices. These policies and practices included being asked by the superintendent not to socialize with community members, being told not to use the first language of the children in teaching, hearing racist comments from other staff members, encountering resistance to adaptation for Indigenous students, and imposing unfair discipline upon Indigenous students. Some of these policies have changed, and effective teachers are partially responsible for those positive changes in policy. Doris described how, when first teaching, she put her career on the line for a disciplinary policy she thought was unfair.

> I had a student in [G]rade 1 who didn't speak a word of English [she spoke only Cree] … She was so shy, she hid under her desk for the first two weeks of school. I almost gave up my teaching career for her because the rule was "You do not stand on the swings." One day a teacher brought her in to the principal to be strapped because she was standing on the swings. I threw a fit and said, "If you strap her when she does not even understand what you are talking about and all your rules, then I don't belong here or in this profession." I started for the door, and I would have quit. I felt that strongly. My principal came after me and said, "We won't strap her. We won't strap her. But you can't be such an old mother hen." But I'm still a mother hen.

This incident illustrates the unique needs of Indigenous children in the school system. It also demonstrates how the commitment, passion, and compassion of teachers, as well as their refusal to comply with unjust policies, can lead to student retention in school.

Characteristics of Indigenous Students

Although the teachers in this study did not use the term *colonization,* they all described situations that were the result of colonization and racism. Teachers noted how they taught for children who live in poverty. Sometimes the students came to school without adequate food. Teachers also saw poverty as restricting a child's access to certain opportunities related to school learning, such as literacy experiences with books or magazines.

In Indigenous communities, colonization imposed a system of external governance and decision making. There was and continues to be resistance to the imposition of external decision making. Standing up for oneself, or *nee-puhistumasowin,* is an important part of self-development for Crees, as is challenging excessive authoritarianism and colonialism. Teachers said that Indigenous children did not respond well to autocratic authority or imposed decision making. Fran explained the connection between the community's experience with colonial authority and the authority vested in the role of the teacher when she said, "[In the Indigenous community,] there has been a stigma attached to authority in general and teachers are seen as an authority figure."

As aforementioned, in addition to the economic and political aspects of colonization, Indigenous children are also affected by the ideology of racism that stereotypes Indigenous peoples and denigrates their cultures and achievements. Fran described the insidious nature of racism in the lives of the children she taught:

> In the mainstream school system, as much as it is changing, there's still an awful lot of Eurocentrism. It's very ingrained in the texts and the audio-visual things students see. The First Nations children have that view of themselves because that's what they have been exposed to ... Other things are really subtle – just sort of infused into life generally, that the students feel put down, they feel inferior, they feel less than ... Some of that is related to the poverty – the prohibitive costs for many [Indigenous] families, like figure skating, hockey, and music lessons – all kinds of things young people would like to do, and they are not always able to do because of the cost. It's so subtle they don't even know they feel that way quite often but it's displayed in various things they do and say.

The teachers in this study believed stereotyping had a negative effect on their students' relationship to school. They referred to many students who had a real fear of "looking dumb" (Owen). Often, students were reluctant to show they did not know something or would not ask a question for fear of appearing stupid to others. Val, an Indigenous teacher, commented that stereotyping in schooling and historical colonial practices made children feel ashamed of being an Indigenous person: "The [schools] really turned [Indigenous students] off their own people, their own language and their own culture, and just kind of wiped it right off. I know a lot of schools are still doing that."

Colonization and racism have produced high levels of social and personal problems in Indigenous communities, such as alcohol and drug abuse, violence, suicide, and medical problems. Teachers in this study were well aware of the high levels of stress in the personal lives of their students – stress that contributed to either withdrawal or acting out behaviours in the classroom. The teachers recognized that Indigenous parents were struggling to do the best they could in challenging circumstances without much support. Several teachers labelled the impact of residential schools as problematic. Most teaching in residential schools was based on the authoritarian teacher-directed practices of *kiskinaumagehin* and very little on the other Cree forms of teaching and learning, such as *kiskinaumatowin* (interactive teaching each other) and *kiskinaumasowin* (self-teaching). Summer visits back to the communities were not enough to balance this rigid structure. The loss of parenting skills by parents who grew up in residential schools meant some children did not have a positive authority figure in their lives. Kendra referred to one aspect of the intergenerational effects of the residential schools: she believed that because residential schools did not engender positive self-esteem in students, as parents, these individuals could not "give something to their kids they didn't have." Parental involvement in the school was hampered by the parents' negative schooling experiences.

While teachers acknowledged the problems faced by their students, they also recognized the positive strengths children derived from their Indigenous culture, such as speaking an Indigenous language, having a sense of humour, and resiliency when faced with obstacles. Many had strong bonds of kinship and maintained close supportive relationships with others in the community. Those who spoke their Indigenous language had the Indigenous knowledge that was embedded in the language. Most had heard many oral stories told by relatives or family friends, since *achimostatowin* (exchanging and telling each other stories) is a favourite pastime of the Cree and other Indigenous groups. These children knew how to focus and listen attentively. Those who participated in traditional activities on the land had a vast knowledge of the natural sciences. Attendance at ceremonies and other cultural events taught students traditional values and cultural pride. Often, Indigenous children were seen as more independent and able to take on responsibilities without adult supervision at a young age. Many children had the resiliency to overcome problems, equipped with positive survival skills Indigenous people have used to help themselves deal with the stresses of colonization and racism, such as teasing, humour, and *kiyam* – letting it go.[3]

While generalizations about the characteristics of Indigenous children were made in this study, it was evident that communities, families, and children are not all affected in the same way by colonization and racism – the effects are uneven. Some communities, especially in the North, have gone through a period of rapid social and cultural change, with an accompanying loss of both language and involvement in traditional activities connected to the land. Some Indigenous communities have embraced cultural revitalization and take pride in their Indigenous heritage and cultural practices. Some are moving forward in the development of self-determination and the local administration of services, decision making, and accountability, while other communities are facing a greater struggle to break the colonial structures of governance. Some families have been able to overcome intergenerational poverty. Some are able to provide access to a wide variety of cultural as well as mainstream experiences. Some have strength of spirit from their involvement in traditional cultural or spiritual practices. There is diversity in Indigenous communities, families, and children. At the same time, the history of colonization and racism has and continues to influence how Indigenous people and their children relate to schooling. A compassionate and respectful approach is a prerequisite to teaching students who have direct experience with the demoralizing and destructive effects of racism and colonization.

The Model of Effective Teaching

The model of effective teaching is a representational configuration of Indigenous education, created to clarify the interrelationships and capture the interactive, cyclical nature of the process of engaging Indigenous children in learning. The complex interrelated processes that occurred in the classrooms of our study are condensed and highlighted to capture the main actions and resulting consequences of those actions. To describe the interrelationships, we use one teacher to represent the actions of all the teachers – that is, the teacher referred to in the singular represents a composite view of all the teachers.

In the model of effective teaching, the four main relational categories of teacher actions – relationship with the student, relationships among students,

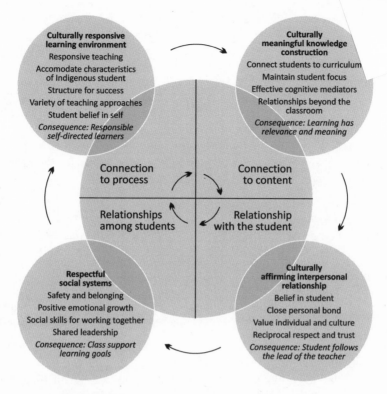

Culturally responsive learning environment
Responsive teaching
Accomodate characteristics of Indigenous student
Structure for success
Variety of teaching approaches
Student belief in self
Consequence: Responsible self-directed learners

Culturally meaningful knowledge construction
Connect students to curriculum
Maintain student focus
Effective cognitive mediators
Relationships beyond the classroom
Consequence: Learning has relevance and meaning

Connection to process

Connection to content

Relationships among students

Relationship with the student

Respectful social systems
Safety and belonging
Positive emotional growth
Social skills for working together
Shared leadership
Consequence: Class support learning goals

Culturally affirming interpersonal relationship
Belief in student
Close personal bond
Value individual and culture
Reciprocal respect and trust
Consequence: Student follows the lead of the teacher

Model of effective teaching for Indigenous students

connection to process, and connection to content – are each represented as one quadrant of an interactive whole. Although the model is based on interviews with and observations of teachers, it reflects the key Nehinuw concepts of social relationships and interactivity. The four main categories are made up of different subcategories. Subsequent chapters describe the specific teachers' actions that make up the different subcategories of each main category. Each category influences the other and, in practice, many of the actions in one category are related to subcategories in another category.

The teacher's actions in each of the four categories produce consequences that connect the student to different aspects of learning. The first and foundational category connects the teacher to the student so that the student becomes more willing to follow the lead of the teacher in the classroom (*kiskinaumagehin*: teacher-directed learning); the second connects the students to each other so that the peer pressure of the class supports the learning goals (similar to *kiskinaumatowin*: teaching each other); the third connects students to the process of learning so that they take responsibility for their learning (similar to *kiskinaumasowin*: self-teaching); and the fourth connects the students to the content of the learning so that learning has relevance and meaning, or *nisitootumowin* (understanding).

The model represents the process of teacher actions that engage Indigenous students, beginning at the bottom right hand of the circle and progressing in a clockwise manner. The spiral begins with the student coming to the learning environment with a teacher who views him as an individual and as a sociocultural, ethnocultural being, and continues around the circle. The development of an effective learning environment for students is represented in the model in a circular format because teaching is interactive and holistic. Actions (*itootumohina,* literally "doings"; *iseechigehina* are actions with impact) in the classroom never follow a smooth trajectory. In reality, the movement of students and teachers can occur in several areas at the same time, with each development impacting other areas of the circle. Because the consequences of teachers' actions in the model are generalized, in reality the consequences identified may not occur for every instance of the action. The local context and circumstances, including the characteristics and responses of students, influence when and how quickly the teacher can undertake certain actions identified in the different categories.

Categories, subcategories, and actions in this model are interdependent and interrelated. Each category is made up of its sub-categories, which in turn consist of specific teacher actions. The specific teacher actions are too numerous to be represented graphically in the model, so the remainder of this chapter provides an overview of the teacher categories and subcategories, while the following chapters provide the details regarding the teacher actions in each of the categories and subcategories. (See Appendix 2 for a descriptive summary of the categories, subcategories, and attributes that make up the model.)

The first step, or Category 1, of the engagement and learning process is the development of a relationship between the teacher and the student who belongs to an Indigenous culture that is or has been negatively affected by racism and colonization. The relationship is thus one that creates a decolonized, culturally affirming interpersonal connection between the teacher and the student.

The first subcategory, "Belief in student," doesn't sound like an action, but it became an action when it was conveyed to students, when teachers demonstrated their belief in the student as a capable person – capable of learning and of changing behaviour. In Cree, belief and truth come from the same frontal stem, *tap-*, and are therefore closely related in Nehinuw thought. *Tapehin* is truth and *tapuhaugeneetumowin* is belief. Flowing from that is *tapuhaugeni-mitowin*, which means believing in one another.

In the second subcategory, the teacher develops a close, personal relationship with the student by showing she genuinely cares for him, which is similar to the Nehinuw concepts of *weechi* (help or support) and that of *otootemitowin* (openness to others). Genuine caring for the student reassures him that the teacher wants the best for him and that she will not do anything to purposely hurt him. Taking this initial stance with children assures them they will not be rejected for who they are, as is the case in colonial relationships of discrimination. Showing humanness means the teacher interacts with students in an informal manner, which signals that she is approachable – that is, the authority inherent in the role of the teacher will not be used in a rigid, dictatorial manner. Informality also allows the teacher to be honest with students and to share her life experiences, both funny and sad. Laughter and the closeness that is possible when people share their emotions build the relationship.

With this closeness and her actions, the teacher demonstrates that she is respectful of the student and of Indigenous peoples, reflecting the strong Nehinuw value of *kistenimitowin* (respect). She expresses interest in the life of the child, his family, likes, dislikes, interests, and life outside of school. The child tentatively shares some of his life with the teacher. In response, the teacher demonstrates value for the cultural life of the child, affirming the Indigenous culture and respecting the social circumstances of the child. When the teacher responds respectfully, the child becomes more willing to be open with the teacher.

Trust is engendered as the power of the teacher is used in a just manner, and teacher actions demonstrate that she expects students to act responsibly. *Mumiseewin* is trustworthy behaviour. *Mumiseetotatowin* is the trustworthy belief in one another and connotes reliance on each other. Boundaries for behaviour are clarified so students are aware of what is expected of them when they interact with the teacher. Firm and fair enforcement of expectations reinforces trust and respect. The reciprocal respect, or *kistenimitowin,* and trust developed in the culturally affirming personal relationship between the teacher and the student mean the student is then willing to follow the lead of the teacher in classroom endeavours. The teacher's use of *kiskinaumagehin* (direct instruction) then becomes effective.

The development of the student-teacher relationship in the first category changes the student's level of engagement in learning. The processes enacted in the first category connect the student to the teacher with the result that the student is now more willing to do things asked of him by the teacher. In Category 2, the teacher connects the student to the class. She does so in a way that creates a social system that acknowledges and respects the students' sociocultural and ethnocultural situation. While in the first category the emphasis of the teacher is with the individual, in this category the focus is on the students learning to enact positive social relationships of *weechihitowin* (supporting and helping each other), *weechiyauguneetowin* (partnerships), *otootemitowin* (openness to others), and *weechiseechigemitowin* (alliances for common action). These first two categories together reflect the Nehinuw view of the importance of both individual and collective relationships in human endeavours.

To facilitate the connection of students to the class, in addition to reassurances in the private, interpersonal relationship of the first category, the teacher indicates publicly, in the social domain, that she values Indigenous peoples and their cultures. The norm of respect for indigeneity (and other differences) is established and enforced for student-student and student-class interactions. When students feel respected, they reciprocate with respect for others in the class. Creating familiarity and acquainting students with their physical and social surroundings engenders a sense of belonging. The sense of safety and belonging in the physical and social environment reduces the need for vigilant self-protection, otherwise important for survival in oppressive and discriminatory environments. When students experience a sense of safety, it enables them to focus on the learning activities of the class.

The teacher also respectfully acknowledges the stresses of children from families and communities affected by colonization. The teacher is attentive to the impact of social issues affecting Indigenous communities and deals with the effects in a matter-of-fact, respectful manner. She strives to alleviate student stress by establishing activities or classroom structures through which the emotional tension in children's lives is given positive expression. The interaction of students in the emotional domain helps them learn to empathize with others, reduces feelings of isolation, and develops bonds among students.

As students give expression to the situation of their personal life, the teacher reinforces appropriate social behaviour. This social behaviour is often developed in group work, where the social skills of listening, sharing, and taking turns are taught and reinforced. Students learn how to treat others with respect and how to ensure they are treated with respect themselves.

Student interaction and sharing in the classroom lead to the development of student leadership and joint authority, which approximates the Nehinuw mode of *kiskinaumatowin,* where students are learning from one another, and *kiskinaumasowin,* which is self-teaching and learning. The teacher uses situational leadership (see Sammel, Linds, and Goulet 2013 for a more detailed discussion of situational leadership): leadership is direct or shared depending on the context, such as communicating high expectations for student learning or the joint construction of class norms followed by the use of direct teacher authority to enforce adherence to respectful norms and expectations. The equitable leadership style in the personal relationships developed in Category 1 means the role of the teacher is shared, when appropriate, with the students in this category. When students assume leadership and share their lives and views in the classroom, they shape the climate of the class and direction of learning. They have joint authority of the classroom with the teacher: decision making is thus more diffuse, arising from both the teacher's and the students' ideas about the class. When students participate in establishing behavioural norms, they are more likely to follow the norms and enforce them with others. The safety and belonging, emotional growth, social skills, and shared leadership and joint authority create a culturally sensitive, respectful social system, and a group identity that supports the norms of the classroom and the goals for learning.

Racism can thwart a child's belief in his own abilities. In the classroom, an Indigenous student can be reluctant to participate if he does not believe he will experience success or that his achievements will be recognized by the teacher. If he tries, he does not want to see his work denigrated. The connections to the teacher and the class that are developed by the processes in the first two categories help draw a reluctant student into learning because through respect, trust has been established in the interpersonal and social system of the class. But the student still needs reassurance that he has the ability to perform the learning tasks with success. Instruction needs to be appropriate for the student's social and cultural situation. The development of the social relationships in the first two categories allows the teacher to enact the different Nehinuw forms of teaching – *kiskinaumagehin* (teaching another), *kiskinaumasowin* (teaching oneself), and *kiskinaumatowin* (interactive teaching each other) – in Category 3 to better connect the students to the processes of learning.

In Category 3, the close relationship developed in Category 1 allows teacher planning to be based on the students' interests and needs. Once learning begins, the teacher pays attention to her students' progress to ensure they experience success. Pacing or the length of time spent on an aspect of learning in the classroom is based on student progress, reinforcing the feeling of joint ownership with the students. Shared leadership is also evident in this category when students bring their knowledge to the classroom, making learning a shared endeavour. Creating space for students to share their knowledge means the cultural life and social situation of the students are represented and valued in the learning environment of the class.

Support for learning is accomplished by addressing the needs unique to Indigenous learners in the class in terms of cultural identity and racism. Language issues are addressed in a way that respects the children's and the community's speech patterns while preparing students for success with English in future schooling. The group skills described in Category 2 are used in this category as well to support the different levels of skill development in the class as peers support one another's learning. Structures or activities that foster the appropriate expression of emotion in previous categories also serve in this category to inform the teacher about the emotional state of students so she can better adjust her expectations for learning that day for both the individuals and the class as a whole.

The close interpersonal bond developed in Category 1 enables the teacher to know the strengths and weaknesses of the student: she knows how to motivate the student and structure experiences to ensure the student will have a successful learning experience. Starting with a student's strength and practising in a safe situation lessens the risk of public failure in an activity. Effective teachers use scaffolding appropriate to Indigenous students. *Scaffolding* (Cazden 1983; Sawyer 2006) is a term based on Vygotsky's zone of proximal development. The zone of proximal development is the space in which a student cannot perform higher level thinking or complete a task on his own but is able to do so with the assistance of a more skilled person. Scaffolding is the support given to the learner that enables him to achieve that higher level of thinking, complete the task, or solve the problem that he was unable to on his own. Effective scaffolding lays down a path for the student to follow or creates a framework to support student cognition in the activity to ensure success.

The teaching approaches develop and reinforce the attributes of previous categories. Mastery learning (Bloom 1971) ensures student success with basic skills. Respect for resources is taught when students use manipulatives and concrete materials. Social skills are reinforced, since students are expected to share materials. Storytelling, or *achimowin*, reflects the emphasis of Nehinuw on the oral tradition. In the classroom, storytelling humanizes and contextualizes knowledge, connecting students to others. Relationships between the teacher and students are strengthened when personal stories are used to illustrate learning. Stories of Indigenous peoples or others in similar oppressive situations help students understand their own social situation and connect the curriculum to the reality of their lives. One-on-one teaching provides the safety of not having to perform in front of others when students are unsure of themselves. It enables the teacher to become aware of the individual's understanding of the learning, thereby reinforcing the attribute of meeting individual needs. The talking circle is a venue for emotional expression, the development of social skills and student leadership, the practice of *achimowin,* and student input into the knowledge construction of the class. The students' leadership of the topics provides the teacher with insight as to how she can better connect the curriculum to the lives of the students. The development of social skills also takes place in group work, which provides for student peer support. Group work, or *kiskinaumatowin* (teaching each other), uses all four domains, as students learn content, interact with one another using the skills and values of *mamuwi-utoskehin* (working together), and enjoy learning together and from one another.

Experiential (Kolb 1984), community, activity- and land-based learning connect classroom learning to the real world and to student life outside the class. This connection reinforces the inclusion of self and culture in the construction of a culturally meaningful learning environment. When learning is personalized, the social and emotional domains become incorporated into learning. Because personalization brings the topic close to the students' experiences, they have strong feelings for it. They are able to express all parts of themselves, personally and culturally. These hands-on strategies alleviate student boredom, bringing life to the learning and enacting the movement inherent in the Nehinuw concept of *pimatsiwin* (life). The classroom and the community become connected, so learning becomes situated in a present-day community with a history that helps students understand their life today.

As the student participates in the learning process and experiences success, he comes to believe in his ability to achieve. The student is thus more willing to engage in learning. The belief in self is reinforced as the teacher sets standards for achievement and clarifies expectations for responsible attainment of those standards. The development in Category 2 of a group identity supportive of learning goals enhances each student's willingness to act responsibly. Culturally appropriate instruction means the teacher incorporates learning activities that develop a positive self-concept and positive cultural identity, which expands the student's belief in his own and his people's abilities. Recognition of achievement reinforces responsible engagement in learning. As self-confidence develops, the student becomes a more independent learner, more willing to take responsibility for his own learning, or *kiskinaumasowin* (teaching oneself). When this self-reliance is combined with the shared leadership of the previous category, it leads to the emergence of a responsible, self-directed learner.

As the student moves into Category 4, the last category of the model, he is now connected to the teacher, other students, and the process of learning. At the same time, given the uniqueness of Indigenous cultures, it is important that resources used in learning are congruent with the thinking and world view of the student. Too often, this is not the case: learning resources have for the most part been developed for use with Euro-Canadian students and based on Euro-Canadian content and structures of thinking. In Category 4, the teacher ensures that the content being taught is relevant to the cultural life of her students, so that they can relate to and understand the material *(nisitootumowin)*.

In the model of effective teaching, the personal relationship in Category 1 means the teacher knows her student – that is, his cultural background and his interests. By having his culture positively represented in the classroom, she is better able to entice the student into participation. The curriculum reinforces who the student is as an Indigenous person, and thus he comes to believe in the curriculum, since he no longer encounters overt examples of Eurocentrism and racism, or if he does, the teacher explains the injustice of that position.

Her personal relationship with the student also allows the teacher to adjust the curriculum to suit the student's interest. Interest in a topic both draws students in and maintains their engagement in learning. The social skills developed in the previous categories serve to sustain engagement in learning because peer pressure keeps students focused on the learning task, as can group work, especially for those students who favour learning in a social context. Working with others is also one way the teacher makes learning fun. Fun brings an emotional aspect to learning, as it heightens feelings that, in turn, assist in the retention of information.

The teacher uses cognitive mediators to support memory and cognition. Because learning is a shared endeavour in the model, the teachers and the students jointly develop many cognitive mediators. When mediators are derived from the students' experiences, they match or are closely connected to the internal cognitive processes of the students. Through responsive teaching, the teacher selects mediators that vary to accommodate the different learning styles of students. The shared knowledge and leadership of the students provide teachers with insight into the mediators that have the most meaning for the students. The more meaningful a cognitive mediator is to the learner, the more it can be accessed by the student's internal working memory to effectively support cognition.

Relationship building in this category occurs both inside and outside the classroom. Teachers connect with individuals, small groups, or organizations through *weechiyauguneetowin* (partnerships) and *weechiseechigemitowin* (alliances for common action) to enhance classroom learning. The community is seen as both a source of knowledge and a network of human resources that, with the development of respectful relationships, will support and reinforce the goals of learning with the student. The cultures of the classroom and the community come together in the relationships with other staff members, families, and community members. Culturally meaningful knowledge construction for the classroom draws from both the Western world of the mandated curriculum and the Indigenous world and understanding of the community and the children.

Summary of the Model

The model uses a spiraling circle to represent the dynamic nature of the process of engaging Indigenous children in learning. Our description of the model may suggest linear movement from one category to the next but, in reality, teacher actions are cyclical, iterative, and recursive. Some of the actions in one category may be dependent on the development of other sub-categories. For example, some approaches, such as activity-based learning used in Category 3, may not be achievable unless the class as a whole is supportive of the learning goals developed through the teacher actions in Category 2. Similarly, before using concrete materials, some students may need to develop respect for the classroom environment to know how to interact appropriately when learning with concrete materials.

The features of the different categories are interrelated. What is an important action in one category, serving one purpose, appears again, sometimes in a different form, in another category, serving another purpose. The same is true for the Nehinuw concepts of interactivity, social relationships, individual and collective determination, and forms of teaching that are emphasized in different categories but also evident in others. For example, *weechi* (support and help) appears in its various forms throughout the model but especially, and initially, with the individual student in Category 1 and among the students in Category 2. Similarly, *kiskinaumatowin* (learning from each other) may be emphasized in Category 3, but it is also an important aspect of developing positive social relationships in Category 2 and connected to the idea of the teacher reaching out to learn from others in Category 4. Thus, the process of engaging Indigenous students in learning takes place over time in a cyclical manner, as actions in one category serve to develop the features in another category, allowing the teacher to proceed to another subcategory or category. The time taken to move through the spiral depends on the context, including the background of the teacher. Though not always the case, it will often take longer for non-Indigenous teachers to connect with Indigenous students, because of the societal divide of racism. Indigenous students see a reflection of themselves in Indigenous teachers, which is often an asset in building relationships. With some children, regardless of the teacher, it takes a long time to develop close relationships of mutual trust. In some classes, student resistance to past colonial instruction is deep, so trust building and group skills have to be worked on for quite some time before responsible behaviour and joint authority with the class is achievable. In these contexts, time is needed to overcome the legacy of colonization, establish trust, and practice the norms of respectful responsibility in the school setting.

In practice, the model flows in a spiraling motion, but depending on the context of the classroom and the teacher's gifts, she may start at any one point. Although most teachers start by building relationships with students, in classroom practice, the initiation of engagement in learning starts immediately, so different teachers emphasize different aspects of the model at different times, depending on their context and their unique approach to teaching in their situation. For example, Owen drew children into learning by engaging the students in games that taught mathematical skills. He built relationships with students by creating an informal, fun relationship of students to the school content. For Wanda, teaching in the inner-city school meant she always had new students arriving in her class. She had to constantly and quickly develop new relationships to draw students into the classroom while simultaneously maintaining the flow of teaching the class. Wanda was Euro-Canadian, and almost all of her students were Indigenous. She developed student mentors in her class so that when a new student arrived, his first connection was with his peers who were also Indigenous; trusting relationships would come more readily with them than with her as a non-Indigenous teacher. The student mentor would initiate the new student into the routines and joint responsibility of the class and connect the child to the physical and social space of the classroom.

This model emerged from what different teachers have highlighted as important in creating effective learning for Indigenous children. The model is a representational configuration of the reality of engagement. As evident in Owen's and Wanda's approaches, there is no one path to follow. Instead, the model provides a conceptual framework that identifies important features to be considered when creating classrooms that successfully engage Indigenous children in learning.

Weechihitowin, Helping and Supporting Relationships: The Foundation

Teacher-student relationships are foundational to engaging Indigenous children in learning. Teacher actions reflect the Nehinuw emphasis on interactive social relationships, especially *otootemitowin* (openness, friendship, diplomacy) as well as *weechihitowin* (being helpful and supportive). Teachers in this study emphasized that close, personal relationships were the key to effectively teaching Indigenous students. In this chapter, we focus on the development of relationships. We begin the chapter with a story from Calvin Racette, who shares his view of the importance of student-teacher relationships that, once built, can produce results in other, unforeseen places, such as a Grade 10 math room.

It Wasn't Math, It Was Relationship Building

Calvin Racette

I have been asked to share a story about my experience in making a math class into a place where students who had a fear of math could be successful. I will provide a context for this story because it began at least a dozen years before it actually occurred. The story began when I was a student in the Saskatchewan Urban Native Teacher Education Program (SUNTEP) in Regina. This program gave me the necessary background and the willingness to enter into classroom situations where populations of Aboriginal students were the norm, and equipped me with the skills to not only survive but also thrive. I was taught and believed I was a change

Calvin Racette with Sherry Germaine, past student who now works with Calvin. *Photo by Keith Goulet.*

agent and my task in life was to work towards making the education system a more affirming place for Aboriginal people. After graduation, I worked at Gabriel Dumont Institute (GDI) as a curriculum developer. While there, I became a student of history and realized the Aboriginal peoples of Canada were systematically colonized and they experienced a process termed by others as "cultural genocide." It is in this context my story finds a setting.

After spending seven years with GDI, I was yearning to go out to a school and get involved with children, since that is what I had been trained to do. I was also a parent of four children and I was fascinated with how they learned and how their schooling was being delivered. I was hired by a rural school division to work as an Aboriginal Stay-in-School Coordinator. I spent the next two years travelling within the school division and working with students considered "at risk" and in danger of dropping out of school. It was here I found my real passion. These students had so many things on their plates and there was very little advocacy for them. Their parents often felt frustrated with the system, and the system appeared to be frantically trying to rid itself of these students in order to make lives calmer. I quickly learned the art of negotiation and realized I needed to pick and choose my battles, and that sharing research and creating a business case for what I believed in was necessary in order to move forward. A business case was based on gathering information and organizing it in a way that made sense and had a logical outcome that appealed to everyone, especially the decision makers and those who held the purse strings.

After two years of that job, I realized there was one school in the division that appealed to me. I had a good relationship with the principal and we shared a similar philosophy of wanting students to succeed. The school was a Grade 7–12 high school with over 400 students. Approximately half of the students were of Aboriginal ancestry, while all of the staff were Euro-Canadian. There were ten First Nation reserves in the immediate area.

I was hired as vice-principal and my journey began. I was informed I needed everyone to know I was not getting an easy assignment. I was to have a teaching load of two senior Native Studies classes, math and English at the Grade 7 level, and Grade 7 homeroom duties with one period a day for administration. When I arrived to begin in the fall, I was greeted by a group of Grade 7 students who had previously failed or were deemed difficult. I embraced these young people as my first group of students. I told them they would be special to me and we would have a great year together.

I was unaware of the clouds at the school that existed with the staff. It appeared there was a great deal of chagrin at the staff level. Although I had taught at the university and in adult education, there were staff members who were concerned about my ability to lead them. There were also those who were concerned because I was younger than them, and although they wouldn't admit it, there were a couple of staff who were outright hostile to me and suggested I got my job because I had a brown face. There were also staff members who embraced me and felt I was exactly what the school needed. The community also had mixed feelings and one of the points I often heard was that I was the first Aboriginal administrator in the school division and, as such, they were taking a chance on me.

At the same time, my Grade 7 students were an amazing mixture. Most had difficulty with math and English but were long on street smarts and charm. I quickly realized a "regular" program would not work, so I drew upon my contacts from the SUNTEP program and the things I learned in SUNTEP to adapt the math and English program to make it work for my students. We did string math, used manipulatives, and studied legends. In short, it was a very interesting and draining year. My students proved to be challenging, but they brought so many gifts to the room that I was honoured to teach them. I had always thought a successful teacher was someone who liked students. It was then I learned that it was not enough to like them; the students needed to believe you liked them. If they believed that, they would work with you and give you some space to prove you were really genuine. I can recall many of the things that made this time special. I spent time taking pictures of students. I displayed them on bulletin boards in my room. My classroom walls were covered with pictures of Aboriginal role models, and reflected Métis and First Nations cultures. The rest of my class focused on Aboriginal content. It quickly became a "nest" or a place of safety where the students would come at break time or recess. As the Aboriginal students felt welcomed, they began to show up regularly for class.

These students all got nicknames from me, since each had his or her own character. They brought to the table a set of values and background history that demanded attention. I spent a great deal of time trying to learn about them to validate where they came from. I also found them generally lacking in respect for themselves and others. This became an area that got a huge amount of attention and we began a process that revolved around respect, both giving and expecting. This began a transformation noticed by others. Teachers asked me what it was that made those students listen to me. I replied, "In order to get respect, you must give respect," and this was our classroom mantra.

I was also very involved in coaching the high school volleyball teams, both boys and girls, and the boys' basketball team, and was the track and field coach. The senior students from my Native studies classes were the older brothers and sisters of many of my Grade 7 students. They were much easier to connect with. They were much better at the respect issues, and I found that treating them like adults was a method they responded well to. They had a strong sense of playground fairness, and they were not concerned by how strict you were, even if you punished them for inappropriate behaviour, as long as you were consistent and didn't let anybody off the hook. These older students helped me groom the younger ones. They used phrases like, "Don't mess with Coach, or you mess with me," or, "You guys listen to Coach, because he is looking out for you." It also helped that I recruited players who lived on the reserves and farms. I wanted a good team, and there were many fine athletes that previously had not been involved, since they were bussed to school. I would ask them to stay after school and would drive them home after practice or games. The parents and I formed a strong connection, as we both knew that students involved in sports led to motivated young leaders.

This process went on for three years, and over the course of these years I had frequent interactions with my first group of students. Many of these were in disciplinary situations, but one of the rules I had was that, no matter what, when the students knew they messed up, they would pay a price. But when it was done, I still liked them and they still liked me. I became known by the students as someone who was tough but fair.

The staff at the school, including those who previously had been on the fence about me, became supporters. As staff retired, I recruited and supported young teachers who would put the students first. This created a positive flow of energy and began to be reflected in the Aboriginal student retention and graduation rates. One area that remained problematic in terms of Aboriginal student success was at the senior math level. Many of the Aboriginal students chose to stream themselves into General Math 10, a class needed to meet the graduation requirements. When the senior math teacher retired, it gave me the opportunity to think about the math class. I noticed that many of the Aboriginal students did not do well even with the general math. I felt I could make a difference with student success based on the relationship I had with these students, whom I had taught in Grade 7, because I still had a connection with them. I also had a bit of a math background, and thought I was ready for the new challenge of teaching the General Math 10. I soon had a classroom of Grade 10 and 11 students who had skill levels ranging from Grades 7 to 11. A couple of the students should have been taking the more academic math class, but they insisted they wanted to come to this class, since this was where their friends were. I quickly found out that the resources selected for teaching the course would not work for these students, and a new approach to teaching was needed. The previous program was quiz- and exam-based, and as a result, the students fared poorly. Confidence was a big factor, and this led to a general dislike for the subject.

One of my teacher allies had worked for many years in the Adult Education area. I asked her for some help, and we put together an assignment-based program. I created sixty assignments ranging in difficulty from Grades 8 to 10. One mark was obtained for each assignment they mastered, calculated at no more than two wrong on any given assignment. I allowed them to work in groups or pairs. I also recruited a teacher associate and we taught, re-taught, encouraged, supported, and pushed the students to complete the assignments. The rest of the marks were based on attendance, effort, and on four exams. However, because the exams were based on the assignments the students had completed, they were able to do the exams successfully. The net result was a substantial increase in the success rate of the students. The first year, over

80 percent of the students succeeded. The second time we ran the program, we had 100 percent success. This was much better than previous years and brought about a strong sense of well-being at the student level. This had an impact on them in their other subject areas as well. Previously, when they had a tough time with math, it had a tendency to discourage them and lead to other decisions that didn't support school achievement. They now began to believe they could graduate and achieve goals that were once private pipe dreams.

I was able to watch the graduation rates rise at the school. I realized the graduates were not able to attend university without upgrading or taking some other math courses, but they had developed a belief in themselves that was positive. They were able to look ahead and see something that perhaps was not there before. I followed the graduation results for a few years after leaving the school. I saw they were still up there. I don't have the answers, but believe the students who came along after were encouraged by the successes of their older siblings. I also believe the staff was able to continue building relationships with the students.

I look back to that time with a strong sense of pride and wonder. Some of the staff I worked with ten to fifteen years ago are still there. I visit with them periodically, and they appear happy to see me. The real joy is when I run into former students. They still refer to me as Mr. Racette. Many tell me that though I was very different from other teachers they had, they liked me. I think back to the successes and I know what it was. It was not because I was a brilliant teacher or a remarkable communicator. Not at all. It was because I took the time to build a relationship with the students. They knew I liked them as people and I enjoyed spending time with them. The willingness on my part to get involved in their lives encouraged them to welcome me into their lives. The friendship and warmth turned to trust and respect.

I currently work in a situation where I am classed as middle management, and I work out of a central board office. Much of my work still involves trying to improve retention and graduation rates for Aboriginal students. I continue to hear the words *literacy* and *numeracy*, and the provincial system keeps talking about a continuous improvement framework. I chuckle hearing all of the buzz words and phrases being used. I know these words have a place and role to play, but the secret is relationship building. The students I have had the pleasure of working with continue to enrich my life. As I said, I periodically run into them. After all, they are still part of my community. I always ask how they are doing and encourage them to be the best they can be. They know I don't have a hidden agenda. They know my feelings for them are genuine, just as theirs are for me.

I thank them for moulding me, in part, to become the person I am today. I am a better parent because of them. I am a better grandparent because of them. The community recognizes the role I played in their lives and has given me a place in the collective memory, and it is there I find security and, in many respects, belonging. I have spent many years in academia reading about teaching and learning and know that Aboriginal education is not a product, it is a process. I have travelled that process, and my students travelled it with me. While looking for the end, I came to realize the end never arrives, because there are new students with similar needs, and my role as a nurturing caring adult is still needed.

The role of the math room, the fear of math, the trust and friendship that began in the Grade 7 class all became building blocks in the students' lives. I am proud to have had the opportunity to meet and work with such a special group of young men and women. Their journey and mine have truly been on a road paved with many special moments that I will always be proud of and hold close to my heart. Marci.

Calvin's story illustrates the impact of personal relationships between the teacher and students on the success of Indigenous students in school. Because he knew his students, he recognized when school programming would not work for them and was able to adapt it so they would experience success. At the heart of this story of success is the importance of trust in overcoming student fear and negative beliefs about their academic abilities. Fear is a powerful block to learning. A trusted teacher, whom you know has your best interest at heart, can go a long way to lead you forward as you face your fears. Calvin built trust through mutual respect, one of the key features of Category 1 of the model, in which the teacher creates the culturally affirming connections between students and herself that are foundational to effective teaching for Indigenous students.

What follows are the details regarding the teacher actions in each of the categories and subcategories of the model of effective teaching. In describing this and other categories of the model, we try to retain the voice of the teachers as much as possible. To illustrate each category, we use the teachers' words by quoting directly from the interviews or by paraphrasing what teachers said.

The school observations and field notes are quoted only as needed when something occurred in the classroom that was not as clearly expressed in the interviews.

Category 1: Relationships with Indigenous Students

Teachers emphasized the importance of close, personal relationships with students as opposed to being distant and formal. As Yvonne said, "You have to develop a relationship with Indigenous students. You can't keep your distance. They want to know you; they want to connect with you. They need to have a sense of belonging." Developing personal relationships was seen by Fran as preceding academics, because the relationships give the teacher knowledge of how to approach the educational material for each individual and the class as a whole. Relationship building in this study was achieved through various means: in one-on-one interactions outside of teaching in the classroom, such as at recess or noon hours; in informal settings, such as coaching or supervision of extracurricular activities; and outside the school in informal community interactions or at community events. Teachers also structured relationship building into their classroom activities. In her classroom with Dene speakers, Val set aside time each morning for "visiting" with the children, when she learned about their personal lives while they practised speaking to express their ideas.

The category of developing relationships has four subcategories: believing in the student; developing close, personal bonds; valuing the individual and his/her culture; and building reciprocal respect and trust.

Believing in the Student

The first subcategory of Category 1 describes the stance of teachers in the development of close relationships with students. In our study, the teachers believed their students were capable learners who had the ability to change any behaviour that prevented them from learning.

Believing in the Student's Ability to Learn

As we've seen, belief in a student's capability is crucial for their success. Val stated it was important also to communicate that belief to the student and to make the student believe it too. As evident in Calvin's story, if a student was not learning, the teacher looked to their instruction for the reason why and sought to use different approaches when one was not working. The strong belief in self and students was evident in the teachers' perseverance. They believed students would eventually be "drawn into the learning" (Fran).

Believing in the Student's Ability to Change

Effective teachers in this study believed students were capable of change. Yvonne described how students were capable of changing destructive, inappropriate behaviour; she had seen the transformation in her students. When a student acted inappropriately, Yvonne conveyed her belief to the student that he was capable of change. She reported that follow-up to the behaviour was needed, to describe appropriate behaviour to the student and reinforce it when it happened.

Students know what people think of them. Unfortunately, negative teacher attitudes are still too prevalent. When a teacher doesn't care, students won't either, and misbehaviour escalates as the frustration of not learning grows. After the inappropriate behaviour of one of her students, Yvonne had a meeting with the principal, the resource teacher, the student, and his parents. After the parents and student left, the principal and the resource teacher placed bets as to how long the student would last. Yvonne was hurt and appalled by the behaviour of her colleagues. "Kids aren't stupid. They know when people expect them to fail." Owen emphasized the importance of the teacher in the child's life – often, the teacher spends more time with the child than the parent during a day.

Developing Close, Personal Bonds

The second subcategory of Category 1 describes the approach of teachers in the development of close relationships with students. The attributes of the subcategory of bonding with students are: genuine caring for students and being open and human with students.

Genuine Caring

Through their words and actions, teachers demonstrated that they cared deeply for their students. They were compassionate; their "hearts were open" to each and every child who came to them and "big enough for all of them to fit in" (Val). Interview participants said a teacher needed to be nurturing and have a lot of patience. Caring was expressed in obvious ways, such as hugs for the little ones or high fives with older ones (Goulet 2005, 13). But it was also expressed by such things as greeting students when they came to school in the morning, to let them know they were welcome and that the teacher was glad to have them there. Yvonne showed she cared about her student when she asked a mother who was moving to another part of the city not to move her son to another school. Yvonne wanted the boy to stay in her classroom, where he was experiencing success, something that had not happened much in his past.

The teachers identified Indigenous forms of cultural interaction and caring communication. They talked about the need for humour in teaching – the ability to laugh at themselves and with the students was seen as key to positive relationships with Indigenous students. Teasing and nicknames were also used. A student would be given a nickname about an incident and then teased about that incident. At the same time, teachers had firm boundaries around teasing and nicknames. Teasing would not be done in a way that would embarrass a student or put him down. Rather, nicknames and teasing were a way of having fun together, recalling shared times of humour, and forming close connections. Many acts of teasing were recorded in the school observations. For example, on one occasion, when a Grade 5 boy was distracting other students from their work, "The teacher commented, 'I think he's doing that so he gets attention. I think he wants a smooch. He has cute dimples. I have lots of girls to volunteer to give those dimples a big smooch.' The students laugh about this and the boy in question grins as he returns to his work" (Goulet 2005, 18).

Here, an open heart meant a teacher continued to care about a child even when the child was in trouble or causing problems. It was important to express compassion and caring to the student especially when he was acting out. Tony commented that a way to show caring when a child was in trouble was to deal with it quickly, impose the consequences, then move on and leave the incident behind, rather than taking the behaviour personally or holding a grudge against a student. Defending students to other teachers also showed caring. Accepting students who made mistakes was closely connected to another aspect of being open – being human.

Showing Humanness
The teachers commented that in developing close bonds with students, it was important to be seen as human by the students, outside the role of teacher. Stepping out of the role of teacher was accomplished by spending time with students outside of academic time. With younger children, Val had students stay after school or at recess to help out with classroom chores. Owen would eat lunch with students and "shoot the breeze" before math club started. The teachers' humanness was also expressed through interactions in the community,

where each teacher was seen as just another adult in the lives of the children. Indigenous teachers who were from the community believed that sharing the same cultural identity, living a common life, and taking part in community events engendered trust and closeness with students.

Showing humanness was also achieved when the teachers were open about their personal lives with students. Teachers shared stories of their family life and opened their personal space to the students. All of the teachers talked about having the students come to their home – for lunch one day on a field trip to show students where the teacher lived off the reserve, for pizza supper at the teacher's house after winning a math contest, to visit over hot chocolate after school, or to babysit for the teacher. When teachers were open about their personal lives, students saw the teachers as regular people. The teacher was not better than the students, but was another human being like them, "having good days and bad days" (Kendra). Teachers shared some of these ups and downs with students, in part, so students wouldn't feel so isolated or alone in facing their own problems.

Mistakes were seen as part of human interaction. Effective teachers were open about mistakes they made with students in order to illustrate that everyone makes mistakes. When teachers made mistakes in the classroom, often they would model laughing at themselves. Val said laughing at mistakes was part of her Indigenous culture, that "self-ridicule and laughter helped others to heal." Ida often asked her students to watch her teaching and let her know when she made a mistake.

Emotions were given expression and were not viewed as something to be avoided in the classroom. Students were made to feel that expressing emotions was healthy and part of being human, whether it was laughter or tears, student or teacher. In this way, students saw teachers as people who, like themselves, made mistakes, had problems, and experienced emotions, inside and outside the classroom.

Like Calvin, other teachers talked about the bonds they had developed with their students lasting for years. An indicator of this bond is that several of these elementary teachers were invited to attend or speak at their former students' Grade 12 graduation ceremony. One teacher was interviewed by his former student when she was in university doing an assignment on a person who had made a difference in her life (Tony). The demonstration of connection was sometimes more immediate; for example, when a kindergarten student dragged a large whitefish in a garbage bag to school as a present for her teacher (Val).

Valuing the Individual and His/Her Culture

This subcategory of "Developing Relationships with Indigenous Students" describes the enactment of the teachers' belief that each child is unique and special. In addition to respecting the child's individuality, the culture to which the child belonged was respected.

Each Student Is Special

How the teacher viewed the students was as important to these teachers as how the students perceived the teacher. Teachers enacted their views by doing things to make a child feel special. When a child was feeling down, the teacher would think of ways to cheer him up, or give him certain tasks to do to take his mind off his problems. Because each student was different, he or she needed to be treated accordingly, depending on his or her strengths and weaknesses. Each student was seen as having a special talent to be discovered, developed, and shared with others. Teachers got to know their students' abilities by observing them, talking to them, and noticing their participation in activities. This knowledge of students' abilities was especially important in determining the level of English-language capability in classrooms where English was spoken as an additional language or dialect.

Respecting Indigenous Culture

Every teacher talked about the importance of demonstrating both a positive attitude towards Indigenous culture and respect for Indigenous people. Indigenous teachers openly shared with students their cultural identity and experiences as an Indigenous person. However, none of the teachers in this study used Indigenous spiritual ceremonies as part of their teaching. One Indigenous teacher mentioned spiritual practices only to indicate that although she herself participated in ceremonies, she was not comfortable teaching traditional ceremonies in school, in part because she believed she was not knowledgeable enough. More commonly, the use of Indigenous ceremonies in the education system was done at the school level, with input from the community, and most often by Elders or community knowledge keepers.

Acknowledging indigeneity was particularly important in racially heterogeneous classrooms. Wanda, a non-Indigenous teacher, taught in an inner-city school with mostly Indigenous students. She would consciously say something positive in front of the class about an Indigenous person the students knew. To the Indigenous students, it acted as a signal that she knew and had respect for

Indigenous people. Then the "children would relax and acknowledge they were Indian."

Building Reciprocal Respect and Trust

The fourth subcategory describes the nature of the relationships. The teachers demonstrated their sensitivity to the lives of Indigenous children by showing respect. If respect was not present, trust did not develop. Respect and reciprocity were features of the leadership style of these teachers that affected the student-teacher relationships.

The Value of Respect

Many of the teachers talked about respect being of utmost importance in teaching Indigenous students. As aforementioned, students were respected as individuals for their uniqueness and their culture, and also as social beings affected by the society around them and the social issues in their communities. Effective teachers were aware of the social problems their students faced. As Ida said, "It helps to know the kinds of lives [the students] live." The emotional state of the child affected how teachers interacted with students. Teachers often listened to students' stories about the stresses in their lives. They demonstrated respect when they responded to the realities of their students' lives with awareness, sensitivity, and understanding.

Honesty was an important aspect of respect. The teachers believed that if you were not genuine with your students, the students would know and not respond. Teachers felt an aspect of respecting students was being honest about their skill development. Val had a student who was eleven and still unable to read. At first, the student tried to cover it up, especially in front of the other students, by acting up whenever it was time to read. When talking to the student alone, Val indicated she knew he could not read, but reassured him she was there to help him learn how. At the same time, Val did not put the student in a situation that would call other students' attention to the fact he was unable to read. Val's actions illustrate the importance of confidentiality and trust as aspects of respect. Trust was also related to setting and enforcing clear expectations and boundaries for performance and behaviour. Students needed to trust that a teacher would be firm in dealing with inappropriate behaviour, impose fair consequences, and follow up.

Respect was both mutual and reciprocal, and tied to responsibility and the development of self-determination. Rather than demanding performance from students, the teachers tried to draw it out of them, showing respect for the student's choice to engage in learning. Drawing students into learning relates to the teacher's belief that students can make the right choices and be responsible for their learning and behaviour. When the teacher treated the students with respect, the students reciprocated. In one school, most teachers would unlock the door for students rather than giving them a key, but Tony would lend students his master key, which was costly to replace. He just said, "I'll trust you with my keys. Don't let me down," and they never did. Trust, responsibility, and mutual respect were inherent in this small act.

Equitable Leadership

As we touched on earlier, mutual respect meant that the leadership style of the teacher was not autocratic. All of the teachers spoke of the need for leadership that was more equitable. In characterizing the kind of relationship needed by a teacher of Indigenous students, teachers indicated that you could not put yourself above the children. A teacher could lead but only by establishing trust so the students would follow. "You can't be the boss looking down at students, like an authority figure. You had to find trust. I worked hard to gain the confidence of the students ... I want to be friends with them, but I also let them know I am in charge. I quickly established I was fair but firm" (Tony). Kendra related her leadership style to her own experience. "I would take the role of the leader rather than an authority figure with the students because I myself do not like authority figures, or have a difficult time with authority figures."

The leadership style was also reflected in the informal language used with the children, particularly by the male teachers. Yet within this informal language, teachers clearly set boundaries and clarified expectations for the students. Owen would tell his students not to "hide in the bushes" if they had not come to see him when he was working individually with them. At the beginning of the school year, he told students they needed to know two things before they could get out of Grade 6: "your times tables and my name." With these words, Owen shared his expectations for student achievement in math, but lightened it with humour.

Consequences of Connected Teacher-Student Relationships

The teachers we observed wanted to be closely connected to their students for a purpose. First, they reported that a personal relationship with students led to improved student attendance. This insight is important, since attendance is tied to achievement and remains an ongoing educational issue for many Indigenous students. When students feel cared about and respected, they want to be in class and come to school. When the teachers showed the students respect, the students could express themselves as cultural beings, proud of who they were and their culture.

Second, personal relationships affected student achievement. Knowing students as individuals meant teachers knew their students' interests, strengths and weaknesses, and the problems in their personal lives. This knowledge allowed the teacher to adjust the curriculum to better meet the needs of students and to "draw students into learning." To Owen, a strong personal bond with students meant he knew their different personalities; thus, he knew how hard he could push them academically.

As we've shown, being human in the classroom is a mutual affair. If the teacher can admit to making mistakes, students can also make mistakes and, if necessary, be given a second chance. In guiding his decision making with students, Tony recalled the people who had given him a second chance when he was "one of those problem kids" in school and tried to focus not only on the negative but also on the positive aspects of the student when imposing disciplinary action. Learning that mistakes are part of the human condition allows students to make academic errors without embarrassment and the fear of being labelled.

A respectful, trusting relationship in the classroom means both teachers and students can take risks with each other in the learning situation. If Indigenous children do not trust their teacher, they will not be open to learning, will be reluctant to try, and will not become fully engaged in learning. On the other hand, as Val said, "once you gain their trust, they will do anything for you, absolutely anything." Students will succeed beyond their teacher's, and often their own, expectations.

6

Weetutoskemitowin, Working Together:
Social Systems

Teachers can connect individual students to the class in a way that creates a social system that acknowledges and respects the students' sociocultural and ethnocultural situation. The first and second categories, when taken together, reflect the Nehinuw concept of a balanced approach between the individual and the collective. In Category 1, described above, we saw that *otootemitowin* (being open and diplomatic) by the teacher facilitates close, personal teacher-student relationships between the teacher and individual students. In Category 2, explored below, the teacher emphasizes *weetutoskemitowin* (working together) by doing activities to develop the values and skills for open, respectful social relationships among students. Students learn from the teacher modelling in Category 1 how to enact *weechihitowin* (supporting and helping each other), which shapes the class into a community of learners.

Angie Caron shared how she develops a sense of community in her classroom. In her story, some of the features of the previous category are evident, such as helping students recognize and share their gifts with others and her belief in students as she supports and prepares them for success in school and in life.

Creating Classroom Learning Communities

Angie Caron

I am a graduate of the Saskatchewan Urban Native Teacher Education Program (SUNTEP) in Saskatoon. Although I am currently a consultant

Angie with the Grade 4 and 5 students from Westmount Community School, Saskatoon, sharing Mom's cookies. *Leftt to right:* Arisha Javed, Zahra Alkashwan, April Jepsen, Angie Caron, Hailey Whitehead, Samantha Ellison, Stella Caron, Natalie Vanidour, Danielle Roberts, and Clement Gagne. *Photo by Keith Goulet.*

for an urban school division, I have been a resource room teacher, a vice-principal in a suburban school, and a teacher in a community school where I taught Grades 3, 4, and 5 for six years. A community school has access to enhanced funding to support the circumstances of students and their families in higher needs communities.

I love being in the classroom. I don't always feel I am the most gifted instructor, but I believe my gift as a teacher is to bond with children. The children I really connect with are often those for whom others have run out of patience. Teachers sometimes take kids' behaviour personally, but none of these kids get up in the morning and say they want to make life rough for their teacher. They simply don't have the tools they need to stay focused and be successful in their learning. All behaviour is purposeful. I try to analyze it and problem solve around it in the hope of helping students meet the need that the negative behaviour is trying to address, in a more positive way.

I think it's important for teachers, and especially new teachers, to know that creating a learning community in a classroom won't happen in a day. Even when you have worked really hard to do this with your students, every day is different. There are good days and bad days for us all, including me as the teacher. I've gone in and apologized to my class and said, "I realize I did this and I don't think it worked for you." Kids appreciate it because then they realize everyone makes mistakes. I'll do that with teaching as well. If kids aren't getting it, I say, "I didn't explain this in a way that was right for you. I'm going to try a different way to see if it works for you." When I make a mistake, they respond with, "That's okay, Ms. Caron." I always encourage them to be as forgiving of themselves as they are of me.

As teachers, we support children in school, but part of our role is to prepare them for the challenges they face outside of school. You can have sympathy and empathy, but as a teacher, you can't use it as an excuse for why students are not successful in their behaviour or their learning. We have to have high but realistic expectations for our students because they will rise to the challenge if we provide them with the tools to face adversity. I want my students to know they may not have choice about their circumstance, but they can always choose how they will respond to those circumstances. As a teacher, you feel badly for kids who are in bad situations, but if you stop there, or try to solve problems for the students, you will not empower them to deal with their own real-life problems. As teachers, we need to provide our students with skills and strategies that will help them develop resiliency so they can overcome the challenges they will face. We also need to be explicit about the transfer of a strategy to a different situation: "You were able to achieve this here at school. How can you use that same strategy at home or out in the community?" My own belief ties into Métis or First Nations world views where young people are encouraged to explore their environment and develop strategies for functioning within that environment themselves. People sometimes misinterpret that as parents not caring – they judge adults negatively who relate to young people in that way as opposed to valuing adult behaviour that develops self-responsibility and independence.

In every school I have been in, I see students who have skills. They may not be achieving on standardized tests using white middle-class norms, but that doesn't mean they don't have skills. It just means we as teachers haven't found ways to uncover the strengths of our kids yet. Sometimes teachers blame parents. I try to take a more self-reflective view. I ask myself, "What am I not doing to enable students to show me what they can do?" If students aren't successful, I don't want to take all the blame, but I do have to take some of the responsibility.

I build a community in the classroom by developing trust and a sense of belonging. That's my first goal at the beginning of year. I tell my students,

"We're a big family. We're spending a lot of hours together, so we have to think about how we want to be in this space." I start with wanting everyone to have a voice. I build trust by listening. To develop voice, I use the talking circle regularly. I start by having them talk about their hopes for the year.

In addition to the talking circles, we get to know each other through various activities. For example, I use a "Me Bag," where students share who they are and explore their own identity. I model the activity by making a bag of objects that represent me – pictures of friends and family, my ball glove, my Métis sash, that I then share with the students to help them get to know me as a person, not just as a teacher. I emphasize that it's not about the number of things or the dollar value of them, it's about the meaning those things have for you. I ask, "Is this something you would be interested in? A Me Bag?" I give them the option to do it and all of them do.

Often, students don't know they have something valuable to say, something to teach all of us. I remember one little boy brought in moccasins his grandma had made for him. It was clear he really appreciated the time and effort she put into making and beading his moccasins. We also learned about how much he valued his relationship with his *Koogom* (grandmother). It made us all think about our grandparents and led to a discussion about how we let our grandparents know we appreciate them. This sharing developed relationships among the students as they got to know one another better. What was really interesting about this was the development of relationships based on knowledge of common values and interests among students, even though many of them had been together for a few years.

I want students to have a strong sense of belonging in the class, so I do a number of activities to help them understand the concept of inclusion. One I have found to be effective is "friendship circles." A friendship circle has two big circles, like a Venn diagram. In one, they describe the uniqueness of themselves, and in the other circle, they include students who are their friends. I begin by talking about friendship. "I know not everyone in the class will be your best friend. Our first temptation is to go to someone you hang out with, but doesn't everybody deserve respect and kindness, and the opportunity to be a part of a group? I want you to get to know others to include them in your circle. See what you have in common. We have to figure out a way to have everyone included. We wouldn't want to be left out, so be aware not to leave anyone else out." I monitor this activity but I try not to intervene because I want the students to be able to identify and then include those students who are sometimes left on the outside.

The students have conversations with other students to get to know them. I model how to start a conversation by asking another teacher to come into my class. I'll share something about me, then I'll get her to share something about herself, like "I have a dog," "Oh, I have a cat." I tell my students to keep talking long enough until they find something in common. When they have their conversation, I monitor and listen in. I ask to join them. I want them to be able to call anyone their friend so they can include them in the activities in the class and on the playground. I also read a lot of books to my class: books on friendship and about ordinary young people making extraordinary differences in the lives of others.

In all the times I have done the friendship circles, there has never been a time someone has been left out. Respect and kindness comes out in our talking circle. Then the friendship circles develop a representation and reminder of what we believe in our classroom. They know it's not kind to leave someone out of the circle, so they try to make sure no one is left out. Inclusionary practice needs to be reinforced. If this is taught and then forgotten about, things quickly slide back into an environment where some are excluded. These activities provide the basis for dealing with our relationships as the year goes on. When a fight develops or someone has been excluded, I ask, "What was your part in this? How could you do this differently to remain a part of the friendship circle and ensure others are included too?"

The community of learners is a common goal we work towards in the classroom. I tell students, "We are all in this together. We're here to support one another." I structure the learning so they have to work together. I choose activities such as Puzzle Island [or other activities from the Quicksilver or Silver Bullet books by Rohnke 1984, 1995], where they have to find hidden pictures and words to figure out what the mixed up letters are in order to solve the mystery by the end of the book. The groups tend to get competitive, so I use it as an opportunity to teach about cooperation. Students are often not used to working with others to achieve a common goal. They often start arguing about who is right, because they believe they know how to solve the problem. Some teams will accomplish the task while other teams are arguing, so I have the team that accomplished the task first share what enabled them to do that. The group usually responds that they listened to each other. I highlight the fact that this group had the time to talk, listen to each other, and still accomplish the task first. I explain that problem solving will often work better "if you work together and don't try to be the boss of each other. Sometimes in life we have to work in a system that doesn't do things the way you would do it. You need to think about what is important and what you can let go of." It is a mini lesson on how to pick your battles.

Everyone should feel good about being in the classroom. I say, "When we act in unkind ways and don't learn from that, we make the classroom an unsafe place for everyone. Your choices affect others. Do you have the right to make this an unsafe place for others? We all have rights but we also have responsibilities attached to those rights." I also talk about rights and responsibilities to facilitate the development of classroom rules and procedures. They will say things like, "We should be able to go to the bathroom anytime we want. We have a right to recess and field trips." We talk about the rights we can implement within our classroom according to the need to function appropriately within the larger school community and within society in general. For each right students believe they have, we have a discussion about what responsibilities go with that right. As soon as you connect that for kids, they know there are responsibilities attached to rights.

Without the development of a sense of community, I have no understanding of how to go into a class as a teacher. A lot of behaviour problems in the class come from the need for power. If you address the students' need for power by giving them a voice in the class, they don't need to exert their power in less desirable ways. Glaser's (1984) work, which addresses the needs we all have for power, freedom, fun, and a sense of belonging, is the philosophical basis of my teaching. I spend time teaching my students about our needs and how we can get our needs met in the classroom and school without infringing upon the needs and safety of others. In saying all of this, I can't always be the teacher I want to be. Sometimes I have to be the teacher my students need me to be at that given time. What tells me what they need is whether the current approach is working for them. For example, how I arrange the room depends on the students. If students choose to sit in groups, they have responsibilities. Sometimes I will ask them, "How is this working?" They often respond with, "We're talking too much, so maybe we have to go back to rows." Sometimes it's them making the decision, sometimes it's me, but together we need to make it work for all of us, including me as the teacher.

When I reflect on my beliefs and my approach to teaching, I recognize the effect that family and cultural values have on my teaching. I think my belief about sitting down and sharing food with people comes from my paternal Métis grandmother who, although she had very little, always believed in feeding people who came to her house. As a family, we carry on those Métis ways, so we get together to share meals to celebrate birthdays, anniversaries, and other holidays. This practice carries over into my work with kids and provides me with a valuable opportunity for building relationships and maintaining a cohesive learning community. I'm lucky – my mom bakes, I bake, Tim Hortons bakes. Even when we have built a community at the beginning of the school year, we need to maintain it. So once a week, we decide what we will do to interact with one another for fifteen to twenty minutes. We may visit and have our snack in the classroom or we will decide to take it outside and play on the creative playground. There is always an emphasis on community and a reminder that all have to be included in the play to maintain the classroom community.

Sometimes, depending on your administrator, these activities can be looked upon as you not being a responsible teacher. As a teacher, I have to explain my philosophy and the relationship of this practice to student learning so that when what I am doing with my class looks different than the norm, it is not misinterpreted. Others may see it as me not doing my job, but I see developing relationships with my students and helping them to build a community of belonging as the most important part of my job because it facilitates effective teaching and learning.

There is often discussion about what we value in our classroom. I share with the students that I value persistence, working hard to achieve goals, and the opportunity to work with each one of them every day. I talk to students about being a learner myself. When we all see ourselves as learners, we have the opportunity to contribute something to the collective that we wouldn't have individually. I tell the students, "You have gifts to share in this class. Everyone has a gift to share. If you are willing to share with us, whether it is building a paper airplane or grooming a dog, I want to learn from you." I like to talk to them about the need to be proud of our gifts, but we also need to be willing to be honest about what we don't know. I will tell them when I don't know something in the hopes that they, in turn, will tell me when they don't know something, instead of being scared to not know or to be wrong. If they don't want to say so in front of the class, I encourage them to come and tell me alone, and we will work after school or at recess together to learn what they need to.

I love working with kids but it challenges my limits every day. I think I'm lucky because I go to school every day to do something I truly enjoy despite the overwhelming expectations and challenges. Every day, someone learns something, and I get to be a part of that. I hope the students know I love teaching and I really care about them, because the relationships I have developed with them over the years have brought so much joy and satisfaction to my life. I've been extremely lucky in my career to work with so many wonderful and gifted teachers and administrators. Each experience has shaped and will continue to shape my philosophy and my practice. I am fortunate to have such an extensive and supportive learning community. Marci!

Who wouldn't want to be in Angie's class where you can visit with friends and relax with cookies and hot chocolate on a Friday afternoon after a week of hard work? We can feel the sense of comfort, closeness, and belonging developed through Angie's deliberate activities to build social skills of *weetutoskemitowin* (working together). In her story, she reminds us it takes time to build a community of learners, and even after it happens, we are still humans working together, so life in the classroom is never perfect. In expecting students to share their gifts, she hearkens back to Category 1, where the teacher recognized each student's individuality. Now, in Category 2, we see individual expression developing relationships among students and as a way to share leadership and responsibility for the learning. Angie's method of getting students to share their gifts and give expression to who they are as individuals and cultural beings foreshadows future categories, in which students make connections between school learning and life outside of school and vice versa.

Category 2: Relationships among Students

As is evident in Angie's story, effective teachers of Indigenous students teach for the intellectual growth of the children, but not in isolation from the emotional, social, and spiritual development of students. (In this book, we use the term *spiritual development* in the way it is often used by Elders when referring to the development of children. Spiritual development is seen as "becoming a good human being" [the late Elder Bea Lavallee].) Like Angie, Ida believed that if a student's social issues were not dealt with, the problems would interfere with learning, because the student would have a hard time focusing on academics when he was trying to deal with the stress of an overwhelming personal problem.

In the chaos and complexity of a group of students coming together with a teacher to form a class, the attributes of teacher-student relationships evident in Category 1 – closeness, respect, believing in and valuing others – are relevant to the relationships developed among the students. In Category 2, the relationship between the teacher and the student is expanded to others, as the individual student is situated in the physical and social system of the class and the school. Whereas in Category 1 the relational focus is with the individual and the teacher, in Category 2, the emphasis is on relationships within the class as a whole. Students learn different values inherent in the Nehinuw social relations of *weechihitowin* (helping and supporting each other), *weechiyauguneetowin* (partnerships), and *weechiseechigemitowin* (alliances) to enable them to effectively work together *(weetutoskemitowin)* and teach each other *(kiskinaumatowin)*.

Category 2, "Relationships among Students," has four subcategories: safety and belonging, positive emotional growth, social skills for working together, and shared leadership.

Safety and Belonging

This first subcategory describes how these teachers created a sense of safety and belonging for Indigenous students within the classroom. In the physical space and in social interactions, the student's needs and culture were acknowledged and dealt with respectfully. Group norms based on respect for the individual and the group were established to guide classroom behaviour and interactions.

Valuing Indigenous Culture

Whereas in Category 1 the teacher expressed respect for Indigenous culture with individual students, in this category, the emphasis is on the class as a whole. In our study, effective teachers validated Indigenous culture by using Indigenous language, respecting cultural knowledge, and reinforcing community values that created a sense of belonging for Indigenous students. The use of Indigenous language in the classroom varied depending on the fluency of the teacher and the students. Where both the teacher and the students were fluent speakers, the Indigenous language was used to visit with students, explain concepts, or clarify instruction given in English. Where children were not fluent, teachers would use phrases the children could understand in classroom communication or as part of the curriculum (Goulet 2005, 20). Others taught children things like the months of the year, colours, and numbers, and used Cree songs in music (2). Even non-Indigenous teachers often used Indigenous language. Doris learned enough Cree to teach the children a word every day.

Teachers also demonstrated respect for the Indigenous cultural knowledge of the parents, grandparents, and community members by including them as resources in the curriculum. The wisdom of family members was valued when making decisions about how to increase the success of a student in the classroom. Community values such as the importance of working together (*weet-utoskemitowin*) were taught as concepts and skills to learn in the classroom.

The use of Indigenous language, patterns of communication, and incorporation of Indigenous knowledge and values in the class created a sense of familiarity and belonging, so that students would be open to learning. This was one of the ways that teachers overcame student shyness and the historical reluctance of Indigenous peoples to be a part of colonial schooling. Both Indigenous teachers, Val and Kendra said that Indigenous students were too often made to feel that to succeed in school they needed to leave behind their Indianness. These teachers believed success in school should not be at the expense of the student's loss of cultural identity; rather, it should be achieved by embracing that very part of the student's identity.

Belonging in the Physical Space

The second attribute of safety and belonging is connecting students to the physical space. Teachers connected children to the classroom and school by establishing familiarity and belonging in the space, affirming the students' right to be there, and providing physical cues that students as individuals and cultural beings were acknowledged and respected in the classroom.

In the inner city, it was particularly important that students become familiar with the classroom and school, because the students tended to transfer frequently among different schools. For young children, coming to a new school in the middle of the school year could be an intimidating experience. Wanda familiarized new students with their surroundings by taking them on a tour of the school. Students were encouraged to smile at and greet the people they met on the tour so the new students had a positive sense of the school community. Students would find out where siblings and cousins were, and get information about when they would see these family members. Being connected to someone they already knew gave the new students a sense of security and safety.

In the provincial school, where many of the Indigenous students came from nearby reserves, Tony told the students more than once that they had a right to be in the school; that it was theirs. "It wasn't the town's school, it was everybody's school, and [the Indigenous students] had as much right to be there as anybody. They never had anybody tell them that before, and that was a first, that they have every right to be here and that is all there is to it."

The classrooms of many of the teachers were decorated in a way that gave children a sense of belonging in that space. Some teachers had children draw themselves or things they liked to do to post in the classroom. Like Calvin, others took pictures of the students and put the photographs on the walls so students would see themselves represented in the room. Many teachers used the physical space to validate the culture of the students. They decorated the classrooms with posters of Indigenous subjects such as role models or art. Some used artifacts like hide paintings or beadwork to decorate the room, while others had Indigenous books on display or Indigenous words posted on the walls (Goulet 2005, 1).

Social Safety

Teachers reported it was important to create a sense of safety by being clear regarding classroom expectations, including the norm of respect. Harriet commented that establishing and practising classroom routines was especially important in the younger grades. Limits were set and consequences were discussed in order for students to know what to expect, and the teacher followed up to enforce expectations. Context was a determinant in the length of time needed by the teacher to establish class norms and routines, because some classes were harder to settle; thus, a wider variety of approaches would be used and for a longer period of time.

In addition to class routines and norms, teachers set up structures where students felt safe to express themselves in front of others. Many teachers used a talking or sharing circle in their class as a safe place where students could share. In regard to personal safety, sometimes it extended beyond the classroom. Ida helped a student make a plan to look after herself when things were not safe at home.

Positive Emotional Growth

The second subcategory is the creation of an outlet for positive emotional expression. Many Indigenous families face hardships and have a great deal of stress in their lives, so emotional safety and security is an issue for the Indigenous students in those families.

Teacher Awareness of Emotional Issues

Effective teachers pay attention to the emotional needs of their students. Teachers emphasized the importance of greeting students and observing their emotional state when they arrived in class. Emily, a Grade 1 teacher, described a student who was frightened of school.

> [A student] was afraid to come into the classroom. He would cry when he came in. His mother would have to literally push him into the classroom. So I greeted him at the door, welcoming [and reassuring] him. I let him know what we are doing, that I am willing to wait for him. I included him in everything. [I made sure he knew] everybody is important and gets treated fairly in this classroom ... I spoke to his mother during the last report card. I told her how much he has opened up [at school], and she has noticed it at home.

Emily was very much aware of her student's fear of school and adjusted her behaviour with him. She took steps to try to make him feel comfortable and safe, with a sense of belonging.

Respectfully Accommodating Emotional Stress

In the classroom, student hardships in life are respectfully acknowledged by teachers. Problems are seen as part of the human condition and so are part of classroom life. Teachers say it is important to be sensitive to the issues, but not to make a big deal about them. Val let students stay at noon or after school when she knew there were problems at home. Wanda said, "[I would tell my inner-city students,] 'We are all here to learn [so let's] look forward to that' as opposed to putting each other down or feeling self-conscious because we're not dressed in the latest clothes (which we all knew about but of course couldn't afford)."

When teachers were aware of a student's problems, they made adjustments in their interactions with that student, in their expectations for the level of academic performance, or in the imposition of consequences in disciplinary action. Owen described an incident with one boy that illustrated adjusting consequences. In his Grade 6 class, when a student was late a number of times, the normal consequence was detention. One particular boy was coming late for class. Because Owen knew there were problems at home, instead of the usual detention, he had the boy work with the janitor. Rather than punishment, the boy was given the grown-up responsibilities of chores to complete with a caring adult. When there was trust and openness in the class, the teachers asked other students who had heard about the problem to be respectful of the student's feelings that day, "to take it easy" (Val) on the individual, knowing he was experiencing difficulty at home.

One of the stresses experienced by children who live with oppression and poverty is the physical strain of not having regular or nutritious meals. Almost all the teachers in this study had food for their students. Even though it was often part of the school program to have some kind of food during the day, a number of teachers kept extra food on hand to share with students who did not have lunch or who had not eaten breakfast. Doris combined her snack time with the sharing circle after morning recess. They would go around the circle once, with each student having a chance to talk, and then students would eat, socialize, and visit back and forth. Wanda used her mid-morning snack time to develop vocabulary around the foods the children were eating.

Expressing Stress Appropriately

Creating a space for emotional growth is important because many Indigenous children have stressful lives. Harriet said the energy of stress spreads from one student to another, like a domino effect. If one student is crying or upset, it affects the other children. Many of the teachers had ways of calming students when energy levels in the classroom got too high. Kendra and Ida mentioned playing music helped to calm students, whether it was powwow, gospel, flute, or classical music. Other teachers talked about doing a physical activity or singing after students had been sitting or focused on academics for some time. Ida had a high number of students who lived stressful lives, so she designed a health program to teach stress reduction and anger management. "I taught them how to do relaxation exercises and creative visualizations to help [the students] sort stuff out. Often they couldn't even identify what was bothering them. I tried different methods to try and deal with anger, either before an outburst or afterwards." Doing deep breathing and visualizations had a noticeable calming effect on students (Goulet 2005, 9).

Other teachers also talked about how students needed to release some of the pent-up emotions created by the stress in their lives. They created structures to promote the emotional growth of their students and help them learn how to express their emotions appropriately in the classroom. The most common forms were writing and talking circles. Talking circles differed depending on the teacher and the group, but mostly they were a time and place for students to talk about feelings while others listened. The teachers not only set the guidelines for confidentiality and respect (no put downs of self or others) during and after circle time but also modelled how to participate and share feelings. Teachers told their students it was all right to cry, especially for young boys, since there was a tendency for boys to hold back emotions and get angry, or if they did cry, to be teased about it.

The emotional issues were not only from home but also stemmed from the community. Yvonne was faced with helping her Grade 6 students deal with two suicides in one year. After the first one, the school counsellor came to class to talk about suicide with her students. Both Yvonne and her students were devastated by the second suicide of a boy who had been in the class the year before. The school counsellor told Yvonne to leave it, not to raise the issue in the class. After doing some soul searching and based on her knowledge of her students, Yvonne chose not to take this advice and came up with her own process to help the children express themselves during this experience. She began by sharing her own experience of the suicide of her good friend's teenage son. She talked about how that suicide affected her, the boy's parents, his friends, and others who knew him. To help the students express how the suicide was affecting them, Yvonne shared how she dealt with a personal loss in her life. Her mom had died when she was very young. As an adult, she wrote a letter to her mom to express her feelings of loss. She then asked the students to write letters to the boy expressing how they felt. Any students who didn't know the boy could write to the parents. When the letters were written, students could share their letter with the rest of the class. Some of the letters expressed sadness, others were angry, while others wrote about memories they had of the boy, such as times they'd shared or funny incidents that had happened. The letters were then taken to the funeral, where they were given to the parents. "I think it was a good way to handle this situation because these kids had really strong feelings, and those feelings needed to be processed. As a teacher, I had to do something to facilitate that ... [The delivery of the letters] brought a sense of closure. Then I felt at peace with it – that I had done my job by helping students express their deep emotions inherent in this situation."

The sharing of *moosihowin* (feelings), emotions, and life experiences with others built bonds among students and teachers as they came to recognize their common humanity. When students and teachers were open about emotional issues in their lives, an understanding of others occurred. Respectful listening, acceptance, and confidentiality built trust among participants that contributed to the development of a positive social system in the classroom.

Social Skills for Working Together

Besides establishing a sense of safety and belonging and facilitating positive emotional growth, teachers, in the third subcategory, connected students to the class by consciously teaching social skills. When planning, in addition to instructional content and methods, teachers thought about the development of the class as a group and identified the routines and group skills children would have to learn to work together effectively while developing responsibility.

Respectful Social Behaviour

The development of respectful social behaviour was taught, modelled, practised, and reinforced. Some teachers used a structured program, such as "Second Step," combined with role-playing to teach skills, while others used specific instructional techniques. Storytelling was used to teach moral behaviour and values upon which decision making was based. The talking circle was used to teach students how to treat others equitably and with a sense of respect. Still other teachers referred to positive adult behaviour to illustrate appropriate actions. Role models from the community and heroes from the larger society were seen as people whose behaviour could be emulated.

Students learned respectful social behaviour in various ways. Emily said her Grade 1 students needed daily reminders to listen to the teacher and to each other. Teachers also asked students to monitor their own behaviour. If there was trust in the group, some teachers enlisted the support of other students to help a student change her or his negative behaviour. Different approaches to conflict resolution were discussed or role-played in some classes. Some teachers made use of the school-sponsored anger management program for students who acted out their anger aggressively or inappropriately (Goulet 2005, 10).

Neepuhistumasowin (standing up for oneself) was another social skill the teachers discussed. Abuse in any form, including racism, was not to be tolerated. Teachers modelled standing up for self when they themselves did not allow abuse from other professionals, parents, or students. Students were taught directly that abuse was not acceptable. Yvonne talked about the importance of giving individual students feedback when their behaviour caused them to be victimized by other students.

Group Skills

Developing appropriate social skills to connect the students to the class was often achieved through group work. Teachers said students needed to have a sense of belonging, of connecting with other students as well as the teacher. Strong social bonds created a positive social climate in the classroom. Relationships were built by the teachers' use of group work, including the talking circle, and by having students help and support other students.

Group work was seen as a tool to develop social skills, so that children would learn how to treat others equitably and with respect. In some classrooms, students really liked working in groups, whereas in others, particularly where there was conflict, group work was developed gradually over time. Students were encouraged to use positive group skills; the values of sharing *(weeta-)* and being open and establishing diplomatic connections or friendships *(ototemiskatowin)* were reinforced. Sharing was related to taking turns using materials, and to sharing knowledge, skills, and ideas with the group. In the higher grades, teachers talked to the students about treating others as they themselves wanted to be treated. Ida made use of work teams in her classroom to teach social interaction and joint responsibility. One of the tasks of the work team was to keep the classroom organized and clean. In her Grade 1 class, Doris talked about the importance of group work in the personal growth of students. She shared with the students her evaluation checklist used to mark them on the development of their social skills. When students were in groups, she observed them to see if they were sharing, organized, and active in the work of the group. She then provided feedback. The talking circle was a particular form of group work used by many teachers to develop close bonds among the students. In the talking circle, teachers emphasized the need for confidentiality and respect.

In addition to the group work and the talking circle, these teachers also encouraged students to help other students. Teachers talked to students about being positive with one another. Harriet said that being positive helped students overcome fighting, as they learned to enjoy each other's company. Being fair and not putting each other down was part of the social interaction lessons. For example, Yvonne reminded students to be fair when choosing teams in the gym. Students were encouraged to make positive comments when someone did something well, rather than complaining when someone missed a shot, especially if the student was not a natural athlete. Once students began to support one another and make positive comments like "good shot," Yvonne reported that the tone of the group changed and students became closer to one another.

Leadership Skills

Creating opportunities for student leadership contributed to the development of social skills in the class. Leadership opportunities for young children included leading class activities such as games or recitations (Goulet 2005, 2). Young children usually enjoyed leadership roles, and teachers saw this as a way to overcome shyness. Being in the leadership role gave students a sense of responsibility that meant they lived up to a high standard of behaviour. In older students, a high standard of behaviour was tied to the notion of "the honour of one is the honour of all" (Ida). Teachers told their students that as individuals they were representatives of a group, so their behaviour was a reflection of the group as a whole. Prior to a field trip, Ida talked to her students about how their actions when sitting in on a chief and council meeting could bring honour or dishonour to their respective families as well as the class. During the visit, the students lived up to her expectations. Their behaviour was exemplary for Grade 5 students as they listened respectfully to the proceedings of a long council meeting. One of the counsellors later remarked how impressed he was with the attentiveness of her students. When Ida passed that comment on to her students, they were proud of the maturity they had demonstrated.

Owen discussed the importance of leadership with his Grade 6 students. They were the oldest in the school and as such he expected them to be role models for the rest of the students. Younger students looked to them for leadership and as models of appropriate behaviour. Leadership was tied to trust and responsibility, because as long as the student worked hard in class, she or he would be given responsibility as a student leader to assist others in the effective functioning of the school as a whole. One of their tasks was to be "school ambassadors," assisting the many visitors who came to the school.

Students were encouraged to help other students learn. Doris, a Grade 1 teacher who felt strongly about this, explained her exasperation with the general expectation in school that children work silently and independently. "I do a lot of activity-based things where [the students] work together in twos or threes and help each other. I don't make them sit in little rows and be quiet – [always trying to learn on their own]. Some people walking by might wonder what the heck is going on in here but I don't worry." The stories of these teachers show that while leadership was used to develop the individual, it was also seen in the context of individual interaction with others and shared responsibility for the development of a positive social system in the class and the school.

Shared Leadership

The fourth subcategory identifies the way teachers enacted their role in the classroom through shared leadership. Teachers used their authority in the class situationally, depending on the context, in ways that invited the students to share ownership for the classroom, while setting and enforcing clear limits and expectations for respectful behaviour.

Situational Leadership

As mentioned earlier, many teachers stated emphatically they were not "the authority" in the class. Although they had authority, they recognized and used their power as the teacher depending on the situation. Authority was used to set academic standards and respectful behaviour expectations and to impose consequences. Teachers held authority in direct instruction. But they also structured activities to develop different forms of student leadership and self-determination, moving from simple to more complex forms of student self-determination as students were ready. Thus, the teacher could gradually share authority with the class, employing hers only when needed.

As mentioned earlier, the teachers created relationships of reciprocity in terms of respect. Fran said that by demonstrating genuine caring for the students, a teacher showed she would not do anything detrimental to the student, which led to the students' trust and ability to follow her. Val had the same experience: by valuing the culture of the students and showing respect for their cultural identity, she gained the students' trust and they then followed her leadership.

Situational leadership was built into the class through student ownership of activities and curriculum and the choice to participate. Many teachers asked their students to "be the teacher," to share their gifts, talents, or cultural knowledge with the class. Teachers were then often able to incorporate student sharing into their teaching. Fran had students take responsibility for an event, such as a fish fry, to raise money for their class trip at the end of the year. She incorporated and taught language arts, art, and math as part of the students' work for this event. Other teachers organized times in instruction when the student could choose when to work independently, with the teacher, or with another student. Teachers' methods encouraged children to contribute content to the curriculum. In the talking circle, the topic was sometimes suggested by the teacher, but more often it was student-directed, such that students shared issues important to them and their lives. The talking circle helped the teacher gain knowledge of her students and the content they were interested in learning, which she could then incorporate into the curriculum.

Joint Authority

Joint authority was evident in teachers' words and actions, and used as part of the teachers' classroom management. Kendra remarked, "It is not my classroom, but our classroom." Doris regularly asked her students how they liked to learn. Wanda asked her students how they could best organize their classroom and learn to work together. Students were then expected to share responsibility for maintaining and keeping the classroom clean.

Teachers viewed classroom management as teaching students decision-making skills and responsibility for their own behaviour. When a student needed to be disciplined, the teacher talked to the student about the choices she or he had made. Kendra said that yelling at students only created more chaos in the classroom, and getting into power struggles may be winning the battle but it was losing the war. Instead, she found a quiet approach: asking a student how he or she wanted to deal with a certain situation worked well once the students got used to it.

At the beginning of the year, most teachers developed the classroom rules together with the students. The class discussed and set limits for what was and was not acceptable. The consequences were planned ahead of time. Student input into establishing expectations and consequences meant that students knew what to expect and had the responsibility to follow through. Like Angie, other teachers developed behaviour norms using values from Indigenous cultures, such as the Tipi Pole Values developed by the Saskatchewan Indian Cultural Centre. Teachers said it was important to establish clear guidelines and expectations at the beginning, with follow-through on consequences, and acknowledgment when improvements in student behaviour occurred. Joint development of classroom rules also helped diffuse conflicts in the class. Wanda said, "If we had agreed to our rules that made sense to us, [the students] abided by [them], or [they] gave us a quick reference to diffuse an argument [when I asked the students involved in the conflict if they were all following the rules]." Once students became used to following respectful norms, they reinforced each other's positive behaviour. When one student changed, that student would influence the choices of others. In this way, responsibility for classroom management to focus on learning was diffused throughout the classroom, rather than resting only with the teacher.

As teachers created opportunities for student participation in the leadership and decision making of the class, the teacher and the class became closer, as they were all moving in the same direction.

Consequences of Developing Relationships among Students

In Category 2, the teachers created a space of safety and belonging by enacting the positive social values of Indigenous communities. They acknowledged and responded to the student's physical, emotional, and social stressors through *kitimagenimitowin* (being caring and compassionate with each other). As students practised *weechihisowin* (helping oneself), *weechihisowuk* (the self-group supporting themselves), and *weechihitowin* (supporting each other) they developed a sense of identity and group unity. Students were proud to be a part of their class. They chose to come to school and did not like to miss class. Even the parents responded. They were encouraged when children came home with stories of being treated fairly and respected at school rather than reports of being teased or bullied.

The conditions for *tipenimisowin* (independence and self-determination) were created as teachers shared authority and leadership with students in the class. Having some independence and responsibility meant the teacher's use of management techniques and interventions were reduced and learning time was increased, as was student engagement in learning.

7

Iseechigehina, Planned Actions:
Connection to the Process

Effective teachers foster learning environments that connect Indigenous students to the process of learning in class. Many Indigenous students approach school as a colonizing institution of exclusion, discrimination, and imposed submission to authority. Based on their grandparents' or parents' negative experiences, the experiences of their older siblings, or their own past experiences with school, Indigenous students are often closed to or resist the teaching and learning process. As we have seen, Nehinuw learning environments balance the self-determination of the individual, the small group, and the larger collective. Since the Nehinuw view of life *(pimatsiwin)* is based on movement, learning environments are often active, experiential, or take place in context. Effective teachers structure their teaching to develop student agency and self-determination. They adapt their teaching to address the issues of colonization and ongoing racism and the effects these issues have on the Indigenous students' past skill development. They respond to students' progress and interests, make accommodations for the characteristics of Indigenous learners, and use a variety of approaches that build on their own strengths and passions and the gifts of their students.

Some of these aspects are evident in Monica Goulet's story of teaching in racially mixed urban schools. Monica's story clearly demonstrates her use of the features of Category 1 and Category 2 as she shows students that she genuinely cares for them and creates a climate for open sharing in her teaching through the use of the talking circle. As mentioned in other teachers' stories, the talking circle connects students to the process of learning to achieve holistic goals such as the social, emotional, spiritual, and academic development of students.

Standing Up to Open Space for Student Voices

Monica Goulet

It has been observed that one's approach in education is profoundly influenced by experiences and world view. As a Métis woman of Cree, Saulteaux, and French ancestry from the community of Cumberland House, I have many experiences that have shaped my approach to teaching.

First of all, I had one of the best teachers in Grade 1. Her name was Miss Libby Newell. She made me feel special and recognized my eagerness to learn. I recall one day I asked her if I could share my love for the Beatles' music with the class. She agreed, and after recess, I proudly went up to the front of the class and proceeded to dance and sing, "She Loves You." In that moment of song and dance, she encouraged me to be me. When I became a classroom teacher and referred to my students as "my boys and my girls," that sense of belonging – of familial and community connection I had experienced in Miss Libby's classroom – was what I wanted to replicate. Although I had dropped out of high school, as a

Talking circle in Miss Bley's Grade 5/6 Class, St. Mary's Wellness and Education Centre, Saskatoon – Dylan Morrissette and Monica Goulet. *Photo by Keith Goulet.*

young adult, I took upgrading to acquire an adult Grade 12. I was fortunate to be admitted to the Saskatchewan Urban Native Teacher Education Program (SUNTEP). At that time, I also overcame an addiction to alcohol. When I was seventeen, I had heard a speaker say, "If you're going to lead your people, you're going to have to do it sober." In a way, teaching is about leading and I realized I wanted to set a good example for my students.

My first teaching job was in an urban high school as the first and only Aboriginal teacher. One memorable event from that school happened when I was on noon-hour supervision by the gym in the hallway. All of a sudden, Wesley, one of my Grade 9 students – probably ninety-five pounds – came running out of the locker rooms with the wrestling coach, Mr. Jones [a pseudonym] chasing after him. His gigantic strides were no match for my little boy. The coach grabbed him by his shirt collar on the front of his neck, lifted him off the ground, and proceeded to bash his head into one of the metal lockers. His head bounced off the locker as I watched in horror. Mr. Jones's anger was so visceral that I could see his veins bulging on his neck and his face was red with rage. My little Grade 9 boy, pumped with adrenalin, got away and began to rush down the hallway. As I gathered my thoughts and emotions, I asked, "What did you do that was so bad?" No sooner had I said this, I realized it was a dumb question. I said, "I don't care what you've done. Mr. Jones had no right to treat you like that." He retorted, "I don't give a [expletive], I'm getting out of this [expletive] school and I ain't comin' back." As he rushed to his locker, I ran to keep up with him. I knew that if he left, that would be the last I would see of him. Luckily, one of my other students was lounging on a table by the lockers, so I said, "Help me keep Wesley here." So he helped me to physically restrain Wesley from leaving. I asked Wesley to look me in the eye and I repeated, "I don't care what you've done. Mr. Jones had no right to do that to you and I am going to help you." That's when his eyes started to tear up. I took him by the hand and I led him downstairs. As we walked to the main office, I saw Mr. Jones pacing in front of the gym wondering what I was about to do. With my boy's hand in mine, I looked Mr. Jones square in the eye and continued walking. Once in the office, I shared with the vice-principal what I had observed. He said, "I'll take it from here." Later, I was summoned to the office and after thanking me and assuring me violence was not condoned and that I had done the right thing, the principal wanted me to know the incident was not race related. Wesley was Aboriginal and the coach was white.

I had a very difficult time with most of my fellow teachers after that. Fortunately, I had two really good teacher friends who helped me survive. The upside was that my students realized their learning and well-being was my primary concern. Wesley stayed in school. The coach was transferred. In reflecting on this experience, I recognize that the strength I needed to intervene in this situation came from observing many of my relatives face challenges, stand up for themselves, and do the right thing. We were always taught to persevere and not to think we are better than anyone else. Our sense of community was modelled and cultivated from an early age.

I needed my perseverance in another school when I was given a Grade 6 class considered to be a "bad group." Initially, I probably spent 90 percent of my time on classroom management. But one of the things I have noticed working with students, especially Aboriginal students, is that they need to have a sense of belonging. To do that, we need to establish a safe climate. At the very beginning of the year, I asked my students to assist in developing a list of guidelines for expected behaviour in the classroom, which applied to me as well. I sat down with them and we generated a list of rules. The rules most important to them were things like no name calling, no put-downs, treating one another with respect. I asked them to be specific: "What kind of put-downs are you talking about?" They didn't want any put-downs about their size, ethnicity, or the clothing they wore. They were pretty comprehensive in their list. The agreed upon guidelines were taped on the wall so we could see them every day.

Since the students developed the rules, they had a sense of ownership for their enforcement. A situation arose when I volunteered to have two other Grade 6 boys from another class take part in a course I was teaching. These boys were two of the leaders who had given this class the reputation of being a "bad group" the previous year. In my own class, we had talked a great deal about racism and colonization as part of the social studies program. I was including Aboriginal content in my teaching when one of the visiting boys made a derogatory comment about Indians. I responded immediately by saying one of our classroom rules was that everyone was to be treated with respect. I asked him to leave and sent him to the principal's office. I spoke to the principal about it and he was anxious for a peaceful resolution, partly because this boy's mother was an administrator in the school system. I said I would take him back, but only if the students supported that decision, and added, "I think it's up to the students to determine whether they want him back in the classroom. We have a job to do and we can't have one student coming and interfering with our learning. So it will be up to them to decide." I went back into the classroom and said, "What do you think? Should we give this boy another chance?" The students clearly knew he had been disrespectful. They had developed the social skills and vocabulary to express their thoughts: "I don't think we should let him back in. He was being racist," and "We didn't like talking in class when he was here because he would put us down." So he had had a really negative effect on those students. With the sense of justice these kids had, they felt like they wanted him to be held accountable for his actions, but they also felt like they wanted to give him another chance. I told the principal, "This is what they have decided. We'll let him come back in, but let him know this is his last chance. If he messes up in any way, he's out. I'm being supported by the students in this decision." So that student knew when he came back in, he had to behave himself, and he did. He was fine after that.

To teach an appreciation for diversity, I used group work with these students. Before I used groups, I did a presentation on "In Group" and "Out Group" dynamics and had students talk about the behaviour of cliques, which is so prevalent in school. I tried to reinforce those ideas when I did my groupings. When there was group work, rather than allowing them to always select who they were going to work with, I would say who would work with whom. In that way, they developed friendships with people they wouldn't normally have been friends with – at least within the context of the classroom.

My primary goal as a teacher was to make the classroom a safe place for my students to fully develop to their potential. I knew I couldn't do that alone; I needed my students to assist in the process. We rearranged the students' desks into a circle and made use of the sharing or talking circle (which was an approved strategy in the Language Arts curriculum) four days out of the week. I had an hour designated for the circle, which we often needed, but sometimes we zipped through in fifteen minutes. Most of the time it was student-directed, although occasionally, I would set the topic, such as the thought of the day out of an affirmation book. Students shared what they wanted to talk about or brought things like a newspaper clipping to class. For example, one student brought in a clipping about Nike exploiting people from the Third World. A lot of the students were wearing Nike shoes. I had them do a written assignment on what they thought about Nike, whether it was okay to do this or not.

Then we had a talking circle. Sometimes I would have them do the writing assignment before they participated in the circle, to develop and reinforce writing skills. Sometimes writing helps kids collect their thoughts. They are able to say a little bit more if they have a chance to write it out first, as opposed to talking off the top of their head.

Another reason for the talking circle was that I wanted the students to be fully aware that I was Aboriginal, and that the integration of First Nations and Métis content in all subject areas was part of my job. To me, the structure of the talking circle was a good way for students to gain an appreciation for what it means to be Aboriginal. I made it clear at the very beginning that the foundational objectives for the circle are that everybody is connected, everybody matters, and everyone has a right to be heard. Those are the underlying beliefs of the circle. The rule is that nobody can interrupt when somebody is speaking. They have to hear one another. In this way, you're teaching the kids listening skills. I've had teachers ask me what to do if some students talk too long and monopolize the circle. As a teacher, you have to show leadership and respond with appropriate guidelines. If it's a problem, you could set a little timer for three or four minutes, so the student knows he or she should finish and it's someone else's turn to speak.

The talking circle developed speaking skills for a lot of the kids. Some of my students were really scared to speak. When it was their turn, they would hold the stone, fidgeting, not able to participate. I used my professional judgment and sometimes prompted them, "Talk about this, what you wrote about," or asked them to just say one or two things. At least if they say something, they are developing their ability to speak. A few times other students would get really uncomfortable or upset when some of these kids were trying to speak. They wanted them to speak right away and viewed them as holding up the circle. The impatient students got somewhat rude. I chided them. "You can't do that," I said. "You have to understand that for some people it's really difficult to speak in a large group." When that happened I would share a personal story or talk about somebody I knew who had a lot of difficulty. I would remind all the students that speaking up can't be taken for granted. That's how I would communicate my support for the person who was having difficulty speaking. I kept reinforcing respect and understanding in the comments I made.

It takes time to develop the climate of trust needed in the circle. I remember one boy in particular who tried to sabotage the circle by continually interrupting or making a nasty comment when somebody said something. I removed him from the circle and put him in the hallway because we needed to have our circle. I only had to do that twice and then he was fine. I believed he could learn how to be quiet and listen to other people. I expected that from him and I communicated that to him. I just let him know I really liked him a lot, which I did. Yes, he was disruptive, but he was also full of life and he had spirit.

I think the talking circle builds a democratic foundation where everybody has a chance to say what they think and feel. The talking circle not only develops critical and creative thinking, it builds personal and social skills, reinforcing important values of respect and sharing. Rather than being teacher-directed, it's student-directed. It allows a place for children to control the curriculum, to be in charge of what's being taught in the school. If we can meaningfully and consistently engage our students and treat everyone with dignity and respect, especially when incorporating Aboriginal content and perspectives, we can create a more equitable space for learning for all students.

Monica's story illustrates how development in each category builds on the next. In her class, she lets students know she really cares for them. Through the joint development of rules and expectations for behaviour, she builds a positive climate in which students can take part in the leadership of the class. Monica's actions demonstrate how important it is to address issues of racism and discrimination in classrooms and schools, especially with heterogeneous populations. She directly and indirectly confronts these issues in the school and in her classroom. Directly, she stands up for herself and her students when racially charged situations arise. Her passion for and belief in the importance of Indigenous content and processes for all students is evident. Her use of the talking circle developed both the individual and the group based on the values of respect and sharing.

Category 3: Connecting to the Process

Because our education system was developed on a European model of schooling, exacerbated through colonization, the hierarchical relationships between administrators and teachers and teachers and students are normalized. Although new forms of more cooperative and interactive modes of teaching have been incorporated, Eurocentric, hierarchical, and individualistic ways of knowing and coming to know continue to be seen as standard. This mode of schooling is in contrast to the Nehinuw emphasis on self-determined, interactive, and collective ways of coming to know through *kiskinaumasowin* (teaching oneself) and *kiskinaumatowin* (teaching each other).

In Monica's story we see her challenge the norm of hierarchical relational teaching through her use of group work and the talking circle, where students learn independent expression and interaction based on equity, as in *kiskinaumatowin*. In the talking circle, students are also developing and practising the oral tradition of storytelling. Both group work and the talking circle open space for student voice and choice in the process of learning, and flatten hierarchical structures to create more equitable participation that in turn fosters student input and responsibility. When space is created for interactivity and reciprocity in the learning process, students are able to bring themselves to the learning, developing themselves as individuals and giving expression to their cultural self.

Category 3 has five subcategories: responsive teaching, accommodating characteristics of Indigenous students, structuring for success, variety of teaching approaches, and student belief in self.

Responsive Teaching

These teachers supported student engagement in learning by being responsive to their students in planning, management, and instruction.

Being Well Planned

Teachers talked about the need to be well planned and spent a great deal of time planning and preparing. At the same time, they found quality planning a challenge when striving to integrate Indigenous content as well as meeting individual needs. Doris expressed the stress of planning:

> Every teacher is not a curriculum developer. You don't have the time. You are supposed to be looking at all the students' needs like "[Do they have] Attention Deficit Disorder, are they this? What can I do for this one and that one?" Meanwhile you're creating a whole curriculum [for Aboriginal students] and making sure you haven't missed any of the skills [for that grade level].

Responding to Students

The above quote also identifies the next attribute of responsive teaching, which is responding to students' cultures, abilities, needs, and interests. Wanda described how she chose stories and other print material that used language her inner city students were either familiar with or would hear used. Teachers were constantly searching for good resources that reflected student interest and ability, and often prepared their own materials. They used the curriculum guides but also adjusted their expectations based on student progress and whether or not students could cover the material quickly. Decisions regarding pacing were based on students' responses to learning – that is, "on how much they're into it" (Doris).

Learning as a Shared Endeavour

Responsive teachers viewed learning as a shared endeavour and enacted *kiskinaumatowin*, where the students learned from the teacher and vice versa. Mutual trust was an important attribute of this reciprocity, because students would not ask questions or show what they didn't know to a teacher they did not trust. Teachers recognized and used the knowledge students brought with them to the class. When Kendra was teaching Grade 1, as her students took leadership, they shared their knowledge of the cultural and natural history of the reserve area around the school.

> One of the students took us to a pile of rocks. We had just finished doing a science unit on rocks. We took rocks back to the classroom and painted them … They taught me about all the different kinds of bugs, and the different kinds of plants … [Another time] when we were outside, one little guy said to me, "Okay, I want you to close your eyes and trust me." So I closed my eyes and he led me by the hand. It was kind of scary because we were [at the lip of the valley]. Finally, he said, "Open up your eyes." I looked over the valley and it was the most spectacular sight I've ever seen. He had taken me to a spot where there was a sun dance ceremony at one time. It was an old spot, and the sun dance poles were still up, with the offerings on the poles. I just stood there. Goosebumps went through my whole body. I looked at him and said, "This is just beautiful. How did you know about this?" He said, "Me and my Grandpa go up there." … It was a wonderful teaching experience [for me and the students] because they just felt so good that they were able to teach the teacher something.

In other classes, students worked together because they liked working with friends and could help one another as soon as one of them encountered a problem, rather than having to wait for the teacher. Sometimes, the students who were closer to the skill and vocabulary level of their fellow students were better able to explain the concept than the teacher. Teachers did not leave the students' teaching of others to chance. Teachers showed students how to effectively assist other students with their work (Goulet 2005, 16).

Accommodating Characteristics of Indigenous Students

In addition to the general practices described previously, the effective teachers in our study used practices responsive to the characteristics of Indigenous students and classrooms.

Contemporary and Traditional Culture

Some of the ways teachers brought the culture of their students into the class will be described in the next category. In this subcategory, the culture of the student was used to create a learning environment that reflected the child's identity as an Indigenous person. To achieve this, teachers sought appropriate human resources from both traditional and contemporary sources. Contemporary role models included Indigenous authors, artists, firefighters, police officers, dancers, and singers. Elders were welcomed to share stories and skills with students. The Elders brought with them their traditional approach to teaching and learning, an approach the children would be familiar with from their early childhood prior to entering school.

Traditional activities included such things as fishing, hunting, and gathering as well as food preparation. Participation with an Elder or in traditional activities meant skills were learned in context in a more holistic manner. For example, fishing requires knowledge of the methods of fishing used by the community in their particular relationship to the land, including their waterways, as well as knowledge of when and where to fish. The activity of fishing has embedded in it the values needed when fishing for sustenance. Students whose families were involved in fishing found familiarity with the activity, so new learning took place within a context of familiarity.

Anti-Racism

Racism is an issue common to Indigenous peoples and affects Indigenous students. Many teachers had an anti-racism stance in their teaching to address this reality of their students' lives. As we saw in Monica's story, she addressed racism in the classroom and school immediately in a way that was firm but fair. In interracial schools, student-student racism can be hidden from the teacher, taking place in the school yard, bathrooms, and hallways. It is important to be aware of this reality and to deal with it as a teacher.

Teachers recognized the ethnocentrism, stereotyping, and bias in the school curriculum and were aware of the effect it had on students. Wanda found an oral language program to be effective but racist in places, so she skipped or adapted the lessons in which there was any bias. In teaching the history of Indigenous people, Val used historical journals but with her own interpretation, using an Indigenous perspective of what the explorers had to say about Indigenous peoples.

Many of the teachers counteracted bias and ethnocentrism by teaching local history. Some teachers involved students in oral history by having them interview family and community members. Teachers included Indigenous or community history because they believed students needed to know the contributions of their people to the development of today's society. Doris designed a social studies program that situated the Indigenous community history within the context of the history of the Canadian West for use with her Grade 1/2 class. In his Native studies class in a provincial school that drew students from nearby reserves, Tony dealt with real-life issues in the community by having students explore the complexity of those issues and discuss solutions in terms of "community solutions as opposed to Indian or white solutions."

Language Development

Language development is important in teaching Indigenous students. Many Indigenous students, especially in the North, speak an Indigenous language as their first language or are only first or second-generation speakers of English. Others often speak a dialect of English. A focus on the development of English and Indigenous language skills was evident in all the interviews and in the school observations.

In one community where Dene was the first language of the children, Val thought it was important to develop oracy in both languages, because the children alternated between Dene and English in one conversation or "code switched when they talked." The students responded to Val's use of Dene in class, because often they did not understand the concept or the content of the lesson until she explained it in Dene. She also used group work extensively so that students could translate for one another. In assignments for which students used written English, she was careful to structure the assignment to make it achievable for "English as an Additional Language" students and to ensure the assignment wouldn't overwhelm them.

Teachers were aware the structure of English is difficult to master. It is even more difficult when students are trying to learn to read in a language that is not their first. Harriet spoke Cree as her first language. Her teaching reflected her insight into the difficulties children faced in mastering the written code of English.

> I tell them how tricky some words are … For example, the word *come* has an *e* at the end, but it doesn't have a long vowel sound, it's a short vowel. So I tell them, "That's why you really have to see the word and know it and learn it, in order to know the difference, to see the difference in it."

Teachers help Indigenous students become familiar with the structure of English in other ways, too. Wanda used manipulative strips on chart paper where words could be rearranged to practise the word order and sentence structure of English. Doris considered language issues in evaluation. She said it was important not to test for English-language ability in the other subject areas because it was not fair for students who were still learning the language.

In addition to emphasizing the structure of the language, the teachers stressed the need to develop vocabulary. This need was partly due to second-language or dialect issues, but it also had to do with the curriculum. School curriculum is designed for middle-class children with middle-class experiences. Many Indigenous children have been exposed to different kinds of experiences than those assumed by the curriculum. Teachers in our study constantly developed vocabulary and often did it in context. For example, when the Grade 5 class was preparing moose soup for a health lesson, one of the students was observed asking, "Teacher, are you going to use that thing you peel potatoes with?" The teacher replied, "A potato peeler? No, I won't use a potato peeler, just a knife" (Goulet 2005, 5). To ensure the vocabulary was appropriate for the students' language abilities, teachers also simplified the language they used in explanations.

Oracy and literacy were emphasized because many of the teachers believed reading and writing were important for success in schooling. In addition to vocabulary building, teachers developed oral language through a variety of means. They integrated the four components of language arts (reading, writing, speaking, and listening) throughout the day and in all subjects. Teachers found music and songs especially effective in teaching oral language, along with chanting, poetry, and choral reading. Children also liked to play word games with flashcards and pictures.

Multi-Level Skill Development

Multi-level skill development is a common characteristic in many Indigenous classrooms. Different skill levels in terms of expectations, programming, and assignments were accommodated in this study. Resources such as books included a range of reading levels. Sometimes, teachers presented the lesson to the whole class and then differentiated the assignments or expectations. One-on-one teaching was sometimes needed to teach basic skills. Group work, with differentiated roles and expectations for individual group members, was another way to engage students whose skills were developed at different levels.

Sometimes the curriculum was restructured, as we saw in Calvin Racette's case study of his math program, or the teacher adapted the method of instruction. In addition to direct teaching for basic skill development, Owen used peer helpers to assist students who had difficulty with math.

> I get peer helpers to sit beside them ... Even if they're doing different work, as long as they are beside them physically, whenever that child needs help, they can help automatically. The ones that don't come and see me, who aren't finished, are the ones that are a little insecure. They might feel more comfortable talking to another student or friend rather than a teacher – because they don't want you to think they're stupid ... When you think about it yourself and someone asks you a question out of the blue at a meeting, if you know what you're talking about, that's okay, but sometimes you have got to hesitate [because you don't know], so how do little kids feel?

In addition to peer support, teachers also offered to work with children outside of class time.

Social and Personal Problems

In our study, effective teachers of Indigenous students made accommodations in their teaching for the social and personal problems experienced by many Indigenous children. Val reported that sometimes just being able to share was enough to "resolve a lot of issues," so feelings were expressed and others could support the person going through difficulties. Providing the opportunity to talk about issues was not enough for some students. When students were under considerable stress and acted out in class, Fran talked about giving them a time out, then easing them back into class instruction when they were ready. In Ida's Grade 5 class, the behaviour of students ranged from physical withdrawal to physical outbursts of anger. A few of the girls regularly came into the class and covered their heads. One girl in particular frequently pulled the hood of her jacket forward to cover her head and face when she sat at her desk. Ida would not respond to this behaviour immediately, but let the student sit with her head covered for a while. Later, when the class was busy doing work, she would go and talk to the girl quietly. Most of the time, but not always, the student would then join the activity of the class (Goulet 2005, 4).

Another student acted out physically when she became angry. Ida worked one-on-one with this student to help her recognize when her anger was rising. Together, they identified alternative behaviours to express anger. Although the extremity of this student's angry outbursts subsided dramatically over the year, she continued to have occasional episodes. When one occurred, Ida made use of the other staff in the school. Sometimes a talk with the school social worker would get the student back on track. Other times, if the student was having a particularly bad day, Ida arranged for her to take work home for the afternoon so she would not disrupt the other students' learning or be roused to further anger in her interactions with others in the school.

Structuring for Success

The second subcategory involves teacher actions to ensure that students experience success in learning. In our observations, we noticed that often, teachers started with the student's strengths to build student confidence. Motivation was important to get students involved. The effective scaffolding of new learning contributed to success that gave students the confidence to proceed to more challenges and to take more responsibility for their own learning.

Starting with Strengths

To draw students into learning, the teachers talked about starting with the students' strengths. A teacher needed to observe her students because all children have different preferred approaches to learning, both individually and as a group. Ida said her students were good at retaining information from oral presentations (as opposed to written text), so she often used that form of instruction. Fran said students who spoke English as a second language or dialect responded to a lesson more readily through the visual arts, because the expectation to respond in written English was threatening. When teaching English writing skills, Fran found students were more comfortable starting with poetry. She believed that since Cree was such a descriptive language, poetry drew on the linguistic strength of her Cree students.

The option to choose enhanced the students' responsiveness. Teachers often used group or other activities for which students could choose how they would participate or what content to use. For example, the class could first choose what book to read. After they read the book, Fran had students respond to the story in groups by making booklets with text and pictures. The group activity required students to do different tasks such as writing, editing, and illustrating. At first, students could choose the task they were most comfortable with. If after a time the students did not choose to take turns doing different tasks, the teacher would encourage them to do so. This approach allowed students who were unsure of themselves in a particular learning task to participate after another student had modelled successful completion of the task.

Practising in a Safe Situation

Earlier categories refer to the importance of safety in the emotional and social realms of the class. In this subcategory, safety is important for student engagement in intellectual tasks. The activities we observed in our study were often structured so that a student did not have to expose what he did not know to others. Not being exposed was particularly important in the beginning, before trust was built between the teacher and student and the individual and other students. Many teachers worked one-on-one with students, paired a student with a younger, less able student, or had students do the performance as a group so that no one person would be singled out. Older and younger students were paired as reading buddies: the older students could read without fear of being laughed at, because the younger students did not know if they were making mistakes. Wanda used a Read-Along process, where all children read together. She said, "Whether you're a good reader or a new reader, it can and does eventually make people feel comfortable."

The development of peer support in the social realm in Category 2 was an important aspect of drawing students into learning. When students were supportive of one another, it lessened the fear of making a mistake in front of another student. Instead of making fun of someone who was unsure, students encouraged other students to try to achieve learning goals. Peer support provided reinforcement for student achievement.

Motivating Students

Teachers used a variety of approaches to motivate students to participate in learning. As in earlier categories, topics of personal or cultural interest often drew students into the learning. Younger children showed enthusiasm and excitement when singing was used to support the development of reading skills (Goulet 2005, 16). With her older students, when the Tribal Council sponsored a storytelling contest, Val came up with a valued prize – a trip to the city to see Tom Jackson – to make the contest exciting and enticing instead of scary. Several teachers in this study used various rewards to motivate students.

Tony let his students choose a cultural enrichment activity (such as watching a video on Indigenous hockey players or doing an Indigenous craft) when their work for the week was done. Owen had students help other teachers and staff members in the school as a reward for completing their work.

Scaffolding Learning Experiences

Teachers used scaffolding to help students learn new information and practise new skills. When students were going to visit the band council meeting to view decision making as part of their unit on governance, Ida identified what she wanted them to look for. Both Fran and Val used scaffolding before students conducted oral community interviews. The teacher provided instructions on how to conduct an interview, and together with her students developed possible questions. Students then practised with one another before they did the interview with community members.

Emily was observed using pictures and diagrams in her teaching. When asked about it, she described how the visual representation gave her students the direction they needed to proceed in new learning situations.

> [In a science lesson a student says,] "I can't draw leaves." So I draw my square that represents the paper they are using. Then I start from the top and work my way down to the bottom. They watch me. "That wasn't hard, Teacher." I say, "I know you can do it too. Now it's your turn." … It's a way to boost them, get them going, get them started with their work.

In Emily's classroom, scaffolding clarified the critical features of the learning task so that students were more confident about how to proceed.

Variety of Teaching Approaches

No single teaching approach was used for every class or by every teacher to effectively connect students to the process of learning. Each teacher used a variety of approaches that included mastery learning, concrete materials, storytelling, one-on-one, the talking or sharing circle, group work, and learning that was experiential, community-based, activity-based, or land-based learning.

Each teacher used strategies that worked for her or him, the students, and the context. Wanda found math workbooks ineffective because too much time was spent deciphering the meaning and format of the workbook and not enough time was given to math experiences. On the other hand, Emily found that sometimes worksheets settled the children if the class was having a hard day. Fran tried learning centres but they did not work, because her students were more social and preferred to work in groups. Doris used one-on-one teaching only occasionally when a student needed help, whereas Emily, who was also a Grade 1 teacher, used this strategy extensively. Although no one teacher used all of the following approaches, there was overlap among teachers in the approaches they found effective for teaching Indigenous students.

Mastery Learning

Teachers used mastery learning (Bloom 1971) to develop student competence in and the understanding of basic skills through review, drill, and practice. They reviewed basic skills in math and language arts daily, often using a fun approach or one in which students competed as teams or with themselves to see how much they could improve. Board work by students was frequently done, especially in math. Teachers stressed student understanding of the processes and concepts of math, along with the memorization of basic operations. Instructing students on how to recognize and understand keywords was especially important for problem solving. Owen said, "[Students have to know the] meaning of words. So we go through [the wording] so they know what the question is asking and they understand how to ... do the questions. In mathematics it's not always the answer that is as important as understanding the process."

Concrete Materials

The use of concrete materials was a teaching approach that sustained engagement when they connected experience to conceptual understanding and symbolic representation. Wanda stressed, "You can't underestimate hands-on activities – getting children to manipulate materials has been a given for me since I started teaching." Ida explicitly taught students how to take proper care of any equipment or materials they used. Doris emphasized the need to develop student familiarity with the materials.

> When I introduce the [Cuisenaire] rods I just let them play with them for the first while. Then we'll put two rods behind our back and I'll say, "Bring out the one that is the biggest" so we get into greater than, less than, [learning] those terminologies they need to know. I'll ask questions like "Is three greater than one or less than one?" So we play quite a bit with [the rods] ... The students have to be really familiar with them [before they use them to learn number facts].

These activities helped students connect abstract concepts and vocabulary to the concrete representations of the concepts. Conceptual understanding was developed and interacting with the materials helped students stay focused on the learning.

Storytelling

Teachers reported that good stories engaged Indigenous children. Oral stories were a vehicle for inclusion of cultural content into the curriculum. Wanda said that reading and telling good stories appealed to the strength of the Indigenous students in her class, since they came from a tradition of oral storytelling. Val reported that her students would sit and listen for hours to oral stories.

Yvonne used personal stories to help students learn decision making in their own lives and how to overcome problems. She used the biography of Martin Luther King to teach English and critical thinking skills, while at the same time, the story of his life was a way to prepare her students for the reality of living in a society still plagued by discrimination.

One on One

One-on-one teaching gives teachers insight into the individual's view of what they are learning. As Emily worked with her students, she observed their performance or directly asked them in confidence if they grasped the concept. Calvin and Owen used one-on-one to teach math because they found it was the most effective way to sustain learning in that subject area. Both had another adult working in the classroom with them: Owen had a special needs tutor, while Calvin had a teacher associate. In Owen's Grade 6 classroom, although one-on-one was the primary form of teaching math, it was combined with whole-group instruction, drill and practice, and peer tutoring. He explained his math teaching as follows:

> There is nothing wrong with things like repetition and drill, in limited amounts. In my class, everybody works at one chapter at a time and they see me whenever they have a problem. That can get a little hairy sometimes. Sometimes I have to stop at page 27 and do it all on the board. But if I can talk to [a student] one-to-one, I can see if they are getting it. After 20 years of teaching, I know when [a student] says "Oh, yeah, I understand" [when they don't. In a one-on-one situation] I can say, "Let's go over it again." We go over it again and again until we understand it.

Owen's description illustrates the time-consuming nature of one-on-one teaching and the complexity of keeping track of each student. At the same time, the effectiveness of one-on-one for both Calvin and Owen was evident because both had measurable success with Indigenous students' achievement in math. Owen's students, over many years, consistently placed in the top ten in the provincial math competition. Calvin's students successfully passed the Grade 10 math course that most Indigenous students had failed in past years.

Talking or Sharing Circle

As evident in the case studies, many teachers made extensive use of the talking or sharing circle in their teaching. Emily viewed the talking circle as reinforcing traditional Indigenous processes and communication patterns in the classroom:

> The main purpose of this talking circle is to deliver the idea of respect and responsibility, respect by utilizing the feather as a symbol of respect. It also reminds the students that in the past Aboriginal people used to have their meetings like this. [I tell them,] "What's the one thing you want to share, because there are lots of us." They have to limit their stories ... [They] learn respect and how take turns. They really like that.

Students were the speakers in the talking circle; thus, the circle differed from the teacher-dominated form of communication common in schools. Students took the lead and could bring their experiences and culture into the classroom. Emily said, "The talking circle is good [for students'] self-esteem, to open up, and to see their stories are important." The talking circle was used as an effective strategy in language arts to develop listening and oral language skills, as well as writing skills, especially where students spoke English as a second language or dialect. The children were eager to pay attention to others, especially when a peer was talking about something exciting, "like what they saw at the circus" (Doris).

Group Work

Teachers told me their Indigenous students liked to work with their friends. Learning was more enjoyable when it could be done with someone else, so group work sustained participation in the activity. In my (Linda's) school observations, the Grade 2 class had a shared reading program with multiple copies of books at different reading levels. Students would read from their own copies of the same book in pairs or small groups. The children were enthusiastic and engaged when participating, and looked forward to reading together. Their talk was animated as they discussed pictures and text. Different pairs or groups would often come over and ask if I would read with them or if they could read to me, even when they came in early before school started (Goulet 2005, 1–5).

For some students, group work was more interesting than other forms of instruction. Fran explained how her students felt when they had to just sit and listen: "In their words, 'That's boring.'" Although some students preferred to work individually, she found most stayed engaged when carrying out a group task.

> They liked [doing group work] because they did it themselves ... If the group work was well laid out and well planned, they knew exactly what they had to do. They had a task, they went about it, and they took pride in it, it was theirs. They had ownership of it. That encouraged the feeling of doing their best, because they wanted to show the other groups they could do well.

Group work sustained student engagement by connecting learning to the social and emotional realms of the child. Students stayed interested because they were actively involved, as opposed to sitting and listening, and were responsible for their own learning. Indigenous students responded positively to the collaborative nature of group work, with its inherent joint responsibility and group achievement.

Experiential and Activity-Based Learning

Experiential learning (Kolb 1984) was based on or applied to the real-life experiences of students. This helped students situate concept development within their cultural realm and allowed them to apply and practise skills in real-life situations. In this way, they were able to better retain the information they were learning. Wanda spoke of how the development of vocabulary and language based on the children's lives validated self in the classroom, especially important in the multicultural and Indigenous classrooms in which she taught.

Many teachers used activity-based learning for academic skill development. To apply real-life math skills, Kendra's students prepared a budget for their fashion show. Fran used the community fish fry to teach math skills, science skills, and vocabulary development, as well as social skills. She said, "I felt experiences such as fundraising would be much more meaningful to the students than doing the same sorts of questions from a math text." As part of this project, Fran had one of the parents come in and talk about fishing as a way of life in the community, as well as about the different kinds of fish. In this way, scientific knowledge and traditional Indigenous knowledge were integrated into the project.

Doris, a non-Indigenous teacher, effectively used role-playing as her activity-based approach. When teaching her Grade 1 and 2 students about the history of Canada, she had students role-play different situations and try to solve the problems they encountered:

> I do the train with the settlers coming. They line their chairs up. They have to decide what they're going to bring with them to this new country, and where they want to get off. ... Then they learn the Aboriginal people got pushed back off the land because farmers and businesses and towns and cities were taking over and Aboriginal people often didn't have the training to do a lot of the jobs. I've had the Grade 6's come in and get these kids out of their desk and tell them they have to find someplace else to sit because the principal said [the Grade 6's] could have their desks. [It illustrates] the white people coming and [taking over Native peoples' land]. They hate it. They're mad at these [Grade 6] kids. But it makes them understand what's happened. I try to develop a pride in where the people are ... where they've come from.

Through an experiential approach to history, Indigenous students learned the hard realities and faced some of the problems their peoples had to deal with during the settlement of this country. They experienced the frustrations felt by Indigenous peoples when solutions were imposed upon them, and better understood what it was like to lose something that was theirs. They could empathize with the feelings of their ancestors and also see how the past affects the present.

Community- and Land-Based Learning

Field trips and experiences on the land were also effective teaching approaches. Wanda took advantage of any field trips that were available, because they worked so well with her students. Ida had her students observe a chief and council meeting as part of a social studies unit on governance, so students could "look at how it's done in action, to see something real." Many teachers implemented cultural camps, often as a whole school initiative. Culture camps can have a profound effect on students and teachers alike as they learn traditional Indigenous knowledge, often from Elders and the land, and take pride in the accomplishments of their peoples. After one of her first culture camps with high school students, where Val emphasized the history of the Dene in the region, she related, "As we were leaving the camp, the students started to cry, saying 'I feel really sad. There's something missing in our life. We weren't taught that. So this is how Dene lived. Why was I not told?'"

Val's and Doris's stories illustrate how, regardless of the teacher's culture or the age of the students, these teachers affirmed the culture of their students while dealing honestly with the history of colonization in Canada. The teaching was done in a way that related history to the lives of the children and to their communities and families today. Their active approach personalized learning for the students. Community history gave the children a sense of their roots, where they came from, and where they belong in the world. In this way, the students were situated in and connected to the learning in profound and meaningful ways. More detailed case studies using these approaches are presented in Chapter 9.

Student Belief in Self

In our study, we observed that the belief in self connected the socio-emotional realm of the student to the intellectual aspects of learning. In order to engage in learning, the student had to believe he or she was capable. The development of belief in self had three overlapping aspects: setting standards for achievement and responsibility, valuing self and one's culture, and public recognition of students' accomplishments.

Setting Standards for Achievement and Responsibility

Standards for achievement consisted of setting expectations, believing in the students' capability, and expecting responsibility from students. Unfortunately, too often in Indigenous education, teachers believe the stereotype that Indigenous students and their parents do not care about school and the students will not succeed. Tony expressed his frustration with what he had seen of teachers' expectations in one school that had a high dropout rate of Indigenous students. "The problem was [the teachers] had no expectations of the [Indigenous] kids. If you have no expectations, you get no results. If you have no standards, you get nothing. Those teachers had no standards." In the situation described by Tony, the students were expected to engage in school learning on their own with no encouragement from or accountability to the teacher.

On the other hand, when a teacher of Indigenous students set high standards and conveyed the belief to students that they could and would meet those standards, Indigenous students responded positively. Teachers followed through with students to ensure expectations were being met and standards achieved. In addition to teacher support, the development of social structures in class discussed earlier came into play when peers provided encouragement as students took pride in their learning. When students in Owen's class were able to solve a math problem on their own, they would "feel good about it" as they explained their solution to the other students. Doris said that as students experienced academic success and gained confidence in their ability to engage in the work, inappropriate classroom behaviour lessened. Kendra developed a budget with students, and then left it to them to find the money for a class trip while she was away. In her absence, the students met with the chief and council and offered to clean the ditches on the reserve in order to earn the money needed. These students responded when they were given responsibility. They appreciated the sense of self-accomplishment when they initiated and implemented a successful idea.

Valuing Self and One's Culture

All teachers talked about the development of self-esteem in their students both in terms of self-concept and cultural identity. Teachers used different approaches for students to explore, give expression to, and develop self-concept. Fran had students make a personal shield with a feather in the middle and four quadrants to represent different aspects of themselves, plotting important life experiences and identifying how those experiences made them who they were and gave them strength. In Kendra's after-school modelling program, practising walking tall helped students feel better about themselves. Ida tied self-esteem to the concept of social responsibility and designed a social studies and health unit around that concept.

Val, an Indigenous teacher, stressed the need to develop the cultural identity of Indigenous students. Kendra, who was also Indigenous, tied the issue of cultural identity to school success:

> In order to get our kids to succeed in school, they have to feel good about who they are as Indian people. They have to know they are worthwhile, and they have just as much potential as anybody else. They have everything intact to be successful, but they need reassurance. They just need someone to tell them their culture is beautiful. They need to be guided, to be shown there's nothing wrong with who they are.

In her teaching, Kendra used art and dance from various cultures to demonstrate the similarities among Indigenous cultures and other cultures. She felt this helped lessen the students' feelings of being different and isolated. Tony talked to his students about building on the success of their community, because both their Indigenous community and the students themselves had so much to offer the non-Indigenous community.

Public Recognition of Students' Accomplishments

Belief in self was reinforced by the public acknowledgment of student achievement. Recognition was usually one-on-one or community based. Often, parents were invited to the school to honour students at school assemblies. Principals recognized student excellence when students entered contests and won prizes or acted in a manner that epitomized respect and responsibility. Public recognition had the most dramatic effect when the students experienced a direct response to their achievement. Kendra's student fashion show that featured Indigenous clothing designers illustrates this point.

> We did the fashion show and it was absolutely great ... Walking in front of a lot of people was a huge risk for them. After the fashion show these kids were absolutely high – a natural high. You could see it in their face[s]; their eyes were glossy and everything. It was due to the pride and the joy in the accomplishment of what they had done.

The risk these students were able to take, the success they experienced, and the resulting pride did much to bolster self-esteem and develop the belief in self.

Consequences of Connecting Students to the Process

In Category 3, teachers connected Indigenous students to the process of learning. In the actions of these teachers, we see the different forms of teaching that develop both collective abilities and self-determination in learners. Teachers used direct instruction (kiskinaumagehin) to ensure students had the knowledge and skills to be successful in learning. They invited Elders, cultural experts, and storytellers who modelled traditional forms of teaching. At the same time, teachers saw learning as a shared endeavour, a process in which teachers and students learned from each other (kiskinaumatowin). In this shared space, teachers became more aware of student characteristics and understandings; their teaching, as a consequence, became more responsive to students' learning needs. Shared learning means students are able to bring their knowledge, including self-defined cultural knowledge, to the classroom. Both *kiskinaumatowin* (teaching each other) and *kiskinaumasowin* (teaching one-self) were evident in the variety of approaches teachers used. When students teach one another and themselves, they take on more responsibility for their own learning processes. They practice self-determination and responsibility to others in preparation for their life in self-determining communities and nations.

8

Weechiseechigemitowin, Strategic Alliances:
Connection to the Content

By connecting educational content to their Indigenous students' lives, effective teachers can make knowledge construction culturally meaningful. Indigenous culture becomes part of the curriculum as the teacher locates and uses traditional, contemporary, national, and local Indigenous resources. The concepts of *weechiyauguneetowin* (partnerships) and *weechiseechigemitowin* (alliances for common action) are important, because it is through these relationships with students and community members that the teacher has access to the lived culture of the children and community.

Melva Herman, a kindergarten teacher, illustrates how she linked the content of learning to her students' culture and language through her connection with the Dene-language teacher in her school. Her photographs of students participating in traditional activities on the land with traditional knowledge keepers highlight the foundations of her language arts curriculum with Dene-speaking students. Melva remains cognizant of the importance of the previous category, connecting students to the process of learning, as she uses situational leadership, striving to follow the lead of her young students to make classroom participation and communication structures more closely aligned with those of the community.

Activities, Pictures, Talking, Listening, Silence: Language Development in a Dene Kindergarten

Melva Herman

Melva Herman in the Dene language classroom at La Loche Community School, Ducharme Building. *Photo by Breanna Laprise.*

I am a kindergarten teacher in a northern Dene community. I am a Canadian of mixed European ancestry and although I have lived in this community a long time, I have not mastered the Dene language. During the height of the whole language movement, I studied at the University of Victoria to become a teacher. I was very fortunate to have instructors who believed whole language truly meant whole language, and included teaching phonemic awareness and phonics when working with children's personal experiences. While at UVic, I also took courses through the Department of Linguistics on teaching English as a second language. I somehow knew I would be teaching First Nations children who still had the gift of their language. I believe it is a great honour to teach these children and a great responsibility to respect their first language and their culture and to develop their fluency and skills in English in order to empower them for future success. Language and culture define us as people. For Indigenous students, it is extremely important to honour and respect their language and culture in order to fully honour and respect the students as people. When the classroom teacher is of a different cultural and linguistic heritage, it is a challenge to fully honour the students' Indigenous language and culture in a way that fosters their language development and learning.

As a non-Dene classroom teacher, I have found it very helpful to collaborate with the Dene language and culture teacher [referred to as the Dene teacher] in planning for the children's learning. I follow a seasonal approach to my year plan outline of themes and so does the Dene teacher. This year, when she put up her signup sheet for classroom teachers to go berry picking, I was the second teacher to sign up. I had wanted to take my class berry picking but hadn't figured out a way to do it on my own with such a large class. I started planning activities to do as follow-up to the berry picking. I met with the Dene teacher and asked her whether or not she had plans for the berries. She replied I could have the berries for my class. I asked if teachers were expected to come along; she said they were welcome but most had opted not to come because they needed the preparation time. I told her I would be coming for sure. I really thought our new teachers would be joining their classes for this experience. To my dismay, I found out that all but one of the new teachers, new to the school, the community, and the culture, felt that an hour of preparation time was more important than getting to know their students in their cultural setting outside the classroom.

Berry picking day came and I was as excited as my students were. We drove in the vans to the berry patch. The children were given cups and instructed in Dene to pick the berries into the cup, then pour them into the pail for the group. They were also told to stay together, warned about the possibility of bears, and shown how to respect the land by picking carefully. As children brought their full cups to the pail, their efforts were praised. All of this discussion was done in Dene. As they picked, the children chatted eagerly among themselves and with the adults, mainly in Dene, but with some English mixed in. I took several pictures of the children at the berry patch. That evening I typed a chant (in English) about berry picking and made it into a big book, using graphics from the Internet and one of my pictures from the berry picking experience. I also printed several of the pictures I had taken. The next day, we followed up the blueberry picking excursion in the classroom. We read the chant several times. We then read a book about blueberries I had co-written years ago that had been illustrated by a Grade 6 class. As it turned out, some of the illustrators were parents, aunts, and uncles of my current students, who were very excited to know the illustrators of the book. After the reading, I passed the berry picking photographs around for the children to look at. As they looked at the photos, they talked among themselves, in both English and Dene, about the class berry picking experience and about other berry picking experiences with their parents and grandparents. That evening, I planned for more activities and decided we would eat berries and cream, since that was mentioned in the chant. Over the course of the next few days, we had several blueberry experiences, eating them with sugar and cream and making blueberry tarts, pancakes, and muffins.

A few days later, the Dene teacher came to tell me she would be taking the children outside to make bannock. I asked if I could come along. She would be working with some Elders at a fire pit in a corner of the school yard, since that handy location would allow time for student participation without worrying about transportation. A traditional Dene cooking fire is rectangular, set in a frame of green logs, and the school fire pit employs a common modern adaptation. The fire pit uses a bathtub to contain the fire. The bathtub is framed with green logs. This keeps the traditional shape and protects the land.

We walked down to the fire pit, admiring the contrast in colour between the lake and the fall leaves on our way. At the fire pit, the Elders had bannock cooking on sticks already, as we wouldn't have enough time to mix it from scratch before the class ended. The Dene teacher gave an oral vocabulary lesson. The children listened and repeated the words. The Elder shared how she had prepared the bannock. Then the children lined up at the table and were asked in Dene whether they wanted to eat their bannock right away or take it home. They responded in Dene and sat down with their bannock. I took pictures in the hope I could use them the next day to evoke serious conversations about their own experiences (Ward 2001).

For the next day's activity, I had prepared writing papers for the students. Each paper had a picture from the bannock making, a box for the child's name, and the caption, "Bannock Making." There were eight or nine different pictures. I just passed the papers out to the students, and because they were stacked as they had come out of the printer, students who were sitting next to each other had different pictures. In the morning class, I handed the pictures out first, and had the students put them on clipboards. Then I gave them time to look at the pictures and talk about them. There was a fairly quiet spell while they looked at their own hand-out, followed by a buzz of talk as they began to discuss the pictures. Most discussed them in pairs, but a few larger groups formed. I did not give any directions for moving or joining up, I just asked them to talk to each other about their pictures and about what they remembered about the bannock making. Not directing them who to talk to or how to move was a conscious decision on my part: I wanted to see what they would do naturally. I circulated, taking a few photos and listening to the students. Most were speaking Dene, a few English, and a few were using both languages. They were all talking about their pictures and about bannock making. Next, I gathered the students into a sharing circle. I explained the use of the talking rock and about passing. We passed the rock. The first student said, "I like the bannock." The next one passed the rock after looking at it for a moment. The third student is normally very quiet in class, partly due to a trauma she has suffered. I waited patiently, her jaw began to move, and she whispered, "Bannock," and passed the rock with a slight smile. Most of the responses were the same, with three of the twenty-one students passing. One girl said, "I taste it, next I liked it." That was the longest response in the morning group. In the afternoon class, the responses were longer and more varied, but we also had more students pass. Six chose to pass out of a total of twenty-three. In the afternoon, we did the talking circle before looking at the pictures, so that might be why more children chose to pass. The longest response in the afternoon was, "It was fun and when we went home I let my mum and dad have a piece and I ate it all."

Following this talking circle, I passed out the papers and the children got to work with their discussions, writing, and drawing. As I moved around the room, I noticed again that most were discussing in pairs, sometimes with a third student observing and listening but not speaking. Discussion was in Dene and English. I was kept very busy going around the class to record their words. For both groups, if students gave me an off-topic response in their written work, I wrote it down for them and then asked them to try adding something about the bannock making to their work. Some did, but some did not. I needed to respect that what they had written was more important to them at that time than what I wanted them to write.

Over the course of the year, the Dene teacher and I had many more opportunities to collaborate. I joined the class for most of the special activities, but not for regular Dene classes. Ideally, there would be a way for classroom teachers to participate in these language and culture classes and to have preparation time, but that would require some very tricky juggling of timetables and budgets, so we need to work within the current reality as best we can. We went with the Dene teacher to snare rabbits, catch fish, go on nature walks, and for outdoor cooking experiences. In every case, I brought my trusty digital camera and took pictures to use in the classroom. Sometimes I simply printed pictures for discussion in class. After we went ice fishing, I printed a small picture for each child to take home in the hopes it would help inspire conversation with their parents about the experience.

It is very important that language and other classroom activities reflect the children's daily lives and their culture (Ward 2001). As the above examples illustrate, I have found using photographs of class activities works well for my students as inspiration for their drawings and writings. As emergent writers, kindergarten children start with drawings to express their ideas and begin to add words as they develop their understanding of letters and sounds (Feldgus and Cardonick 1999). In the past, I would often follow up an activity by having the children draw and then dictate to me or a tutor what their drawings were about. I often had children who did not make drawings or their drawings were not related to the topic. Upon reflection, I felt that in most cases they were just having difficulty understanding what was expected of them or remembering the activity if the drawing was being done the next day. I decided to add a small photo to each child's page and see what would happen. The first time I tried this, I was very worried. Would the photos stifle the children's creativity? Would they try to copy the photos? I was very pleased with the results. The children did not try to copy the photos. They drew their own pictures and were very eager to have someone come and write their words for them. I also found the children's responses were much more closely related to the topic. I have continued to use photographs of activities on writing papers for the children, and have been very pleased with the quality of the children's oral work while they discuss the pictures as a pre-writing activity and with their actual writing/drawing and the stories they dictate for me to scribe for them. I also use photographs to make matching cards for concentration games and to make three-part nomenclature cards for teaching vocabulary.

Last winter's rabbit snaring experience turned into a class research project for the school-wide science fair. We had a display with drawings and writings by the students, a snare, some branches, and of course, photos of our experience, including close-ups of the rabbit before and after being skinned for soup. As we worked on the project, the children told many tales of family members snaring rabbits. Through collaboration with the Dene teacher, I was able to extend the children's learning in a culturally relevant manner. Using the materials I made with my photographs meant the learning could continue even when the Dene teacher was not with the children. I also gave the Dene teacher copies of my photos to use with other classes.

In summary, there are four key things to consider here. First is the importance of classroom teachers collaborating with language and culture carriers to involve the children and extend cultural activities into the classroom. Teachers need to value the inclusion of the language and culture enough to give up some of their preparation time in order to participate in key language and culture activities or take the time to organize them with members of the community. Second, now that I have suggested that teachers give up some preparation time, I am going to suggest they prepare more materials! That may seem like a paradox, but not really. Teachers always need to prepare materials, but we must use preparation time wisely. Materials that reflect the children's language and culture are far more effective than those that do not. Third, teachers need to be aware of cultural differences in dialogue rules (Ward 2001) and respect those differences in the classroom. In my practice, I was already accepting repeat responses, but in the past, thinking I was being encouraging, I was probably coming across as coercive when encouraging students to speak rather than pass the rock in the talking circle. The fourth key is to trust the students when they are speaking their home language. Trust that for the most part, if you have set up the lesson, they will be talking about the topic. Of course some will stray off topic, but isn't that often what we as adults do? Yes, I have the advantage of understanding some Dene, so I could check, but we also need to let go and trust our students. I have often heard it said during professional development and staff meetings, "But if they are all speaking Dene how will I know if they are talking about school work?" Classroom teachers need to develop a sense of trust with their students, set up their lessons carefully, provide appropriate mediators to prompt discussion, prepare the classroom environment, and then let go and trust the students. Collaboration, awareness, and trust are very powerful teaching tools in cross-cultural situations.

In the above story, we see children using their experiences with traditional community-based activities to develop their oral and written language in both Dene and English. We see how the implementation of land-based activities identified in the previous chapter is used effectively in this classroom. Children's initial experiences take place in a culturally familiar milieu where they develop their home language. Through the use of Melva's pictures to support memory, this culturally familiar experience is built upon in the classroom to further develop the home and English languages used to describe that experience as the students move from the familiar to the less familiar and, through oral expression, to build on the students' strength in the oral tradition. In using content familiar to the students, the complexity of the learning is reduced: students can focus on language rather than on decoding unfamiliar content. All of us are naturally curious about how we look in different situations, so Melva's pictures act to stimulate and hold student interest. Familiarity with the land-based activities allows students to easily connect the content of the classroom to the content of their world, thus giving the learning meaning in their lives.

Category 4: Connecting to the Content

As we have said, the curriculum often ignores, omits, or denigrates Indigenous peoples, cultures, languages, knowledge, and understandings. In Category 2, *weechiyauguneetowin* (partnerships) and *weechiseechigemitowin* (alliances for common action) are used to develop the students' ability to work together. In Category 4, the focus is on partnerships and alliances to develop the teacher's ability to shape the curriculum to meet the needs of Indigenous students. To draw Indigenous students into the learning, effective teachers strive to integrate Indigenous content across the different areas of the curriculum, giving the students material to which they can relate when they recognize themselves and their people in the content. Teachers then maintain student focus by presenting or structuring the learning so it is fun and interesting. Culturally appropriate mediators are used to assist the cognitive functioning of students, extend their memory, and direct their thinking. Relationships with others outside the classroom are developed and used to support student learning.

Connecting Students to the Curriculum

In order to initiate and sustain engagement in the curriculum content, teachers included representations of the cultural and personal lives of the students. When thinking about program planning, they said they started "where the students were at" (Val). In addition, the shared leadership identified in previous categories allowed students to contribute to the educational content.

Representing the Cultural Self in the Curriculum

Including elements of the students' culture in the curriculum showed them that their people were present, respected, and valued, and facilitated the students' connection to the educational material. Appreciation of the traditional lifestyle of the community was consistently reinforced. Elders were used as sources of Indigenous knowledge, which they imparted through stories or teaching about traditional practices. Including Elders as part of school programming also demonstrated respect for the knowledge of the community. Like Melva, many teachers developed their year plans around seasonal activities in the community. For example, Val's plans included berry picking in the fall, caribou hunting in the winter, and fishing in the spring. The required reading and writing skills would be taught using content based on these activities. Most teachers had their classes make bannock, often with an Elder who also told stories.

Teachers emphasized the importance of using both traditional and contemporary culture so students saw the value of their culture in the present as well as the past. Several teachers talked about using contemporary Indigenous musicians, authors, and professionals in their teaching. In his Grade 7 language arts program, Tony found that his students responded well to traditional legends. Contemporary culture was presented when he showed his students the beginning of Indigenous movies, then had his reluctant writers write their version of what happened in the story before watching the end of the movie. Because students could relate the content of the movie to their own lives, they were better able to express themselves in writing.

Teachers were constantly searching for culturally appropriate materials to make the curriculum more relevant to the students. Many Indigenous students live a different lifestyle from that represented in resource materials, and inappropriate resource materials can interfere with the ability to learn. In my (Linda's) school observations, I often saw Grade 1 students stumped when trying to identify pictures in their phonics books. They would ask the teacher, ask each other, and ask me. One student who came to me didn't recognize a wig, a well, or a walrus. He thought maybe the picture of a watermelon was a pickle (Goulet 2005, 2). A pickle was a part of his lifestyle, whereas wigs, wells, walruses, and watermelons were not familiar to him. In striving to practise consonant sounds, these children spent much of their learning time trying to identify the content of the material instead.

Teachers were resourceful in seeking out cultural materials and, over time, most accumulated collections of relevant materials and internet sites. But because there were never enough good relevant resources, teachers borrowed materials from other sources such as other schools or the provincial library. Sometimes, as is evident in the next section, teachers adapted, changed, or created their own curriculum to make the content more culturally relevant.

Personal Self Is Part of the Curriculum

Having a personal relationship with students meant the teachers were aware of the characteristics and interests of their students and were able to use these to connect students to the curriculum. They also paid attention to and took note of students' viewpoints. Kendra's decision to start a modelling program was based on the students' interests.

> Some people were apprehensive about the program because it was focusing on models and models are beautiful. But with these kids I found, because of their self-esteem issues, it was easier to start with outside stuff, because that's what kids at that age see first. I really wrestled with the idea for a long time, because I don't like to focus on physical attributes of a person. But for these kids I had to use it to pull them in. It worked. It worked because they are very self-conscious about their physical appearance at that age level.

When starting the program, Kendra was not quite sure how to proceed, so she started by asking the students who their favourite model was and what they liked about that model. Although the modelling in our society focuses on physical attributes, entrance to Kendra's modelling program was not restricted in any way, including physical appearance. Her slogan "If you have the guts, then you can have the glory" meant students of all shapes and sizes experienced the pride of being models in her fashion shows that showcased Indigenous designers.

Teachers found ways to encourage students to take the lead and ownership of the direction of the curriculum. In Wanda's class, students developed and wrote their own booklets to be used in the reading program. Other teachers focused on the individual strengths or talents of each child. Students were encouraged to share their knowledge with others. In Kendra's class, a student who was a particularly gifted artist was asked to teach art to the rest of the class, which made learning fun but also made the student feel good about himself. Cultural knowledge was seen as a strength to be shared, so students would teach other students, for example, how to jig or share stories of hunting and life in the bush. Through sharing special skills or knowledge, children came to see themselves as having something special, something unique to them, and recognized they were valuable enough to spend time learning about it in the class. They became represented in and connected to the curriculum in the class.

Maintaining Student Focus

Maintaining student involvement in an activity was an important aspect of connecting students to the curriculum. When students were interested in and enjoyed what they were doing, they remained engaged.

Fun in Learning

The emotional and social domains were important aspects of connecting students to the content as teachers strove to make learning fun and interesting. There is a misconception that when learning is fun, it is somehow trivialized. But when students had fun, they remembered what they learned and had a positive emotional connection to learning. Although fun was stressed when students did repetitive tasks like memorizing times tables, fun was often inherent when students were challenged to use higher-level thinking. In younger grades, teachers often appealed to the children's imagination. Val took a "trickster" approach when teaching basic information to her students: having planned a school tour, she hid the gingerbread cookies her kindergarten class had baked together. The students then enthusiastically toured the school in search of the cookies as they imagined their "gingerbread men alive and on the run." Doris liked to start her lessons with "Pretend I am" to arouse student thinking and stimulate curiosity. She often followed those words with role-play, so students could use their imagination and visualize the situation, as opposed to using only verbal instruction, when learning is processed through the structure of the English language.

Teachers strove to make competition fun in the classroom, with oneself, other groups, or adults. Competing with oneself occurred in timed tests of basic skills for which students would track results to measure their improvement over time. Owen said making it "fast and furious" and giving it a name like "Math Maniacs" made repetitious memorization more enjoyable for students. Competition with adults took the form of students challenging their parents or other adults to do the same work they were doing. Students felt smart and competent when they were able to do something that was challenging to their parents. At the same time, parents were informed about the progress of their child. Competition with others or other groups most often took the form of a game. Games helped students stay on task and, again, made memorization or repetitive activities more fun. Harriet's students played sight-word Bingo to develop their skills.

Interest in Learning

As we've seen, when students saw their teacher, themselves, or their community reflected in the learning material, it created a personal or emotional connection to the content, which sustained engagement in learning. Fran recalled what made learning interesting to her as a student and applied that format to her teaching. If she could connect the learning to something that happened in her life, she would share her personal experience with the children. The personalization of learning kept the students' attention.

Doris situated students in the learning by combining problem solving with imagination. When reviewing the concept of community in her Grade 1/2 class, she started the lesson by telling the students that because the earth was too crowded, they were going to have to move to another planet and start a community there.

> We started out with "Where will you go?" One group said they would build their community on Jupiter. "Why is it your choice?" "Because it's not too close to the sun." "What kind of services would you need?" There was a discussion about that. "We would use candles." Somebody said, "If there's no air there, will a candle burn if there is no air?" [One student's] grandpa works at the dam [on the river] so he knows you can make power with water. So he said they're going to make power with water. They are going to have heat with electricity too. The thinking process and problem solving was wonderful.

Evident in this lesson is the children's interest in being challenged to use their imagination, to combine their scientific knowledge with their own and their families' experiences, and to come up with solutions to problems, all the while reviewing the features of the concept of community.

Effective Cognitive Mediators

An important way teachers connect students to the content of the class is through the cognitive mediators (including materials) teachers choose for their teaching. Mediators are those things in learning that mediate between our external world and the internal world of memory and thought. Cognitive mediators such as teacher questioning were used to focus attention or stimulate recall, while mediators such as diagrams were used to highlight specific features or consolidate learning. Cognitive mediators were chosen to suit the learning styles of the students. Teachers co-created some of the cognitive mediators with students so that they were both culturally relevant and connected to students' experiences.

Support for Cognition

Teacher questioning is one example of the kind of cognitive mediators used in the classroom. Fran prepared different sets of questions for stories at various reading levels for her Grades 4, 5, and 6 students. The questions helped students focus on points that were key to their comprehension of the story, a reading skill students needed to develop. She also used questions to help students remember different aspects of an oral report when they first started presenting. "I would ask them questions when they did their reporting to get them accustomed to saying what had to be said." Emily said, "Sometimes students have a hard time getting going on a story, so I motivate them by asking probing questions [like,] 'Who did you play with?' They will name the friend. And I ask, 'What kind of game did you play?' Then they remember and ... away they go."

Cognitive mediators were also used to organize and consolidate learning. Doris used diagrams to clarify similarities and differences when studying different types of communities. After reading and talking about communities of long ago and today, she used circles to represent each. "When you do the circles, they overlap, like a Venn diagram. We brainstorm the similarities and differences. There's a lot in the middle. The children can see that [communities of the past and present] still have a lot of the same needs." In this case, the visual representation organized and structured the content of learning for students by providing a visual representation to illustrate that over time some of a community's needs change, while others remain the same.

Support for Different Learning Styles

Cognitive mediators supported a variety of learning styles. In addition to the use of modelling or demonstrations in her teaching, Emily was observed using diagrams, pictures, or other graphic representations of concepts. She believed that visual representations gave students "the real picture" so they would have a "visual idea" of what they were learning. Several teachers emphasized the visual approach but used oral and kinaesthetic methods as well. In phonics instruction with her Cree students, Emily had children concentrate on the feel of the shape of the mouth for the different sounds in English. She used a visual chart of the various mouth shapes and sounds to help students distinguish the different sounds. This approach connected the oral, visual, and kinaesthetic aspects of the sound to the letter. Emily said this combined approach "seems a lot easier for them to understand and comprehend. In their phonics [by itself], it's just a lot of words. So I really stress the sounds and the feel of the different sounds. This chart really benefits students in terms of keeping it in their short-term and long-term memory. They remember it."

When teaching number facts with primary students, Doris started with concrete materials and had children represent the number facts using Cuisenaire rods first. The students would practise their number facts with the rods until they became good at it. They then held the rods behind their backs, pictured the number fact in their heads, and did oral examples. They would then move on to the written representation on practice sheets. Doris summed up the process. "A lot of Indigenous kids are visual learners and some are oral. I feel [teaching is most effective] by having them do it, by having them visualize it, and by having them hear it. Then we do the practice sheets."

Culturally Meaningful Mediators
The most meaningful cognitive mediators were emotionally evocative or personal or were fun, interesting, and related to the students' lives or generated by the pupils themselves. Val's class of older students in a northern community studied a story of a plane crash in which cannibalism was involved. Some years later, a movie based on the story was produced. After one of the students had seen the movie, he told Val he was disappointed that the movie had missed a certain part of the book. Although years had passed since he had studied the story in Val's class, he remembered its events in detail. He had found the story so compelling because it had taken place in the North, and the social taboo of cannibalism, strong in the moral beliefs of northern communities, had been broken in the story.

Cognitive mediators were meaningful when students created the mediators themselves, because they were derived from their cognitive understanding. Used over time, mediators helped students remember and conceptualize. When learning about the concept of community, the students in Doris's class created a mural together to illustrate the different aspects of community. The mural was then hung in the hallway for the rest of the year so "every time they walk by it, they can remember." Since the students themselves generated the pictures in the mural, they understood the meaning of the pictures. In this way, the mural connected students' life experience to school knowledge. Similarly, Harriet posted a list of sight words that were reviewed orally every day and used by students when they were writing in their journals. The list was comprised of words from Dolch sight words and words generated by the students during their daily sharing. The word list helped students move from what was known orally to a written representation of familiar words, while introducing new Dolch words that were outside the students' cultural experience but needed for reading school material in the future.

Relationships beyond the Classroom

Support for student learning did not occur in isolation, in the classroom alone. Teachers strove to build networks with others to share the role of the teacher, incorporating *weechiyauguneetowin* (partnerships) and *weechiseechigemi-towin* (alliances for common action) in their practice. Teachers established relationships with families and parents of the pupils, other staff at the school, and community members to help connect students to the content of learning.

Parents and Families

As we have seen, teachers are part of an educational system that has not always been a positive force in Indigenous communities. Teachers, whether Indigenous or not, are seen as part of that system. Val reported even though she was from the community, being a teacher and educated set her apart from the community in the eyes of some parents. She had to demonstrate to these parents her respect for and capacity in traditional cultural practices such as hunting and skinning an animal. Meeting parents informally at community events was an important part of parents coming to know and trust teachers.

Teachers and schools planned for ways to draw parents into the school to try to overcome negative experiences the parents may have had with the institution of schooling. Some schools emphasized the community school concept and organized school-sponsored events that brought parents into the school for non-threatening and fun activities, such as a volleyball league, a family dance, or a Christmas-tree decorating night. The school was open for the parents to use. Owen said that when parents used the school outside of school hours, they became more comfortable in the building and were less reluctant to come during the day. It also provided an opportunity to recruit parents as volunteers.

In addition to school-sponsored events, teachers initiated non-threatening contact with parents. Val had a "Meet the Teacher" night where she explained her program for the year, asked parents about their child, and sought information from parents regarding knowledge or skills they might be willing to share in her classroom. She also initiated educational nights when parents gathered to do crafts, share stories, or learn about the history of the community. Owen invited one of his students, a winner in a math contest, and the child's parents to his home for supper. Ida would pop in to parents' homes for coffee, just to visit, especially in the fall. These stories demonstrate the importance of involving Indigenous parents in the education of their children. When parents knew the content and skills students were learning at school, they were able to support learning at home. A team approach involving the home and the teacher was important, especially in problem solving when a student encountered difficulty or was subject to disciplinary measures. If the parents were part of the decision-making process, they would understand and be more inclined to support the consequences imposed.

To achieve a team approach, open and ongoing communication with parents was needed. In the inner-city school with its migrant population, Wanda always had new students and new parents, so regular, ongoing communication was needed with parents to clarify programs, expectations, and routines. Because inner cities were not always safe areas for children, it was crucial that the parents and teacher were clear about arrangements for the children's movements between home and school. Ida phoned parents and sent notes home on a regular basis. Sometimes, she would send a note to make a positive comment about a child, so the parents could be proud of what he or she was accomplishing at school. As a result of these actions by the teacher, the parents felt more positive towards the school and conveyed this attitude to their children.

Teachers also recruited family members to assist with teaching. Sometimes parental support was just making sure the student had a quiet space to do homework. Some teachers suggested resources for use at home so parents or siblings could support student learning. Owen encouraged students to involve their family in fun ways to learn basic math skills, and made them miniature flash cards to take home. These teachers encouraged learning from whatever source worked best for the student. Owen said, "Sometimes [a family member could] explain [the concept] to the student better than I could. So the student tells me [how his parent explained the solution] and then I can explain it that way to [another student] over here. So it's a learning process all around."

School Staff
As is evident in Melva's story, teachers also sought support beyond the classroom from other staff in the school. When teachers had a positive relationship with other staff members, the staff were responsive to the teachers' requests for assistance. Principals supported program initiatives, approved budgets needed

for unique programming, and were involved in the public recognition or honouring of students' achievements.

In our study, teachers supported one another in their classroom management, and were used as a reliable source of information for resources that worked well with Indigenous students. New teachers learned effective organizational and discipline techniques from experienced teachers. The school in which I (Linda) observed had a classroom exchange among teachers for in-school time outs. When students were being very disruptive in their own class, they took their work to another teacher's classroom. Being with a less familiar group of students often worked well to settle the student (Goulet 2005, 17).

Other staff members were also used to support student engagement in learning. Indigenous staff in a school provided leadership and support for cultural programming and Indigenous language teaching, especially for non-Indigenous teachers. If the school had a social worker, counsellor, or Elder, they assisted in resolving serious student social problems. School staff also supported the development of leadership and responsibility when teachers assigned students to assist the school secretary, janitor, or other school staff. Fran, a non-Indigenous teacher, had students practise their interviewing skills with the school janitor. Because he spoke both Cree and English, the students could practise in the language they would be using in the actual community interview. Teachers relied on school librarians to identify resources and allocate funds to purchase culturally relevant teaching materials. When he was an administrator, Tony deliberately developed a relationship with the school bus drivers, meeting the buses every morning and afternoon. The drivers were from the reserves from which the school drew students, and were aware of what was happening on the reserves; thus, they were able to provide Tony with pertinent information regarding the students' lives at home.

Elders, Knowledge Keepers, Community Members

As we have mentioned before, Elders and other community members were respected for their expertise in Indigenous languages and knowledge. Val emphasized that it was important to develop relationships with others in the community who have traditional expertise, so that when the teacher asks them to share in school events, they know the teacher and are prepared to work with her. Elders came to the classroom to tell stories, share traditional skills and knowledge, or to talk about community history. In some cases, they also acted as personal support to the teachers. Yvonne frequently sought the advice of Elders, which was especially valuable when she was unsure how to proceed with students who were experiencing serious emotional trauma.

The teachers in our study also made use of community resources to support the students' involvement in school – for example, they had professionals such as dental therapists and firemen come to teach health and safety. Yvonne had a student who she thought would benefit from an older female role model, and referred her to the Big Sisters organization. After finding a Big Sister, the student did much better in her school work.

Reciprocal relationships with community organizations were particularly evident in community events. Often, the school participated by sponsoring a dance or putting on a performance at a community event, which then encouraged school and student participation. One school organized a community carnival in conjunction with elections for chief and council on the reserve, so that student volunteers got to experience the democratic process of selecting their community leadership, which tied back to their unit on governance in social studies. Tony reported that attendance at the regular community cultural celebrations sponsored by the Tribal Council helped reinforce students' positive cultural identity.

Consequences of Connecting Students to the Content

The teachers' actions in this category connected students to the content of learning. Through *weechiyauguneetowin* (partnerships), teachers are able to learn more about the lived culture of the students and their community as well as the personal interests of students. Establishing alliances and building collaborative approaches with community people *(weechiseechigemitowin)* provides the building blocks that will lead to the vision, principles, and practice of mutual respect and co-determination. When students see their teachers and school staff working with parents and other community people, it is a strong signal that the old, disparaging colonial system is being dismantled. When students see themselves and their people in the curriculum, connections to their own world are strengthened. Learning thus has relevance, meaning, and understanding *(nisitootumowin)*.

9

Breaking Trail: Stories Outside
the (Classroom) Box

Despite progress in many areas, schools and teachers continue to experience a lack of success with Indigenous student achievement. Too often, educators forget standardized tests are culturally biased, established to measure the norms of white, middle-class Canadians. As educator Sarah Longman asks, "Why do we keep measuring the weaknesses of Indigenous students rather than their strengths?" Sometimes, the results of standardized testing cause school systems to focus on the literacy and numeracy of Indigenous students, using materials prepared by large education companies. These resources have their place in fostering literacy and numeracy, but other, more innovative, holistic approaches need to take their place in our education systems as well.

If students do not attend school, they can't achieve. If students are present in school but not engaged in the learning process, they won't achieve. Improved achievement for Indigenous students is a goal for all involved in education – parents, teachers, administrators, and students alike. But we must be thoughtful and reflective in charting the path to get there. Melva's story in the previous chapter demonstrated her use of cultural activities to strengthen student engagement in oral and emergent writing activities. In this chapter, we highlight the stories of two teachers who are addressing the challenges of Indigenous education through innovation. Both move outside the confines of the classroom to achieve holistic goals for their students. Their stories are followed by a description of what happens when community experts or Elders are brought into schools on a regular basis, bringing with them changes needed in schools to make them more supportive of Indigenous student learning.

Bonnie begins the storytelling in this chapter by sharing an account of a community-based learning project. Both the parents and the curriculum identified the importance of learning the value of *weechihitowin* (supporting or helping each other). Bonnie discovered that getting students out of the classroom to experience learning in service to and by interacting with others on their own was an effective way to instill those values in her students while preparing them for *tipenimisowin* (independence or self-reliance).

Collaboration, Reflection, and Changing Teaching Practice for Cultural Relevance

Bonnie Werner

I teach Grade 7 in a community high school in a northern town. I spent ten years working as a teacher for the local First Nation and now have been teaching at the provincial public high school for twelve years. Although I am a non-Indigenous teacher, I have always tried to adapt my teaching to make it more culturally relevant for the students I teach. Each year is different, but many of my students face profound academic challenges, having been diagnosed with a variety of learning disabilities. My class is ethnically and socially mixed, with most being Woodland Cree

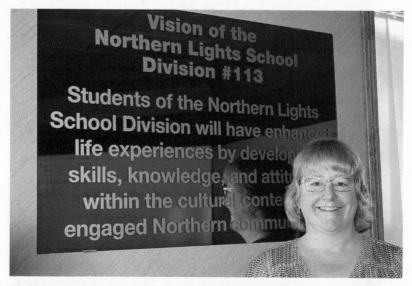

Bonnie Werner, in front of the Northern Lights School Division Vision Statement that she was striving to implement in her community-based project. *Photo by Keith Goulet.*

and Métis students. Many of the students live below the poverty line or are on social assistance, while several other families have six-digit incomes.

In thinking about improvement to my teaching practice, I decided to focus on collaboration. I wanted to address obstacles that impede the academic success of First Nations students. Because my school is designated as a "community" school, active connections with the community are encouraged. I began to work more collaboratively with other staff members, families and community members.

To strengthen the incorporation of First Nations content in the curriculum, I engaged the Cree-language teacher, the teacher librarian, and one of the Métis teachers at my school to find ways to teach about historical and current events using First Nations world views. The Office of the Treaty Commissioner (2002) in Saskatchewan had developed a kit that contained a variety of resources to assist teachers in teaching about the treaties. In a collaborative manner, the other teachers and I went through this resource and found many ways to incorporate authentic First Nations world views in our social studies and language arts lessons. The kit explained how many First Nations children are oral learners, so I changed my evaluation for some of my language arts activities to focus more on oral presentation rather than relying so heavily on the written responses. This focus on oral speaking also reinforced the "speaking" strand of the English language arts curriculum. The Treaty Resource kit also explained how the world view influenced many of the ways First Nations people entered into treaty negotiations. I used these ideas to present a more equitable view of the treaty negotiations, one that respected both the European and First Nations perspectives. Working with these knowledgeable teachers as well as other First Nations colleagues, I was able to find and use a variety of resources to enhance how I teach about the historical and current events that impact First Nations people.

One of the initial changes I made to my teaching was to engage the parents, grandparents, and older siblings of my students in a discussion about how to have students genuinely build positive self-esteem. I was challenged by Brendtro, Brokenleg, and Van Bockern's (1990) words: "Young people cannot develop a sense of their own value unless they have opportunities to be of value to others." Much of what I am required to teach in Grade 7 gives very little opportunity for students to develop that sense of value. Brendtro, Brokenleg, and Van Bockern's (1990) Circle of Courage states that meaningful learning for adolescents should encompass the four quadrants of the circle: Belonging, Mastery, Generosity, and

Independence. More often, I reinforce individualism and mastery of a certain set of skills over generosity and unselfish behaviour. This disconnect between what I believe is important learning for adolescents – to become self-actualized contributing members of our society – and what is actually practised day after day in the classroom, caused me concern. Talking with the students' parents revealed that many of them shared this same concern. They wanted their child to participate in classroom assignments, earn good grades, and feel good about learning. But more importantly, they wanted their young adolescents to be mature and responsible while maintaining their sense of individuality.

Students often seem to be apathetic and they can be defeatist, feeling they have little power to change their life or the community. I wondered if getting the students out into the community would be a positive way for them to see they could be involved in changing the community. I believe making positive life choices comes from students' feelings that the choices they make can impact their community and their life. When they feel they have no power, they can become passive and more easily convinced to get involved in unhealthy behaviour. I wanted to begin to empower my students to effect change in the community, while improving my teaching of values like generosity and independence through the implementation of service-learning projects.

I thought volunteering in the community, or service-learning projects, may be a good way for students to feel proud about contributing to the community while gaining positive work skills. At the time of this project, I had only twenty students, which meant the management of this type of individualized assignment was possible. I started this project by speaking with the parents on report-card night. In general, the parents thought it would be a positive activity for their children. I then had several planning lessons with my class in which we examined some of the benefits of volunteering. We looked at all the volunteers who touched our lives, and discussed possibilities of where and how students could volunteer. We discussed the individual nature of this project, and even though some of them wanted to work in groups, I told them when they were out in the real world of the community, they would often be required to be independent when completing a task. I was concerned if they approached this project as a group, their behaviour might not be as mature as it would be if they worked on their own. In the past, I found it more difficult to get community people to welcome groups into their workspace, as many people are uncomfortable around groups of teenagers. Another reason why I chose to have them work independently is that several of my students could be quite dependent on their "group" and had shown reluctance to take leadership because that would involve questioning the status quo in terms of who has power in their circle of friends.

After much discussion, we made a list of things they would like to do. We classified activities as being possible or impossible within the one-month timeline we had set for doing the projects. Students' volunteer activities ranged from assisting with the Atoms hockey team, to fundraising to build a seniors' home on-reserve, to helping private citizens and the local elementary schools. More than half of the students made contacts with people in the community to volunteer without my help, as I had encouraged them to do so. I assisted others in respectfully making contacts with the people for whom they wanted to volunteer. I shared the grading rubric with the class so they knew this was an important part of their Health/Guidance grade for this term. I sent notes home to parents with the list of activities and the dates and times students would be volunteering. I informed my administrators about the nature of the service-learning projects, and although they cautioned me about making sure the students were supervised, because of insurance liability, they were supportive. Over a period of several weeks, most of my students were able to complete the required hours of volunteering. I requested a signed note from whomever they were volunteering for so I could verify the students had done what was expected. The response from the students was very positive.

From the oral accounts I received from the community members, I learned the students were well behaved and completed the tasks set before them. Two parents phoned and said they were impressed with their child's work. The community school coordinators at both of the elementary schools were happy with the jobs the students did while in their schools and expressed gratitude to me for giving them help at this time of the year. Some of the people sent detailed notes about what the students did, and some just signed a paper. In terms of making a positive connection with the community, one of the community school coordinators asked for more volunteers, suggesting she might hire some of them for pay.

Most importantly, the students showed they valued the experience by the kinds of things they wrote in their summaries for their career portfolio. Working with the school guidance counsellor, we set up an in-class celebration to honour what the students had accomplished and to ceremoniously place their written documentation in their individual career portfolios. The students were so proud when they presented their projects in front of the class. They were using words like *perseverance, patience,* and *fun* when describing their projects. After the student presentations, I looked around the room as the guidance counsellor was praising their work, their presentations, their generosity, and their responsibility; the students had big smiles on their faces. This holistic learning experience did indeed cover the four quadrants of the Circle of Courage, allowing the students to feel like they belonged to a greater community and had mastered valuable skills, shown generosity, and developed some independence from their teacher, parents, and their peer group.

Taking the time to sit and talk with parents and other educators to examine what constitutes "best practice" has had a profound impact on me and my teaching. I learned in this community, where Indigenous and non-Indigenous people live, work, and learn side by side, that the values of collaboration meld with the traditional values of the Woodland Cree. Opening myself up to truly listen to others' opinions about what they think will work for my students has involved a shift in how I've always done things. Sharing the decision-making process transformed my practice and allowed students to achieve a more holistic understanding of the concepts. Engaging in discussion with other teachers allowed me to build a sense of confidence and community I hadn't experienced before in my two decades of teaching. Many professionals in school get nervous when talk turns to the spiritual realm, but through shared decision making as a teacher, I began to understand that the things I do in my classroom are interconnected with everything else.

Bonnie's story illustrates how *otootemitowin* (openness to others) leads to the development of effective educational *weechiseechigemitowin* (alliances for common action). For Bonnie, as the teacher, she learned valuable lessons about her own teaching practice, and found strength and courage for innovation in the collaboration with other teachers, parents, and community members. For the students, the community projects served to engage students in holistic learning, providing them with meaningful work experience while they practised the value of *weechihitasowin* (supporting and helping others). The experiences, oral presentations, and written reports achieved curriculum goals in both Health and Language Arts. From this experience, the idea of in-dependent action as self-support *(weechihisowin)* becomes an integral part of student development.

In the next story, Cheryl describes what happened when she moved her class out onto the land. She outlines how the land affected the students, their sense of who they were, and their attitudes to learning.

Lessons of the Land: Learnings for the Heart

Cheryl Morin

I am a Woodland Cree from the Peter Ballantyne Cree Nation (PBCN), which consists of eight communities spread out over three hundred square kilometres and comprises one of the ten largest bands in Canada. I have chosen to live and work as an educator in Pelican Narrows, which is the largest community in PBCN with a population of about three thousand people. Approximately 60 percent of the community's popula-tion is under the age of twenty-one. The land we live on encompasses an area referred to as the Precambrian or Canadian Shield. For me, this land holds a special spiritual significance: it is filled with culturally sensitive and significant areas because of the ways the Woodland Cree live in harmony amid the multitude of beautiful lakes and rivers, rock hills, and mixed forests that house our buried ancestors, medicinal remedies, organic materials, and stories. The land is like a data bank that holds the informa-tion I want to learn about in order to enrich my students' lives. I want them to know how the Woodland Cree people lived in their traditional territories for centuries by respectfully using traditional ecological knowledge.

In my heart and soul, I have needed to balance my Western education and upbringing with my ancestors' cultural and traditional knowledge, beliefs, values, and practice. It has been my intention to get to know my relatives, learn to speak the "Th" dialect of the Woodland Cree language, and satisfy my lifelong quest to learn and practise the traditional skills and cultural knowledge of my Woodland Cree paternal grandparents. I also want to find my place within the larger context of the Woodland Cree community and culture because I was raised in many different rural, urban, and northern communities as a child and adolescent. I want to be able to provide my students with essential skills from the land needed by my ancestors to understand their lives, practices, and attitudes. It is

Cheryl Morin kayaking on the Churchill River. *Photo by Krystal Vaudreuil.*

important to learn that our spirituality drives our success. To be thankful and give thanks to the Creator for giving us life and providing all that the earth supplies is to live according to the laws of the land based on humility, reverence, and a respect and understanding that we are keepers, not owners or exploiters, of the land. By learning on the land about the land with knowledgeable others, we can improve ourselves by becoming more self-disciplined, better informed decision makers, and environmental advocates. We can create our own personal action plans to ensure our future continues to have our ancestors' cultural and traditional sites intact for generations to come. Knowing our place in the interconnected realm of life also helps us to appreciate the benefits of using the land wisely as we learn to understand the consequences of not keeping our practice or attitudes in harmony with all other living things.

I presently teach twenty-three Grade 7 students. I have been teaching in the same school for seventeen years and have experience working with and learning from students from Grade 3 through Grade 9 as well as Alternative Education classes for high school–age students. I am responsible for teaching all core subjects. All of my students speak Woodland Cree as their first language, so English is their second language. Basically, they are my Woodland Cree culture and language teachers and I am their English teacher.

By Western standards, our large community of approximately three thousand has few services and even fewer employment opportunities found in the schools, the band office, health centre, and Child and Family Services. Our band schools receive federal funding from Aboriginal Affairs and Northern Development. As a result, I feel we are underfunded and impoverished in terms of school resources – technology, library services, extra-curricular activities, qualified staff, and professional development opportunities. Our community today suffers from the extreme consequences of colonization, resulting in various sorts of dysfunctional behaviour and thinking. Throughout the residential school era, our Woodland Cree Nation communities had hundreds of children taken away. On the plus side, we have access to a natural, significant environment consisting of hundreds of interlinking waterways, forests, and natural outdoor treasures, like the Churchill River, which has been named a national historic site and has been a super "river highway" for hundreds of years, allowing all sorts of people to criss-cross the country. Our combined traditional knowledge of environmental land use has allowed us to clothe, nourish, shelter, and educate ourselves while learning to be holistic and flexible.

I hold a number of positive beliefs in my heart, spirit, and mind that keep me focused and intent on moving forward. First and foremost is my belief that the large number of youth in our community are an untapped asset, full of potential. Youngsters are open and willing to try new ideas and alternative practices if they have guidance and receive reassurances that they won't be left defenceless. They appear to bounce back with happy smiles that soon overcome sad or angry moments even if their whole life is in an uproar. Mostly they are willing to listen, discuss, and attempt to make small incremental changes. I think they understand nothing good will happen if they don't make an effort to create change. I also believe a child has the power to influence others, especially in his or her circle of peers or family members. Essentially, I regard myself as a mentor and role model whose responsibility it is to create support networks and guide and help motivate the children to discover who they are and what gifts they have, by providing opportunities for them to grow, learn from their experiences (positive and negative), and prosper. Our outdoor environment is the perfect place to experience a spiritual reawakening, learn about our abilities, and draw out our dreams in order to turn them into action. Our responsibility is to preserve its most basic principles – to heal and be able to sustain ourselves holistically.

I also believe the Creator has given every group the antidote to life's ailments and societal dysfunction, if they choose to utilize their natural environment in their area. If the cultural knowledge is re-implemented into our daily practice of living and working in concert with others, we can find our own answers to aid in the recovery of our spiritual, mental, physical, and emotional anguish. We must reassess the value of our local Woodland environment, which holds the key to becoming holistic in our actions, ideas, and words, and learn to respectfully reconnect with our spiritual, emotional, physical, and mental selves through the meaningful practice of incorporating the lessons and values our land base has to offer us presently and into the future.

Many students in school are labelled upon entry and they quickly live up to the expectations of adults, whether that be in a negative or positive light. Taking the children out of the four-walled classroom expands their awareness of where learning can occur – places such as the playground, the local pond, the rock caves, or a campfire spot. On the land, the layers of students' beliefs about their "negative school abilities" begin to be questioned as they successfully master new outdoor skills; the negative attitudes and behaviours begin peeling away. In addition, students who spend time outside become relaxed and are more apt to become open to discussing how one is able to increase skills and strategies for dealing with others who may try to deflate their self-esteem or abilities through a misuse of power. Many local hunters say they need to get back to the land to restore their sense of internal peace, because the land is a calming place that brings a balance back into their thinking and behaviour after suffering the overwhelming burdens of society. My class has also learned from our female and male Elders, and I from my father Philip, different gender perspectives about the land and its uses. We have learned the land is so much bigger than ourselves. It is we as people who have to adapt to the land, not vice versa. We have to be aware, open, and willing to navigate with our hearts through prayer and ceremony, through communication and working relationships with others who will help us learn how to get through the natural trials and tribulations of changing conditions and weather experienced on the land and waterways. As in the field of science, where observation, communication, and action are key factors, so it is for survival and maintenance in our local environment.

We are very fortunate to live and go to school in close proximity to our outdoor environment. Within one hundred metres we can be near the forest or a pond and are within walking distance of our lake. It is essential we use the environment not only as a teaching resource but as a centre for discovering, reconnecting, and reclaiming ourselves.

My students' behaviour quickly changes from unsettled and noisy to calm and patient when we take our studies outdoors. To find historical connections between the land and our relations, I constantly ask all of my students to enquire of their grandparents and other relations as to what kind of activities and feelings they had as children when they were away at their traplines and fish camps. Many students have reported that "traditional life" in the wilderness brings a feeling of serenity and peace to one's heart and spirit and allows a person time to think in a relaxed and spiritual state because the pace of life is more relaxed and less controlled by others. Learning outside also requires the individual to be accountable and responsible for their own behaviour when they believe, accept, and are willing to be the guardians of the land. My students have all told me nature has a place for everyone and everything and they feel good and important in calm and open settings. The unconditional acceptance is not without the hard work of overcoming the unrelenting force that weather and lifestyle conditions bring to the people of the North. You can never expect something without giving something back or offering something up. For example, the sweetest blueberries can only be found very low to the ground and requires the person to use back muscles that often hurt for a period of time afterward; however, the reward of a tasty, nutritious treat is well worth the effort.

We especially like to utilize our local environment when our physical classroom temperature gets very hot since our school infrastructure is poorly ventilated. We have spent many hours outside learning various academic concepts in all subject areas. On many occasions, despite my planned lessons and intentions to learn about particular concepts, all must be set aside when normally "distracted" classroom students become very interested and focused on what the environment is presently creating for us. I refer to this as reading the land and learning from it as it offers up its lessons. For example, the fall migration brings flocks of various types of migrating birds like sandhill cranes, Canada geese, speckled geese, snow geese, and trumpeter swans, among others. One day, as we were making our way outside for an art lesson, over one hundred migrating snow geese were flying high above. Some students began calling the geese very loudly. Then it looked like these students were running away from our group. I later learned they did this to compensate for the wind as it was blowing towards them, and they were trying to get upwind from the geese so the wind would carry their calls towards them. The boys quickly succeeded in the difficult task of calling those geese down to our school field, and told their classmates to lie down in the long grass and just watch. While observing the geese, our conversations and imaginations became quite animated and intrigued as we discussed the changing leaders in the vee formation, the positions of various other geese in the vee, the flyway patterns of various other birds, the habits of migrating birds, and the considerable bird behaviour knowledge people have to entice a huge flock of geese to settle on a patch of grass for others to see. Conversations also led to the conservation of geese, morals or lack thereof in young hunters, and contaminated geese from mine site areas, among other interesting topics. Also evident were the competency in skill areas such as communication, team work, diligence, and perseverance as well as a mission accomplished so adeptly that we could notice the beautiful coloured markings on different snow geese's wings. After forty-five minutes had passed, without any prompting from me, the students took to their art lesson of drawing and shading their new waddling subjects eating the field grass. From the series of second-floor school windows, other teachers saw my class lying down on the grass and would later chide me for letting them "run wild then sleep" during school time.

In this situation, I had to be flexible and aware of the change in attitude and interest level of the male students, who normally find school work difficult and boring. They assumed the role of teacher because I was willing to set aside my plans and let "nature" take its course. I was also very aware not to make the students the total centre of attention in a loud or overly attentive manner, so as not to embarrass them. If the other students had not been willing to watch the geese, they still could have completed their art assignment. These boys demonstrated critical and creative thinking, mastery, and independence, in addition to a display of many skills any hunter or northern Woodland Cree parent would find pleasing.

My students also show a positive sense of pride and belonging when we discuss how brilliant our ancestors were as they were able to navigate long distances at night without getting lost, locate and use traditional medicines to treat maladies in a holistic and environmentally friendly way, find everything they needed to live within their traditional territory without damaging or disrespecting their local environment, and share their skills and knowledge with most who travelled throughout their homelands. By sharing the outdoor teaching arena with Elders, local family members, and other resource people, the students find validation in coming from families with an enormous amount of confidence, skill, and knowledge, which is just as worthy as an academic degree from any institution. Students also require opportunities to share what they know in a location they feel an integral part of. The land gives us room and time to create connections between our innermost beliefs about ourselves and our exterior creative capabilities. My students need to hear there is a reason for their existence, because so many of them have been raised to believe otherwise.

My strength lies in knowing and sharing our history of colonization and how to question our colonizing practices. It is also in having an arsenal of strategies to try to decolonize our thinking while appreciating that the practical application of our collective traditional knowledge, values, and skills counteracts our colonized actions and behaviours. We are an integral part of the land. It defines us as a nation and helps us to identify our place and roles in a non-judgmental setting.

Our relatives have taught us that the land gives us specific place names that identify for us certain land forms and stories to help us find our way. One of our favourite local places is the largest rock hill, located at Opawikoscikan, or "Narrows of Fear," between Mirond Lake and Pelican Lake, which was a traditional crossing for various tribes from long ago.[1] We go there to pick berries, take class photos in various seasons, think, locate interesting plants, and see the layout of the land. Over the months my class has gone there, various relatives of my students have offered stories about the location, which my students eagerly love to share with their classmates. One elderly grandmother told her grand-child long ago that young men used to go to this site for vision quests and prayers for guidance. Students have approached me to say, "I have a story and I want to tell it on the hill." The way the students share their stories, with glee and confidence, shows me they believe "our hill" is a special healing place where good things are offered and freely given. It is not an easy climb to the top, as we have to take a winding trail over steep rocks, fallen trees, and through tangled brush, and whatever reason we give to go there means a bit of a sacrifice on everyone's part.

This hill has empowered students to seek out other stories from family members. I regard this as drawing out the culture and Indigenous know-ledge from older people who may have gone to residential school. When their grandchildren say, "Please tell me a story," the act unconditionally validates the older generation and their knowledge. Relationships are promoted; the gift of story is given.

The transmission of lifestyle through story and practice cements relationships, creates a set of values that guide behaviour, and ensures cultural longevity. In sharing this with my students at our special hill, they have indicated to me that they never tire of our hill, because there are so many new stories to recreate as they view the changes in the landscape, themselves, or their own interpretations of their thoughts about different things or difficult topics not easily shared in a confined classroom space.

The land has provided my students and me with many gifts and opportunities: peace and serenity to be able to listen to our heart strings in order to become in tune with our interests and emotions; to find and build courage through successfully achieved activities like building picnic fires, catching fish, painting the scenery, and completing a long arduous hike, which helps us to think we can do anything if we give ourselves a chance; to create new positive personal beliefs by being allowed to pray and daydream about ways to create what we want in our life; to overcome our fear of failure in life by allowing ourselves to paint a picture of success; to grow our desire to do good for ourselves and others; and to know that the skills we master from lessons learned on, from, and about the land are necessary and needed to play a pivotal and valued role in the world we inhabit.

In Cheryl's story, we see the congruence between education, the world view, and the identity of her Woodland Cree students when the land becomes the mediator of learning. She describes the change in behaviour, as students relax and become more open to learning. The late Clara Pasqua, a Saulteaux Elder from Pasqua First Nation, said "A person doesn't feel so closed when they get out onto the land. A transformation happens when you get out of the enclosure of square buildings, the pavement and concrete sidewalks of the city ... The students are more open and (she points to her heart) – open to their surroundings, to themselves, to others and to learning – when they are out on the land" (quoted in Goulet and McLeod 2002, 362). In this land-based learning environment, away from the pressure of the colonial institutional relationships, they can just be and feel a part of this world. The calming influence of being in nature, being a part of it, allows students to let go of the negative stereotypes Indigenous peoples are subject to on a daily basis in Canadian society. The guardedness of Indigenous students and the preparation for resistance to oppression can be wearing, and cause students to be closed in order to protect themselves. In contrast to the constant vigilance required in schools, knowing how to interact in a safe way in the natural environment gives students a sense of competency, openness, and willingness to engage.

The land is more than the environment for open learning; it becomes the teacher as the geographical formations, rivers and lakes, plants and animals, and specific locations hold stories from the past, as in the naming of Pelican Narrows as Opawikoscikan, or, the Narrows of Fear. When she describes her Anishinaabe community of Namekosipiink (Trout Lake), Kaaren Dannenmann talks of the web of interconnectedness among people, place, past, present, and future and the importance of the land in making historical connections through place-based stories. "Every rock, tree, blade of grass tells a story of those who long ago walked these trails. It is said that the clear, cold waters of Trout Lake carry the memories of my grandfathers and grandmothers" (Haig-Brown and Dannenmann 2002, 456). In Cheryl's story, the land connects the students to the ancestral knowledge of their peoples. She validates local Indigenous knowledge as a valued source of education in the curriculum. Students' competence and identity is further developed as they share their land-based knowledge and skills and take pride in gathering stories from their relations to share in school.

Learning on the land becomes a process of healing as students connect to their past, imagine a future, and situate themselves in the present. As students become more open, they develop bonds while they collect and share family and community stories and stories from their own lives – bonds crucial to the positive and authentic development of their identity as Indigenous peoples. Peter Hanohano describes being Indigenous, saying, "It's a collective, it's a group, it's a community ... It's built upon the interconnections, the interrelationships, that bind the groups ... but it's more than human relationship. It's our relationship to the land" (quoted in Wilson 2008, 80). When they are introducing themselves, many Indigenous peoples situate themselves first by where they from, then to whom they are related. Lewis Cardinal said, "Who I am is where I'm from, and my relationships" (quoted in Wilson 2008, 80). Through their activities and sharing while out on the land, students come to know the interconnected realm of life that impacts all aspects of their being.

Cheryl's story clearly demonstrates how she builds the identity of her Woodland Cree students and engages them in learning activities through their close proximity to the land. But what of those students who are living in the urban environment? Like any group, Indigenous cultures are diverse. When an Indigenous teen was asked by his mom where his new friend was from, he replied, "Oh, Mom, we don't ask that question anymore. We're urban Aboriginals"

(J. Episkenew, personal communication with authors). At the same time, urban Indigenous students need to know who they are and where they are from in terms of their own history and the history of their peoples. This belief was clearly articulated in the Indian Control of Indian Education (NIB 1972, 9) paper:

> Unless a child learns about the forces which shape him: the history of his people, their values and customs, their languages, he will never really know himself or his potential as a human being. Indian culture and values have a unique place in the history of mankind. The Indian child who learns about his heritage will be proud of it. The lessons he learns in school, his whole school experience, should reinforce and contribute to the image he has of himself as an Indian.

As mentioned in both Bonnie's and Cheryl's stories, one way to achieve the goal of identity development and to support student achievement is by having Elders come to the classroom.

Elders Come to School to Teach Us All

Linda Goulet, Russell Fayant, Sarah Longman, Joanne Pelletier, Shauneen Pete, and Calvin Racette, with the Late Elder Ken Goodwill

Front row: Elder Betty McKenna, Calvin Racette. *Back row:* Russell Fayant, Linda Goulet, Sarah Longman, Shauneen Pete (absent: Joanne Pelletier). *Photo by Keith Goulet.*

In a recent collaborative research project with an Elders in Residence program in an urban school division, we examined the impact of the Elders' presence on the schools (Fayant et al. 2010; Goulet, Pelletier, et al. 2009).[2] The Elders, from the different First Nations cultural groups in the area, were identified and approached by the school division's cultural liaison person, who is an *oskapehis* (Elder's helper) and so had spent time working with many different Elders. It was arranged that they would visit the schools regularly, usually once a week. These Elders are both traditional and contemporary: some have knowledge to perform ceremonies, while others do not designate themselves as Elders but as koogoms or mosooms (grandmothers or grandfathers). All have a wealth of life experience and Indigenous knowledge to share with students.

Our research examined the impact of the Elders on the schools from the perspectives of the Elders, students, and teachers. According to the participants, the socio-emotional environment of the schools changed when the Elders were there. Students told us people in general were "nicer" (elementary school focus group, March 4, 2010) and "more respectful" (high school focus group, March 10, 2010) when the Elder was in the school. Besides improving social relations, Elders supported student retention and achievement by developing the identity of Indigenous students (Elder circle, November 20, 2009), creating a sense of belonging, improving student engagement in learning, goal setting, and supporting students when they experienced problems or crises.

Through these actions, the Elders create a space where Indigenous ways are valued, thereby giving Indigenous students a sense of belonging in urban schools. As Dennis Omeasoo said, "You don't even have to say anything. You just have to be there. An older Indian in the school makes [Indigenous students] feel better ... All it is, it's just a presence so they don't feel alone in the majority of mostly non-Indian students" (Elder circle, November 20, 2009).[3] The sense of belonging is further developed as Elders share cultural knowledge and address issues of colonization and racism in their teaching, creating an awareness of our shared history from an Indigenous perspective in a way that validates Indigenous students while being sensitive to Euro-Canadian students. The "older Indian" in the school engenders respect for Indigenous peoples from all students. As a Euro-Canadian high school student said, "I think our Elder is really helpful in bridging the gap between Aboriginal and non-Aboriginals because her perspective is really valued in our school" (high school focus group, March 10, 2010).

The importance of this impact cannot be underestimated. Racism is one of the main reasons cited by Indigenous students for dropping out of school (Schissel and Wotherspoon 2003; Silver et al. 2002). Racism is only one legacy of our colonial past. Attendance, retention, and achievement are all impacted by the personal and social issues faced by Indigenous students. Often, assistance with problem solving is more crucial than assistance with academics. Students shared stories of Elders helping them with academic work at school, but perhaps more importantly, all the students emphasized the importance of the Elders' view of them, and their role in assisting the students as they navigated the "rapids of their river of life" (Betty McKenna, Elder circle, November 20, 2009). They felt that the Elders genuinely cared for them and had the time and patience to listen to them in a non-judgmental way; thus, students were more open with the Elders than they tended to be with school staff. One Indigenous high school student experienced the suicide of a close friend. It disrupted her life in such a deep way that it caused her to lose interest in her future, which was reflected in her failing grades and lack of achievement. The Elder who visited her school helped her through her grieving and reminded her of her life goals, including high school graduation and university attendance. The student said,

When I first met with Elder Betty last year … I didn't have any ambition to go on and go to school. She talked to me about the importance of education and it just reflected a lot of what my grandparents said because I spent a lot of time at my grandparents' house … She really put me back on track to graduate and stay focused on my work. (High school student focus group, March 10, 2010)

This student's grades are now back up and although it will take her an extra semester, she is re-engaged in school and committed to graduate from Grade 12, with a goal to enter a university program. Other students stated they wouldn't still be in school if it wasn't for the support they got from the Elders. Life in urban schools can be hard for many Indigenous students. The Elders can and do help the students succeed in dealing with their many challenges.

Students find the teaching style of the Elders engaging and interesting, especially when they personalize information for students or share cultural values through storytelling. Elders are often able to connect the curriculum to the student in a way that enhances meaning making, understanding, and thus retention of information:

> When she [the Elder] teaches us it's interesting and you can remember it. Every time she comes she brings something new. (Elementary student focus group, March 4, 2010)
>
> We've been learning about residential schools for the past two months ... Instead of your teacher telling you what residential schools were, the Elder can tell you better because they were there. It makes you really believe what happened ... Like, in our class the teacher talks about when or how it was. Koogom Val, she tells us more ideas about it – like who was in the residential school and if we know them, if they're in our family. (Elementary and high school students focus group, March 30, 2010)

Elders don't just affect students; they also impact teachers and their practice. Teachers said the Elders gave them support both personally and professionally. The Elders had a way of building close relationships with the teachers that were non-judgmental, so the teachers felt they could share issues with them about their teaching and their life outside of school. Elders modelled *otootemitowin* (openness and acceptance) with teachers. This respectful openness engendered trust from the teachers, some of whom came to see the Elders as *weechiyauguneetowin,* or partners in the teaching-learning endeavour. Productive, friendly relationships provoked transformative thought and reflection on practice for the teachers. One teacher commented:

> I can't separate the professional and personal impact of the Elder. Every time I talk to the Elder, it's like a magic moment. She pulls me back down to reality and keeps me grounded. As teachers, we always tend to think in terms of the curriculum ... but she reminds me of reality. In doing so, she changes my actions. (Quoted in Goulet, Pelletier, et al. 2009, 10).

As indicated in the above quote, teachers' practice and philosophy changed when they worked with an Elder on a regular basis. Elders helped teachers integrate Indigenous knowledge in the different subject areas by modelling for the teachers and encouraging them to take risks.

The modelling also reminded teachers of methods of instruction, such as storytelling, that may be more engaging for students. Elders also often used more equitable forms of classroom communication and interaction, which encouraged quiet students to participate: "The Elders introduce different ideas for teaching, such as the talking circle. The talking circle approach ensures that children who might not normally speak in the class have a chance to share" (teacher, quoted in Goulet, Pelletier, et al. 2009, 11).

As they work with Elders, teachers begin to rethink their taken-for-granted practices and relationships. The Elders remind them to think holistically and teach the whole student - to expand beyond academics: "For me as a teacher, the academics are always there, but now [after working with the Elder], I focus more on the social. I want my students to be happy. I want them to have a good day when they are in my class" (teacher, quoted in Goulet, Pelletier, et al. 2009, 12).

Being happy just a consideration of the whole child: students are more open to learning when they feel good. Elders remind the teachers of the importance of feelings in the learning process, modelling values and activities that support student engagement in learning. One of the Elders, who had expertise in teaching jigging and square dancing, believed that children need a break from book learning to be active and have fun. Elder Norma Jean Byrd said: "We need the experiential along with book knowledge if we want balance. Students need that integration. They get tired of [book] learning. If they can, have fun, then go back [to book learning] again" (November 20, 2009).

These Elders' words reinforce the importance of Indigenous values such as balance in life that are also needed in learning. They emphasize the holistic nature of learning as they talk of bringing life (*pimatsiwin*), movement, and experiences into the classroom. Teachers and students having fun together brings joy and life to the classroom and builds connections with each other.

Elders also address issues of relationships, content, and process. Using Indigenous ways of being, they model the respectful, non-judgmental approach to social relationships for teachers and students. Their expertise in Indigenous understandings allows them to model the integration of Indigenous content across the curriculum. Elders teach to the whole child, considering the feelings of the students and helping to connect the curriculum to the life of the child.

Elders influenced teachers' beliefs, professional practices, and relationships with students. Teachers reported that Elders had a kind of magic about them. When teachers speak of Elders' "magic," what they may be referring to is the Cree concept of *kisewatisihin*. The pre-stem *kise-* refers to someone who has achieved a very high level of respect. For example, *kisehiyuk* is the term reserved for the most elderly in the community. When a person has the quality of *kisewatisihin*, they possess the characteristics of great kindness, respect, caring, and compassion. They exude love, a combination of spiritual peace and love for everyone and everything around them. In their presence, a person has a sense of spiritual and emotional calmness.

Concluding Thoughts

These case studies illustrate the reiteration of ancient teaching methods: learning in the community, on the land, and with Elders. Other innovative approaches can also improve the instruction of Indigenous students, such as storytelling (Archibald 2008), using the arts (Goulet et al. 2011), including multimedia technology (Baker 2008), and trying new technologies to explore traditional knowledge (Hull 2002). These methods have all been shown to engage students in learning. The potential for improvements in teaching practice lies in the gifts, imaginations, and volition of all of those engaged in education, those who can look to the past and recreate Indigenous ways in the present and for the future.

10

Ininee mamitoneneetumowin, Indigenous Thinking: Emerging Theory of Indigenous Education

"Try to learn your culture and get an education. When you have these two things, then you'll be strong" (Saskatchewan Indian Federated College 1989). These words of the late Elder James Ironeagle, repeated in the teachings of the late Elder Willie Peigan, highlight the challenge facing educators of Indigenous students. How can we as educators ensure that Indigenous students experience success in school? How can Indigenous students access the benefits of Indigenous understanding as well as Western knowledge in a Western education system without the process being an act of colonization?

Situating the Story

We have come a long way in finding solutions for effective Indigenous education. We celebrate the many Indigenous peoples who are now teachers and administrators in education systems and making the changes needed to better serve Indigenous students in schools. Many Euro-Canadian educators are examining their white privilege and learning about and incorporating Indigenous pedagogies in their teaching. Appropriate curricula have been developed, and many helpful resources are now produced by Indigenous artists, writers, academics, educators, and government departments. Work is moving forward in Indigenous language teaching. Policy development is taking place. Partnerships are being forged among teachers, with community members, and among school systems to better meet the needs of Indigenous students.

Unfortunately, as we have said, inequity and racism are still pervasive aspects of our schools and society. The long-term effects of displacing children from their families and social systems though residential schools and a schooling system that disparaged and rejected their cultures, language, and heritages are still with us today. There continues to be unequal distribution of resources in education as well as in society in general. Too often, we forget that a significant part of our government funding comes to us through resource revenues from the land – land that is the traditional territory of Indigenous peoples. Although fellow Canadians in different provinces have had access to the principle of equalization (the fair redistribution of revenues to poorer provinces), such is not the case for Indigenous peoples. For example, First Nations schools receive approximately $6,500 per student per year in band-controlled schools, yet when a student who is a band member attends a provincial school, the First Nation is charged more than $10,000 in tuition (Pratt 2012, 11). This inequity worsens as provincial rates rise while federal funding remains the same. Equitable funding is urgently required for the gains needed in Indigenous education to occur. Because many of the inequities in Indigenous education are systemic, Rita Bouvier (2001, 52) says, "the issues that confront people [living in poverty] belong to all of us." In addition to political action, Bouvier calls on governments to ensure their economic and social policies support initiatives to improve Indigenous education. Sufficient support for First Nations' education is imperative. Provincially, in this study, several of the non-Indigenous teachers taught in community schools. They were strong advocates of the policy that supported schools in impoverished communities with extra resources. Real equity can be achieved in Indigenous education only when a principle of equalization is adopted, so that we have equality in staff salaries and benefits as well as infrastructure, including up-to-date technologies; quality curriculum resources, including those that support Indigenous languages and cultures; specialized programming to support students with special needs; and access to specialized programs to expand student life choices in science, sports, and the arts.

Although funding and policy change are desperately needed, we cannot lose sight of the gifts Indigenous children bring with them to the classroom. Poverty restricts choices and access to the many goods and services that students know others have. Many of the teachers commented that students are often made to feel inferior because too often our society emphasizes access to material wealth while forgetting the assets of their indigeneity. A story by Métis educator Rita Bouvier (2001, 51) illustrates this point. When she was visiting a class of Māori students in New Zealand, a little girl asked her a question that caused her to stop and think. Bouvier wrote,

> After sharing a few comments about myself and the land I had come from, [a little girl] asked me the same question three times before I answered her. The question was, "Are you rich?" [I finally replied with], "Yes, oh, yes. I am very rich." I went on to list the names of my extended family, my friends, my son, to which she responded, "Like you, I am very rich."

Indigenous students need to hear and see affirmations of their assets in their learning. Both Melva's and Cheryl's stories of land-based teaching are examples of methods that could be used as an introduction to a more intensive look at Indigenous land concepts, historical changes and present-day challenges, and community accomplishments to counter the materialistic, consumer-oriented messages students are exposed to in the media and broader society.

Indigenous Students as Individual and Cultural Beings in Social Positions

Assumptions cannot be made about Indigenous students' social positions or cultural practices. Although poverty is a reality in the lives of many Indigenous peoples, for others it is not. Many Indigenous peoples are doing well economically. Students also come from a wide variety of cultural and linguistic groups. Communities, whether urban, rural, or northern, are undergoing rapid social and cultural change. In some communities, traditional occupations of hunting, trapping, and fishing are no longer able to sustain as many people as they once were. In others, self-determination has given rise to the development of First Nations involvement in business ventures and service delivery. In many communities, there is a rejuvenation of traditional practices and a renaissance of cultural expression. At the same time, all are affected by the larger Canadian and global culture. Individual Indigenous students will identify with and express their connection to their languages, cultures and traditions, and communities in myriad ways.

Teachers can prevent students from feeling stereotyped by treating them as individuals. Leonie Pihama, Fiona Cram, and Sheila Walker (2002) state that in education there is a tendency to categorize all Indigenous people into one monolithic group, not recognizing the diversity of Indigenous cultural groups and situations. A stereotypical view imposes a certain identity upon the child and does not give autonomy to the individual to express his culture as he chooses.

Both Indigenous and non-Indigenous teachers in our study noted that when they stepped into the role of teacher, they became identified with the school and its authority. However, one of the contradictions of schooling is while it can be an institution of colonization, it also has the potential to decolonize (Smith 2000) and support the development of self-determination for Indigenous students and their communities. The teachers' stories in this book provide us with examples of how teachers are drawing upon their own knowledge and on the understandings of Indigenous peoples to create and build practices that, despite the inequities, serve Indigenous students in the classroom and help create pathways for their success.

Indigenizing and Decolonizing Education

The model presented in Chapter 4 offers one conceptual framework for indigenizing and decolonizing Indigenous education. Although teachers used different approaches, they all built close, personal relationships with their Indigenous students based on genuine caring, reciprocal respect, and belief in the students' abilities. Positive social relationships among students developed group and leadership skills that created a place of belonging and safety where emotional expression was the norm. Teachers used a variety of teaching methods congruent with traditional Indigenous practices and that met the unique needs of their Indigenous students, so that the students developed a belief in their abilities as learners and connected to the process of learning. Teachers also connected students to the content by ensuring that students and their communities were an integral part of the educational process. Close relationships with the teacher, respectful relationships among students, and connection to the process and educational content created culturally meaningful learning environments in which Indigenous students were engaged.

Holistic Teaching

Teachers used a holistic approach in creating culturally meaningful learning environments, an approach that considered the socio-emotional, physical, intellectual, and spiritual domains of learning. As in the model of effective teaching, in which development in one category positively impacts development in another category, in practice, the four domains of learning are interrelated in the process of teaching. However, to understand the effect of each, it is useful to examine them separately to highlight the features that contribute to effective teaching practices.

Intellectual Domain

When teachers connected students to the learning content, the emphasis was on the intellectual domain. To facilitate student success, teachers contextualized learning, addressed the needs specific to Indigenous children, and ensured that their students mastered the basic skills. They used *achunoogehina* (legends), *achimohina* (stories of people, living beings and entities), and *ahtotumohina* (stories of events and happenings), the different forms of storytelling that relate to the oral tradition of Indigenous peoples, to connect the intellectual to the other domains. Teachers also used a variety of interactive teaching approaches to develop mutual understanding between themselves and their students, and among students. Understanding was enhanced through *weechiyauguneetowin* (partnerships) and *weechiseechigemitowin* (alliances for common action) when others were called upon to share their knowledge, experience, and guidance.

When children and their cultures were given expression in school, as was the case in the talking circle and with experiential and activity- and land-based learning, the cognitive mediators available to the child had meaning. All three of these approaches reflect the Nehinuw views of learning. The talking circle builds on the oral tradition of the Nehinuw. Children learn values of respect and patience while developing their storytelling (*achimohina* and *ahtotumohina*) abilities. Experiential and activity- and land-based learning emphasize the importance of movement inherent in *pimatsiwin* (life) as well as that of *pimachihitowin* (interactive generation of lifemaking with the world around us).

Because they are based on traditional forms, the above teaching approaches tend to draw upon the strengths of the Indigenous student, enabling him to participate in culturally meaningful knowledge construction and to move beyond rote knowledge to *nisitootumowin* (understanding).

Physical Domain

In Graham Smith's (2000, 66) articulation of principles for Māori education, he includes the mediation of socioeconomic and home difficulties. In the physical domain, the teachers in this study accommodated the physical needs of their students, particularly in regard to the social conditions faced by many Indigenous students. They created a safe place, provided food, attended to student stress, and changed the pacing of the lessons based on the actions of the students. The creation of a safe place was key; safety is an issue in our society because many children are "not safe physically, educationally, economically, or spiritually" (Brendtro, Brokenleg, and Van Bockern 1990, 34). The issue of safety for children is compounded when communities face difficult social stresses. Although safety was an aspect in all four domains, it is highlighted in the physical domain in terms of the creation of a place of belonging for Indigenous students.

Many Indigenous authors write of the importance of land or territory in Indigenous education (Ah Nee-Benham 2000; Bouvier 2001; Hampton 1995). Eber Hampton (1995, 39) likens the importance of land or territory for Indigenous peoples to that of creating a place of belonging for Indigenous students: "A sense of turf, a place that is Indian, a place ... to be one's Native self is essential to well-being." Though physical, this is also a safe psychological space, because the students' sense of connection to the physical space includes the sense of psychological safety and belonging. Keith reflects, "I believe I was one of the lucky ones with a school in the community, so I experienced the traditional way of life and learned to live off the land. Although school focused on only Western knowledge and ways of being, I experienced hunting, trapping, gathering, and fishing, immersed in Nehinuw life outside of school." A strong connection and attachment to the land was nurtured through these processes and activities.

The importance of a sense of place for Indigenous peoples is situated in a colonial history that displaced Indigenous peoples from their land. Rita Bouvier refers to the common experience of the "dispossession of land" as a tie that binds diverse Métis peoples (Bouvier and Ward 2001, 178). Dispossessing Indigenous peoples of their land, whether through scrip or unfulfilled treaty promises, continues to be a sad chapter in Canadian colonial history. In addition, the government policy of extinguishing treaty and Aboriginal rights through a policy of enfranchisement in exchange for a small piece of private property and the supposed right to vote was duplicitous. One of the most destructive aspects of residential schools was taking young people away from their physical and social place. Not only did the operation of residential schools split apart the bonds between parents (and grandparents) and their children, but it also abruptly removed children from their land base. This policy thus severed the strong traditional connection the children had to the land.

Although the Nehinuw recognized individual use of land, they did not have the concepts of private property or individual land ownership. Instead, the Nehinuw had collective authority over the land, stated as *nituskeenan* or *kituskeenuw,* meaning, "our land, our country." People are connected to *nituskeenan/kituskeenuw* (our land): the unity of the people is tied to this collective territory.[1] In describing destructive changes to the land (and plants and animals), Elder Henry Roberts from the Woodland Nehinuw nation of Lac La Ronge expressed, "I feel it right here. It hurts me right here." He pointed to his heart, indicating his oneness with the traditional land of his nation.

Land-based seasonal activities with students restore connection to the land, develop social bonds, knowledge, and skills, and teach cultural values in context. Land-based learning is therefore not only a return to land for the purposes of learning; it is also a statement on the importance of Aboriginal title to the land and the duty to consult and accommodate in traditional territories.

Whether out on the land or working with others in the classroom, as was evident in many of the methods used in the case studies, physicality was important. As evident in their term for *life, pimatsiwin,* movement is seen by the Nehinuw as foundational. To the Nehinuw, movement and action are part of their philosophy and belief systems, including learning. The practice of having children sit still all day to pay attention in school is outdated. Recent medical research identifies physical inactivity as the fourth leading cause of death in the world (Coyne 2012). Given the high rates of diabetes among Indigenous populations, regular movement, daily physical activity, and interaction with the world around us are imperative.

Movement relates to the other domains as well. The latest neuroscience research points to the importance of movement in cognition and brain development for all children (Breithecker 2011, para. 5–6). As Breithecker states: "The commonly held opinion that movement detracts from attention and concentration is no longer valid. Movement is an anthropological need and a basic behaviour for [children] to support a well-balanced physical, mental and emotional development." Given the centrality of movement in the Nehinuw concept of life, and the evidence of the latest medical and neuroscience research, as educators, we need to imagine new ways to activate students in the learning process.

Socio-Emotional Domain

Since many aspects of the socio-emotional domain will be presented later in the discussion regarding the foundational aspect of relationships and values, this section deals with the importance of emotions, evident in our findings, because emotions are not often considered when teaching focuses primarily on intellectual development. Western educational theory tends to trivialize emotion, advocating objectivity and unemotional detachment in professional relationships. In Indigenous education, Odawa scholar Cecil King (1993) believes teachers of Indigenous students need to learn how to effectively deal with emotions in teaching. The stories of the teachers in this book reflect the belief that emotions are an important aspect of the learning process. Caring and compassion need to be hallmarks of educational endeavours, as is evidenced in the experiences of our effective teachers. Yvonne's students expressed a range of strong emotions when given space in the classroom to deal with the suicide of a fellow student. Pride was evident when Bonnie's students completed their community service projects. Fran and Doris described the enjoyment of group work, while Cheryl's students shared laughter and tears at their special place on the land. When they discussed the importance of fun in learning, these and other teachers were aware of the power of emotions to assist with memory and cognition.

As teachers, we are often reluctant to bring emotions into our classrooms, but they are important not just for memory and learning, but for the relationships between the teacher and student and among fellow students. The interconnection of emotion and thinking is expressed in the Nehinuw term *mooskateneetumowin*. *Mooska-* is a crying out or the showing of outward emotion, and *-teneetum* is the word stem for thinking and cognition. It is used to describe someone who is experiencing emotional conflicts that bring about emotional cognitive stress, which affects a person's thinking and makes it hard to focus on learning. The word combines both emotion and cognition. At the same time, when teachers express their emotions, it demonstrates to the learner that the teacher is vulnerable and is "as human as the learner" (Freire 1998, 48). Paolo Freire (1998) states that the emotional realm is important for understanding in the intellectual realm, especially in examining social and historical process. Understanding our feelings helps us make connections to broader social issues and deal with the impact of colonization.

Spiritual Domain

In 1972, the National Indian Brotherhood stated that children need to know themselves and their potential as human beings. Becoming a good human being occurs in relationship with others and the environment. Judie Bopp et al. (1984) described spiritual development, or becoming a good human being, as developing one's gifts and coming to understand who one is in the world, with a sense of identity, purpose, and volition. When the teachers in this study got to know their students as individuals, they did so in part to know how to develop each student's unique talents and gifts. The model of effective teaching depicts how the teachers fostered individual identity and group support as students developed confidence, the belief in self, and thoughtfulness of others.

Cultural identity, or the belief in one's own peoples, is shaped by a sense of the history of those peoples. Indigenous students need to know their history without "avoiding the hard facts of the conquest of America" (Hampton 1995, 32). The teachers in this study brought local history and the history of Indigenous peoples into their classes. They conveyed to students that the poverty and social problems they faced were not their fault and encouraged them to explore issues of social justice.

Cultural values develop students spiritually. In addition to *tipenimisowin* (developing authority over oneself), *neepuhistumasowin* (standing up for oneself), and *neepuhistumagehin* (standing up for others), an important value in Nehinuw thinking is *saseepeneetumowin*, which translates as "one perseveres," or one has long-term stamina in their mind, or has the stamina of determined, focused thinking. These values are embedded in how we as Nehinuw see and name ourselves. The Nehinuw word for Indigenous people is *Ininiyuk*. If I use the word *inineesiw* to describe someone, I am saying he or she has a great deal of initiative and the skills to carry things through. He or she is a self-starter. To be *Ininiw* is to be self-determining as a person and as a people – to be strong as an individual within a reciprocal relationship with the collective, including *kituskeenuw* (our land/world). In this study, spiritual growth developed the Indigenous students holistically in their relationships with others. The spirit of students was raised and enhanced by the energetic demands of self-determination and working together.

The Interconnection of the Four Domains

Although the division into the four domains is useful for insight into the complexity of effective teaching, Indigenous peoples typically see the different domains holistically, as interacting with one another in learning, as is the case in classroom practice. Physicality, the emotional state, thinking, and interactivity are emphasized in learning. Therefore, although the socio-emotional domain is where decolonizing relationships were initiated, to Saulteaux Elder Clara Pasqua, for example, teaching from the heart meant that students had an emotional connection not just in their social relationships but also with the content and methods that were used.

Nehinuw scholar Willie Ermine (1995) asserts that Indigenous epistemology is about making connections and synthesis. He refers to the importance of inner reflection, reflection in which "the experience is knowledge" (104). Walter Lightening (1992, 232), another Nehinuw writer, states, "Learning is not a product of transferring information between a teacher and a student. It is a product of creation and re-creation, in a mutual relationship of personal interaction, of information. It is not just a cognitive (mental) act, but an emotional thus physical act. Learning is felt." Working interactively brings about holistic learning, where sensations are felt and given expression through the act of creation. Energy stirs, awakens, and moves with the physical movement of the body. As in *pimatsiwin* (life), movement and sensations make us feel alive.

Linda Goulet et al. (2011) use an embodied interactive approach with First Nations youth to explore concepts of leadership and decolonized relationships. Through relationship-building exercises, theatre games, and dramatic storytelling, youth give bodily representation to their lived experiences, then examine and reflect on the choices they have made. The words of one student are very telling about how movement, combined with shared authority, is different from her usual school experiences of learning: in the drama workshops, she feels a sense of freedom. When asked what she meant by freedom, she replied:

> In class, it's you have to be quiet, you have to listen, you have to sit down and do your work. But [in the workshop] we're having fun, we're learning what we want to learn, we can take in whatever we want. [In the classroom] it's just basic: you got to learn to spell this word, you got to learn to write this certain way. [In the workshop] we can take in what we want, right? So that's what I mean by freedom. (Quoted in Goulet et al. 2011, 56)

Many cultural activities, such as drumming, dancing and singing, involve interactive embodiment. However, if the teacher is unaware of the concepts embedded in the activity, such as math concepts in hand games, she may not be able to make the connections to the math curriculum (Sanders 2012).

Embodiment in cultural activities, when done as a group, can bring students to a place of decolonization. Lorna Williams and Michele Tanaka (2007, 13) used the construction and installation of a Thunderbird/Whale house pole as the central aspect of their cross-cultural course for diverse students. The cultural and collective nature of the work brought about respect for and a deep understanding of the Indigenous world and each other. Students reported strong feelings of attachment to and investment in the learning, the project, and each other through actions that created *kamucwkalha*, "the energy current that indicates the emergence of a communal sense of purpose."[2] Similarly, Denise Nadeau and Alannah Young (2006, 90) use traditional song along with other embodied forms of expression, such as dance and drawing, to "restore the sacred vitality" that reconnects Indigenous learners with their inner self,

Grade 5/6 students passing the stone in the talking circle (Anthony Wee-Eng, Tinisha Ferrier, and teacher Jocelyn Bley). *Photo by Keith Goulet.*

their spirit, the earth, and others and thus creates "a feeling of being fully alive," educating bodies and spirits for self-determination.

In their review of the literature, Angelina Castagno and Bryan Brayboy (2008) call for a focus on self-determination, racism, and Indigenous epistemologies in the study of culturally responsive teaching for Indigenous youth. In the stories presented here, teachers achieved meaningful connections as they wove cultural ways of being with decolonizing practices to engage Indigenous students in learning. These practices opened spaces in which the students could express their lived culture and develop authority over themselves. Decolonizing practices were enacted, and social relationships reflected those of the Nehinuw. Relationships were less hierarchical since leadership was shared between teacher and classroom. Issues of power relations, authority, and responsibility were discussed, and the practices of self-determination and co-determination were encouraged.

Relationships Are Foundational

Nehinuw philosophy emphasizes the interactive dimension of life; we are dynamic beings filled with the creative power of life. The interactivity of individuals and groups stresses the embedded nature of life – of students and teachers in the classroom, in school, in the community, and beyond. We are interacting living beings, influencing and being influenced by, creating and being created by, life around us. To the teachers in this book, the development of interactional relationships with and among students and others was central to the teaching-learning process. The nature of the interaction was as important as making the connection.

The Enactment of Nehinuw Relational Concepts

In the teachers' stories, such as Anne's, we saw teachers practising *otootemitowin* (openness and acceptance) in their relationships. In English, teachers expressed their interactions as being respectful to the child as an individual and as an Indigenous person, so the child felt validated, accepted, and welcomed by the teacher. What was also very apparent was the openness teachers showed to Elders and community members. Students were aware when mutual respect was developed between their teachers and their own people. The implementation of this important relational value *(otootemitowin)* meant the students chose to follow the teacher's lead.

As we've seen, as in Angie's story, teachers connect their students to the learning environment through relationships based on *weechihitowin,* the act of reciprocal help and support. The student develops and experiences responsibility through the interactive processes at the three levels of social support: *weechihisowin* (self-support or self-help), *weechihitasowin* (one supports or helps others) and *weechihitowin* (helping each other). In building these relationships in the classroom, teachers support student development and learning, encourage students to support others, and promote student authority and independence in the development of an environment conducive to learning.

In enacting *weechihitowin* (helping each other), respect is the core value teachers use to guide behaviour, beliefs, and decision making. As asserted by Verna Kirkness and Ray Barnhardt (1991), respectful, reciprocal relationships foster responsibility and create relevance for Indigenous students. An important concept in Nehinuw philosophy, respect is conveyed in two different words: *kistenimitowin,* respectful reciprocity between people, and *kisteneetamowin,* respect for the world around a person, including cultural creations, inanimate entities, ideas, processes, and artifacts. These concepts, which were evident in the teachers' actions throughout our study, convey the expectation of respect for all around you: the people, the processes, and the content. Elder Peter Waskahat (quoted in Cardinal and Hildebrandt 2000, 16) affirms these foundational values of the traditional Nehinuw system of education:

> We had our own teachings, our own education system teaching children that way of life, and how children were taught how to view, to respect the land and everything in Creation ... Talk revolved around a way of life based on these values. For example: respect, to share, to care, to be respectful of people, how to help oneself. How to help others. How to work together.

Elder Waskahat connects respect and individual responsibility to interactive reciprocity, as he refers to the values enacted in sharing, caring, and working together. In Nehinuw social relationships, one needs both *kistenimisowin* (self-respect) and *kistenimitowin* (reciprocal respect for each other). *Weetutoskemitowin* (working together) and sharing require some form of interactive reciprocity, which was evident in the way teachers structured their classrooms and developed social skills.

When a person acts respectfully, he learns responsibility because respect involves valuing self and others. The late Elder Bea Lavallee, from the Piapot Nehinuw First Nation, clarified how respect relates to individual responsibility when she observed, "Every day we make a choice as to whether we're going to have a good day or a bad day. It is up to each of us as individuals to be respectful, to make the right choices, and to take responsibility for those choices" (personal communication, September 4, 2003).

The actions of the teachers in this study served to honour others when they were engaged in and developed relationships reflective of Nehinuw concepts that, in turn, changed teachers' practice. *Weechiyauguneetowin* (partnerships) and *weetutoskemitowin* (working together) were developed and used by teachers when they were confronted by a teaching issue or when they sought to improve their professional practice. In Calvin's case study, others helped him change the structure of the curriculum and the implementation of his redesigned program. Melva changed both the structure and content of her teaching as she partnered with the Dene language teacher to develop land- and culturally based activities. Monica achieved these goals by making students partners in learning. Cheryl partnered with students as well as the environment – everything that gives life, including *kituskeenuw* (our land) and *keesik* (sky or universe).

Weechiseechigemitowin (alliances to create a common action) were also used by teachers to connect to others and the community. Bonnie said her teaching practice changed fundamentally and for the better through her alliances with teachers, administrators, parents, and community members. The curriculum project described by Lily – which brought together Elders, teachers, other school staff, community artists, and musicians – helped Lily recognize and value her own Indigenous knowledge as a teacher. In the final case study, alliances with Elders that embodied *kisewatisihin* (respectful, compassionate presence) clarified teacher and student thinking, reminding both of the importance of caring, consideration, and compassion for self and others in education and in life.

It is vital that the school and community recognize the importance of community involvement in education and the involvement of students in the community. Co-determination in education happens when school leaders and teachers actively strive to overcome colonial relations that separated Indigenous communities and schools. Whether urban, rural, or remote, communities are vibrant places for student learning to take place. On the land, in service to others, or in community research to solve real life scientific or social problems, learning in community develops students' knowledge in context and can make a contribution to the community – bringing real meaning to learning.

When Indigenous communities become "true stakeholders" (Klug and Whitfield 2003, 274) in the education of their children, creative problem solving is possible. School boards can share responsibility for the ongoing education of their teachers. Communities provide venues for teachers to become familiar with positive features of the culture, arts, stories, and history of the community and to identify Elders and knowledge keepers who are willing to bring the Indigenous language, knowledge, and understandings into the school (Tsannie 2001).

Just as educational problems cannot be solved by pedagogy alone, education alone cannot solve the serious socioeconomic problems facing Indigenous communities. Social transformation is needed to resolve socioeconomic issues. At the same time, education plays a crucial role. As Paulo Freire (1998, 37) reminds us, "It is true that education is not the ultimate lever for social transformation, but without it transformation cannot occur."

The Enactment of Nehinuw Concepts of Teaching

One of the key concepts in Nehinuw philosophy is action by the self or directed towards the self. As described in Chapter 3, independence, responsibility, and self-determined action are inferred by the medial stem *-iso* or *-ato*. As children grow, they are expected to develop decision making skills and take responsibility for their actions. *Eti tipenemisot* is the transition one makes in becoming independent, in having measured authority over oneself and becoming a self-determining person. The role of education is to support children in becoming responsible decision makers in their actions. The teachers in this book strove to meet this goal in ways that reflect three Nehinuw forms of teaching: *kiskinaumagehin* (teaching others), *kiskinaumasowin* (teaching oneself), and *kiskinaumatowin* (teaching each other).

When teaching others *(kiskinaumagehin)*, teachers modelled responsible decision making in their direct instruction. Students were not abandoned to an irrelevant curriculum, spoon-fed information, or expected to learn all by themselves. Teachers provided responsive leadership in the social relationships, physical environment, content, and process of learning to ensure the learning environment was culturally congruent with their students' backgrounds. Doris made extensive use of direct instruction. In math, she used manipulatives, so students learned the concrete realities of basic math concepts before visualizing them, learning the verbal representation and creating the symbolic representation of the concept. She was familiar with the provincial curriculum but created her own social studies program to teach young children the history of settlement in Canada while encouraging imagination through role-playing. She often started her teaching with, "What if … " while ensuring students' understandings of their world were given expression in the classroom.

In addition to direct instruction, teachers created the conditions for self-learning *(kiskinaumasowin)* by developing student skills and competence. Responsibility for self was advocated and practised in the classroom. Learning was structured to build student confidence in their abilities. In teaching themselves, students understood how to take action by themselves and for themselves. The effective use of *kiskinaumasowin* (teaching oneself) was evident in Calvin's math class, for which he created a series of assignments that students did on their own. Initially, his students were not confident in their math abilities, so self-teaching provided them with privacy, taking away the fear of "appearing dumb" to their fellow students and the teacher, so they could engage with the math material. The math program was organized into sequenced, achievable parts; this enabled students to incrementally experience success and gain confidence in their ability to learn math. At the same time, Calvin continued to support students with direct instruction as needed to individuals and the class as a whole.

In interactive, relational thinking, one must move beyond the self to the consideration of others. Students learned to share their knowledge, understandings, gifts, and skills through *kiskinaumatowin* (teaching each other), as is evident in Melva's use of photographs to stimulate student-student discourse in language development. Teaching others solidifies self-learning and fosters creativity, validating the student's unique gifts and ways of interacting with the world. The inclusion of students' contributions to the curriculum demonstrates the value of that knowledge to others and fosters pride and confidence in sharing one's gifts. The power of the teacher is dispersed when students assume the role of teacher.

As students contribute to the learning, they also contribute to classroom decision making and thus develop a sense of self-determination but within a relational view of teaching and supporting others. This was evident in Monica's use of the talking circle. *Kiskinaumatowin* (teaching each other) was also in Cheryl's approach to having students share their Indigenous knowledge, understanding, and skills when she took them out on the land, where they opened up to learning from and teaching each other. In addition to the demonstration by students of hunting skills to call geese to land in the school playground, the geographic locations they visited evoked questions to be asked of relatives to deepen students' Indigenous understandings, which they could then share with others in the class. Sometimes, this knowledge was so special it was shared through stories only at their special place on the land.

In many Indigenous cultures, the autonomy of the individual is an important value, tied to the development of individual responsibility within a collective consciousness (Hampton 1995). The development of this value was achieved as teachers implemented in their instruction the three Nehinuw concepts of teaching.

Addressing Power Relationships

Decolonization is about restructuring power imbalances in relationships (Bishop 2003, 2012). The classroom is part of and influenced by the broader social context. Ruth Paradise (1994, 60) asserts that teachers and students are social actors who live within historical, social, and political contexts, but every classroom constructs its own particular social arrangement of "domination or respect." Decolonization rejects domination where authority remains external to the individual and there is no representation of Indigenous peoples' understandings or ways of being. Instead, the professional distancing for teacher objectivity in Eurocentric schooling is replaced by a close, personal bond that demonstrates respect and caring for the student by the teacher.

The responsible use of power by the teachers was a complex issue in this study, because in the interviews most described themselves as not being "an authority" in the class, while at the same time they were "tough" and "strict." The complexity of the teachers' positive use of power lies at the heart of decolonization in education. These teachers used their authority to set expectations for both respectful behaviour and academic engagement and to impose limitations within a context of equity. When teachers said they were not the authority in their class, they were referring to the authoritarian misuse of power inherent in power relationships associated with the colonizing role of the teacher in classroom interactions. Fyre Jean Graveline (2002, 21) refers to the complex tension between equity and limitations when she says, "Power with, not power over."

In examining the issue of authority in teaching, Paulo Freire (1998) analyzes power in the teaching-learning relationship, exploring the contradiction of freedom and authority, of developing voice and critical reflection within limits of respect for others, and the development of discipline and democratic practice. To Freire, democratic leadership balances freedom and authority. Authority is power that can be used to silence students and impose one's views upon them. Or power can be used to set ethical limits on the exercise of freedom. In this study, ethical limits were established and enforced when respect and other Nehinuw values were used to guide the actions of both the teacher and the student. Nehinuw values meant the teacher did not abuse power. She acted in the interest of the student in a way that maintained the right of the student to develop his own voice. Power was used to ensure the voice was an ethical or respectful one that did not "falsify the truth" (Freire 1998, 66) and was not irresponsible in its expression and used to silence, belittle, or hurt others.

Similar to Freire's view of the exercise of power, teachers used situational authority (Sammel, Linds, and Goulet, 2013): they were strict in enforcing the enactment of positive values in the classroom, but when appropriate, they shared authority jointly with students or expected students to take responsibility for teaching themselves or each other. *Shared leadership* was the term used to describe how the teachers dispersed power in the classroom when the role of the teacher was shared with others. Power was dispersed in curriculum decision making when students and community members were invited to share their experiences and to bring Indigenous meanings to the learning. Contributing to the knowledge and the decision making of the classroom situated students in leadership positions, which created more equitable relations between the students and the teachers. Dispersed power through shared leadership occurred gradually, as teachers guided students in taking on more responsibility in classroom interactions.

Creating equity in power relationships decolonized the learning environment through the development of student freedom and expression. As noted earlier, *tipenimisowin* is used primarily for youth as they learn how to do things on their own. Independence and authority over oneself require freedom to develop, but also have the connotation of freedom with responsibility. Without freedom, as occurs in colonial relationships, the self is restricted, creativity stymied, and development stunted. On the other hand, *tipenimisowin* allows for self-determined action and self-expression to develop one's own decision making, to tell one's story, and to enter the process of decolonization. Shared leadership in this book created space for community members and Indigenous students to take action, tell their stories, and, through their expressions and actions, assert their identity and authority. These actions and stories connected learning to their history, time, place, and lives, and thus were relevant, bringing meaning to and inviting engagement in the learning.

To exercise authority over oneself, one needs to be able to stand strong when facing a challenge. Too often, in the past, when Indigenous peoples stood up for themselves and others, the heavy hand of excessive authority was imposed to stop their actions. *Neepuhistumasowin* is the Nehinuw concept of standing up for oneself while *neepuhistumagehin* is standing up for others. It is recognized that in some circumstances one needs to compromise or negotiate a middle ground, but there are also those situations in which one must take a position and stand firm, especially in the context of empathy, compassion, and fairness. There needs to be space in the classroom for students to develop *neepuhistumasowin* and *neepuhistumagehin*. Learning these skills can help students stand up by themselves, and with and for others, to the bullies and injustices they encounter in and out of school and also later in life.

Self-determination is both a political and social goal of Indigenous peoples. Even though *self-determination* is often the term used politically to describe Indigenous authority in decision making, as explained in Chapter 3, determination of actions takes place within different levels of self-determination, co-determination, and societal determination. In the classroom, self-determination is enacted at the individual student, group of students, and teacher level; co-determination, when the teacher, the class as a whole, and other partners participate in decision making; and societal determination, when the teacher uses the institutional power vested in the position of teacher to create partnerships and alliances to improve education for Indigenous students and to stand up for changes needed in schools. In these interactive processes, students develop academic and social skills that balance the freedom and restraint required when working independently and together with others. Students learn to exercise responsible authority over themselves *(tipenimisowin)* and to stand up for themselves *(neepuhistumasowin)* and others *(neepuhistumagehin)* as future participants and leaders in self-determining Indigenous communities.

Ininee Mamitoneneetumowin (Indigenous Thinking)

In summarizing what is needed in Indigenous education, Ojibwe educator Thomas Peacock stated, "I think we need ... to get to the serious job of turning our education systems upside down and inside out to meet young people's

Jaycee Misponas taking water samples in land-based learning. *Photo by Linda Goulet.*

needs" (Bergstrom, Miller Cleary, and Peacock 2003, 183). Indigenous concepts are developing new theoretical understandings in Indigenous education: the Māori development of schooling based on Kaupapa Māori is creating educational success for Māori students while rejuvenating the Māori language. Changes to classroom teaching for Hawaiian children are being implemented based on key Hawaiian concepts and practices of learning. Indigenous concepts such as those of the Lil'wat described by Lorna Williams (2012; Williams and Tanaka 2007) provide new ways of thinking about the learning process. Nehinuw relational concepts have the power to transform practice with their emphasis on interactive processes. The interactive dimension of life as enacted by teachers changes the position of the teacher as the only expert in the education of the Indigenous child. Hierarchical, paternalistic relationships of the colonial past are replaced by interactive, more equitable social relationships that serve to create learning environments conducive to the success of Indigenous students.

Teachers who work with Indigenous students need to examine colonization and self-determination in both theory and practice. Just as it is important that prospective teachers of Indigenous students be knowledgeable regarding the theory and impact of colonization, we also need to recognize the enduring nature of cultural ways of being. As we have seen, Indigenous languages, knowledge, and understandings provide the key to meaningful, engaged learning. Indigenous philosophies, knowledge systems, and social relationships can be used to create new educational systems that are successful for Indigenous students.

At the 2012 American Education Research Association meeting in Vancouver, Canada, Māori scholar Linda Tuhiwai Smith reflected on the conference's theme "To know is not enough." In her presidential address, Smith stated that learning is indeed beyond knowing. This view is exemplified in the Nehinuw concept of life and learning. For the Nehinuw, it is not enough to know or attain knowledge; one must learn by self-discovery, interaction, or be directed in coming to understand. While the Nehinuw and English views of understanding are similar, their roots are different. In the case of the Nehinuw, understanding is attained by actually doing something about what you know.

In Nehinuw thought, land is a great source of knowledge and understanding. *Kituskeenuw* (which translates as "our land") reflects the embedded and holistic nature of Nehinuw thought. Unlike the everyday understanding in English, where land is seen mainly as geographic features, in Cree *kituskeenuw* includes everything around us: the land and its features, the plants and animals, the air space and the waters. All peoples of the world learn through observation of and interaction with *kituskeenuw,* the world around us. While observation is important in Nehinuw philosophy, the emphasis is on the processes, activities, and interactions with *kituskeenuw* and *keesik* (the sky or universe). This view relates to learning by doing, but is a much more complex concept. *Nisitootumowin* translates as "understanding," but it is also tied in with "meaning." The word stem *nisi-* is used in the related word *nisituhinum,* which translates as "s/he recognizes something," so it can be related to the English verbs of *observation, perception,* and *recognition,* as well as *meaning* and *understanding.* The latter part of *nisitootumowin, itoota,* is "to do, to carry out an activity, or to act." To the Nehinuw, then, understanding is a dynamic interactive process connecting thought, action, and meaning. Whether relating to life in general or to the acts of teaching and learning, action and interaction combined with reflective thought are integral to Nehinuw understanding. Action and interaction create and recreate understanding within the self, with people and other life force entities, with our tools and technology, as well as with *kituskeenuw* (our land/world) and *keesik* (sky/universe). Little understanding occurs without action and interaction.

This view urges us as teachers to breathe life into our teaching, our relationships with our students, the content we teach, and the methods we use. Teaching needs to become real – tied to the life around us that includes the present, past, and future, not just the past in its glorified or Eurocentric rendition, but also the reality of the hardships, challenges, and triumphs of ordinary people and the contributions of all people, including Indigenous peoples.

Sometimes we focus on the issues or problems to solve, but at the same time we need to be able to identify strengths of the past that provide us with our gifts in the present. Our gifts are what we can use to address and resolve today's challenges. Above all, as the teachers in this book have shown, we need education for hope – hope that we and our students and community members are capable people who, through our individual and collaborative efforts, can create innovations for positive change in Indigenous education as we enact *kee-chi-giskinaumatowin*, the striving for excellence in our teaching and learning, with and for each other.

Appendix 1: Cree Orthographic Chart

The writing for Cree in this book is a phonetic, non-macron system rather than a macron-based phonemic system. This writing system is based on the actual pronunciation, speech, and lived experience of Nehinuw speakers and Elders. Many of the Nehinuw Elders learned to read the complex Cree language words in their prayer books, hymn books, and bibles using a writing system similar to the one used in this book. This writing system is also reflective of the historical dialect at the community level. Because it does not use macrons, it requires no special keyboard, programs, or adjustments for typists or publishers – or texters! The words used for illustration in the following charts are from the "N" Cree dialect pronunciation spoken in Cumberland House, so the pronunciation varies for some of these words in other Cree dialects. The following is a simplified description of the Cree sound system to be used as guide to the pronunciation of Cree words in this book.

Cree Consonants

	English pronunciation	*Cree pronunciation*
t	tan	tansi (how are you?)
ch	cheap	cheeman (canoe)
k	kiss	kinipee (hurry)
b	ebb	nibebeem (my baby)
d	sled	n'danis (my daughter)
j	Major	n'jiyau (my cousin)
g	bag	nigosis (my son)
m	miss	misit (foot)
n	nap	napew (man)
p	pen	poona (make a fire)
s	sit	seepee (river)
y	yes	yapew (bull moose)

Note: The consonants *p, t, ch,* and *k* are used when they occur at the beginning of a word. In our "N" dialect, most of time, but not always, when these consonants are in the medial or final position in a word, they are pronounced as the voiced consonants *b, d, j,* and *g,* so the spelling in this book reflects this. For example, *neeginan* (our home), *uskeeg* (pail), and *sigak* (skunk) all use a *g* in the medial or ending position. Note the word for skunk, *sigak,* remains spelled with a *k* at the end of the word and that *uskeeg* retains the k in the middle, because that is how it is pronounced. An attempt is made to replicate the actual oral pronunciation. The interchange of the pronunciation of these consonants also varies when the structure of the sentence changes. For example, when making a statement, a word like *kiskeneetum* (s/he knows) becomes *nigiskeneeten* (I know it). The first k of *kis* changes when it is used in the medial position in *nigis,* but the medial k of *ken* doesn't change to a *g* sound, because it is preceded by a consonant.

Cree Vowels

Although the sounds are not exactly the same, this chart is provided to illustrate the closest approximation of English/Cree pronunciation. Within Cree there are more sounds than those represented here, but for practicality and simplicity, the writing system used in this book limits the spelling to these approximate vowel sounds.

	English pronunciation	Cree pronunciation
a	ask	astum (come)
u*	up	upi (sit)
i	it	misit (foot)
ee	see	seeseep (duck)
e	Esther	nete (over there)
o	book	mostos (cow)
oo	moose	moosa (moose)
au**	Paul	iskautem (door)

* When *u* is used at the ending of a word in Cree, the pronunciation is difficult and confusing for people who are used to English endings and writing systems, so an *a* is used instead. So, for example, in the word *koonu* (snow), pronounced as in *up,* the *u* is changed to *a,* as in *koona.* It is also used at the beginning of words, such as in the word *usum* (feed him or her) which is spelled as *asum.*

** This is one of the examples of dialect variation. The *au* sound of the "N" dialect changes to a *wa* sound in some of the other Cree dialects, such as the "Y" dialect in southern Saskatchewan; for example, the word for *door* is *iskautem* in the "N" dialect and *iskwatem* in the "Y" dialect in the south.

Appendix 2: Model of Effective Teaching for Indigenous Students – Categories, Subcategories, and Attributes

1. **Relationships with Indigenous Students:**

   Developing Culturally Affirming Interpersonal Relationships

   Believing in the Student
       Believing in the student's ability to learn
       Believing in the student's ability to change
   Developing Close, Personal Bonds
       Genuine caring
       Showing humanness
   Valuing the Individual and His/Her Culture
       Each student is special
       Respecting Indigenous culture
   Building Reciprocal Respect and Trust
       The value of respect
       Equitable leadership
   Consequence: Student follows the lead of the teacher

2. **Relationships among Students:**

   Establishing Respectful Social Systems

   Safety and Belonging
       Valuing Indigenous culture
       Belonging in the physical space
       Social safety

Positive Emotional Growth
    Teacher awareness of emotional issues
    Respectfully accommodating emotional stress
    Expressing stress appropriately
Social Skills for Working Together
    Respectful social behaviour
    Group skills
    Leadership skills
Shared Leadership
    Situational leadership
    Joint authority
Consequence: Class supports learning goals

3. **Connecting to the Process:**

Creating a Culturally Responsive Learning Environment

Responsive Teaching
    Being well planned
    Responding to students
    Learning as a shared endeavour
Accommodating Characteristics of Indigenous Students
    Contemporary and traditional culture
    Anti-racism
    Language development
    Multi-level skill development
    Social and personal problems
Structuring for Success
    Starting with strength
    Practising in a safe situation
    Motivating students
    Scaffolding learning experiences
Variety of Teaching Approaches
    Mastery learning
    Concrete materials
    Storytelling
    One-on-one
    Talking or sharing circle
    Group work

Experiential and activity-based learning
Community and land-based learning
Student Belief in Self
Setting standards for achievement and responsibility
Valuing self and one's culture
Public recognition of students' accomplishments
Consequence: Responsible, self-directed learners

4. Connecting to the Content:

Constructing Culturally Meaningful Knowledge

Connecting Students to the Curriculum
Representing the cultural self in the curriculum
Personal self is part of the curriculum
Maintaining Student Focus
Fun in learning
Interest in learning
Effective Cognitive Mediators
Support for cognition
Support for different learning styles
Culturally meaningful mediators
Relationships beyond the Classroom
Parents and families
School staff
Elders, knowledge keepers, community members
Consequence: Learning has relevance and meaning

Notes

Chapter 1: Where We Are in Indigenous Education

1. In this book, the term *Indigenous* is used to include First Nations, Métis, and Inuit peoples who are each recognized as distinct groups. *Aboriginal* encompasses these distinct groups in the Canadian constitution, and is commonly used in Canada. The term *Indigenous* is also used more broadly in the international context to include those First Peoples of the Americas, Pacific, and other regions. In the United States, the original peoples are referred as *Native Americans* or *American Indian*; these terms are thus used in that context. Where possible, the name of the specific Indigenous nation is used. Because different terms such as *Indian* and *Native* have been used historically, references in cited documents are maintained as presented by the original authors, as are terms used by teachers in their stories and interviews.

2. The terms *Euro-Canadian* and *settler Canadian* are used to designate those of the dominant settler society. Settler societies are those colonized by Europeans who became politically dominant over Indigenous peoples and developed the country with regard to class and race. Settler colonists are all of those who come to a colony or colonized country in order to benefit from the spoils of colonialism (Memmi 1965). Because we live in a racialized society, the term *white* is also used to represent those from the dominant group in our society. All terms are problematic because they are not inclusive and because different people do not benefit equally from the colonial process.

3. *Nehinuw* is the ethnonym or self-designation for the people called Cree (in English) who live in western Canada. In this book, the terms *Nehinuw* and *Cree* are used interchangeably because of the historical and contemporary use of the term *Cree*. *Nehinuwuk* is the plural form, while the language spoken is Nehinuwehin. In western Canada, the dialects are "N" and "Th," as well as two subdivisions of the "Y" dialect, a plains "Y" and the "Y" of the northwest. The dialect used in this book is the "N" dialect of the Cumberland House Nehinuwuk.

4. In this book we italicize Cree words and word stems as a device for easier reading. A phonetic writing system is used rather than the more abstract phonemic system with macrons and circumflexes. This writing system is more accessible to those who have not studied Cree linguistics, such as the Elders and the general public (see Appendix 1 for orthographic chart and explanation).

5. For a full definition, see Wikipedia, "Indigenous education," http://en.wikipedia.org/wiki/indigenous education.

6. A talking circle is an Indigenous pedagogical approach whereby participants sit in a circle and pass around an object in one direction, and only the person holding the object can speak, while others listen. The talking circle "encourages dialogue, respect, the co-creation of learning content, and social discourse" (First Nations Pedagogy Online, para. 1).

Chapter 3: What to Build Upon

1. Cole (1996) uses the term "cultural artifact" in his explication of cognitive mediators, but we use cognitive mediators because in Indigenous education, cultural artifacts are too easily confused with the historical and contemporary cultural material creations of Indigenous peoples.

2. This story is based on speaking notes for the keynote address "Learning from Elders" by Lily McKay-Carriere, at the Stirling McDowell's Learning from Practice conference, Saskatoon, Saskatchewan, November 21, 2009.

3. This research project was funded by the Dr. Stirling McDowell Foundation for Research into Teaching.

4. Sometimes the goals of expressing uniqueness in Indigenous languages and of doing comparative analysis between Indigenous and European languages can lead to over-simplification. The terms *animate* and *inanimate*, though commonly used in Cree linguistics, are problematic in that they reduce the complexities of the Nehinuwehin grammatical structure to an overly simplified living and non-living duality. It is also said that the Cree language is verb-based. Indigenous languages need to be examined in their totality, not only as subsystems based on nouns or verbs or other grammatical structures and devices. Although we do utilize specific grammatical structural arguments, our major point of reference and focus is based on Nehinuw educational concepts and teaching practice, rather than linguistics. For a more thorough discussion of the Nehinuwehin structure from a Nehinuw perspective, see Goulet, forthcoming.

5. *Pimachihowin* is an example of Cree "action nouns," nouns that refer to "the act of."

6. *Waso* actually refers to an animate being or entity, whereas *wastew* refers to artificial light coming from various sources, such as a flashlight, lamp, or electrical lights. The latter are classified as inanimate.

7. The story of the naming of the north wind was retold by Elder Danny Muskwa in the presence of the author during the May 14–16, 2007, Conference on Indigenous Knowledge in Education at Banff, Alberta.

8. In Cree, there is no generic word for grandfather and grandmother. They are relational terms: *noogom* (my grandmother), *koogom* (your grandmother), and *oogoma* (his or her grandmother); *nimosoom* (my grandfather), *kimosoom* (your grandfather), and *omosooma* (his or her grandfather). In recent usage, people use *koogom* as a generic word for "grandmother" and *mosoom* for "grandfather."

Chapter 4: How to Get There

1. In the following chapters, for the purposes of brevity and clarity, the teacher is referred to as "she" and the student as "he." If we were writing in Cree, we wouldn't be faced with this problem.
2. In this book, some teachers are identified by pseudonyms, while others who shared their case studies used their real names. In citing evidence in this chapter, the responses of the teachers are often summarized. Where direct quotes are used, the name of the teacher precedes or follows the quote.
3. *Kiyam* is a Cree word meaning, "It's okay, so what? Let it be." *Kiyam* means that whatever social pressure is coming at you from another person, it is something that you can choose to ignore and from which you can be independent.

Chapter 9: Breaking Trail

1. The "Narrows of Fear," or Opawikoscikan, which is the Cree name for the community of Pelican Narrows, is so named for a historical incident when the Dakota raided the community, attacking at the river narrows when the Nehinuw men were out on a hunting or trading trip. The captured children were left on an island, while the women were taken south in canoes. The Nehinuw men caught up to the Dakota and freed the women.
2. This case study is based on two collaborative research projects funded by the Dr. Stirling McDowell Foundation for Research into Teaching.
3. The participants in the Elder circles gave us permission to use their names when quoting their words to acknowledge their authorship of the oral narrative.

Chapter 10: *Ininee mamitoneneetumowin,* Indigenous Thinking

1. There are two *we*'s or *our* in Cree. One is inclusive while the other is exclusive. *Nituskeenan* is the exclusive form that excludes the listener from the *we* or *our* while *kituskeenuw* is inclusive of both the speaker and the listener. The former is used when we are talking to people from outside our territory and the latter for those who are part of our territory.
2. Lorna Williams (2012) explains that the Lil'wat concept of *kamucwkalha* has a deeper, more complex meaning than is translated here. She notes that it also means that everyone has a voice; that everyone's voice has a space; that the more one's unique attributes are honoured, the stronger the group. The root of the word means "belly button," so connectivity is key.

References

Absolon, Kathleen E. (Minogiizhigokwe). 2011. *Kaandossiwin: How we come to know*. Winnipeg: Fernwood Publishers.

Acoose, Janice. 1995. *Iskwewak – kah'ki yaw ni wahkomakanak: Neither Indian princesses nor easy squaws*. Toronto: Women's Press.

Adams, Howard. 1989. *Prison of grass: Canada from a Native point of view*. Rev. ed. Saskatoon: Fifth House Publishers.

Ah Nee-Benham, Maenette K.P., with Joanne E. Cooper, eds. 2000. *Indigenous educational models for contemporary practice: In our mother's voice*. Mahwah, NJ: Lawrence Erlbaum Associates.

Aikenhead, Glen. 2006. *Science education for everyday life: Evidence-based practice*. New York: Teachers College Press.

Alberta Education. 2007. "The First Nations, Métis and Inuit school: Community learning environment project – Promising practices report." Edmonton: First Nations, Métis and Inuit Services Branch. http://education.alberta.ca/media/164304/sclep%20promising %20practices%20report.pdf.

–. 2008. "Promising practices in First Nations, Métis and Inuit education: Case studies #2." Edmonton: First Nations, Métis and Inuit Services Branch. http://education.alberta.ca/ media/859897/promising%20practices%20case%20studies%20two.pdf.

Alo, Pamela L., Iwalani Hodges, and Jay M. Taniguchi. 2012. "Ha'akea: Learning from our communities." Paper presented at the American Education Research Association annual meeting, Vancouver, April 13.

Archibald, Jo-ann. 2008. *Indigenous storywork: Educating the heart, mind, body, and spirit*. Vancouver: UBC Press.

Baker, Carmen. 2008. *Aboriginal student achievement and positive learning outcomes in Canadian schools: Promising practices*. Report for the Canadian Council on Learning's Aboriginal Learning Knowledge Centre. Issued by the Aboriginal Education Research Centre, University of Saskatchewan, Saskatoon, and First Nations and Adult Higher

Education Consortium, Calgary. http://www.education.gov.sk.ca/ablkc-k-12-literature-review.

Ball, Jessica, and Alan Pence. 2006. *Supporting Indigenous children's development: Community-university partnerships.* Vancouver: UBC Press.

Banks, James A. 1989. *Multicultural education: Issues and perspectives.* Needham Heights, MA: Allyn and Bacon.

–. 1996. "The canon debate, knowledge construction, and multicultural education." In *Multicultural education, transformative knowledge, and action: Historical and contemporary perspectives,* ed. J.A. Banks, 3–29. New York: Teachers College Press.

Barber, Elizabeth W., and Paul T. Barber. 2004. *When they severed earth from sky: How the human mind shapes myth.* Princeton, NJ: Princeton University Press.

Barman, Jean, Yvonne Hébert, and Don McCaskill, eds. 1987. *Indian education in Canada.* Vol. 2, *The challenge.* Vancouver: UBC Press.

Battiste, Marie. 2000. "Maintaining Aboriginal identity, language, and culture in modern society." In *Reclaiming Indigenous voice and vision,* ed. M. Battiste, 192–208. Vancouver: UBC Press.

–. 2002. "Decolonizing methodologies and research: Engaging Indigenous communities." Paper presented at the World Indigenous Peoples Conference on Education, Morley, AB, August 7.

–. 2005. "Indigenous knowledge: Foundations for First Nations." *WINHEC Journal.* http://www.win-hec.org/docs/pdfs/Journal/Marie%20Battiste%20copy.pdf.

–. 2013. *Decolonizing education: Nourishing the learning spirit.* Saskatoon: Purich Publishing.

Battiste, Marie, and Jean Barman, eds. 1995. *First Nations education in Canada: The circle unfolds.* Vancouver: UBC Press.

Battiste, Marie, and James [Sákéj] Youngblood Henderson. 2009. "Naturalizing Indigenous knowledge in Eurocentric education." *Canadian Journal of Native Education* 32 (1): 129–30.

Bell, David, Kirk Anderson, Terry Fortin, Jacqueline Ottmann, Sheila Rose, Leon Simard, and Keith Spencer. 2004. *Sharing our success: Ten case studies in Aboriginal schooling.* Kelowna, BC: Society for the Advancement of Excellence in Education.

Bennett, Robert. 1997. "Why didn't you teach me?" In *First person, first peoples: Native American college graduates tell their life stories,* ed. A. Garrod and C. Larimore, 136–53. Ithaca, NY: Cornell University Press.

Bergstrom, Amy, Linda Miller Cleary, and Thomas Peacock. 2003. *The seventh generation: Native students speak about finding the good path.* Charleston, WV: ERIC Clearinghouse on Rural Education and Small Schools.

Bilash, Olenka. 2004. "The rocky road to RLS in a Cree community in Canada." Paper No. 606, 20, University of Duisberg, Essen, Germany, Linguistic LAUD Agency.

Binda, K.P. with Sharilyn Calliou, eds. 2001. *Aboriginal education in Canada: A study in decolonization.* Mississauga, ON: Canadian Educators' Press.

Bishop, Russell. 2003. "Changing power relations in education: Kaupapa Maori messages for 'mainstream' education in Aotearoa/New Zealand." *Comparative Education* 39 (2): 221–38. http://dx.doi.org/10.1080/03050060302555.

–. 2011. *Freeing ourselves.* Rotterdam, NL: Sense Publishers. http://dx.doi.org/10.1007/978-94-6091-415-7.

–. 2012. Te Kotahitanga: Making a difference in Maori Education. http://tekotahitanga.tki. org.nz/.

Bishop, Russell, M. Berryman, T. Cavanagh, L. Teddy, and S. Clapham. 2006. "Te Kotahitanga Phase 3 Whakawhanaungatanga: Establishing a culturally responsive pedagogy of relations in mainstream secondary school classrooms." Wellington: Ministry of Education. http://www.educationcounts.govt.nz/__data/assets/pdf_file/0004/9922/Te_Kotahitanga_Phase3.pdf

Bishop, Russell, Mere Berryman, and Cath Richardson. 2002. "Te Toi Huarewa: Effective teaching and learning in total immersion Maori language educational settings." *Canadian Journal of Native Education* 26 (1): 44–61.

Bloom, Benjamin S. 1971. "Mastery learning." In *Mastery learning: Theory and practice,* ed. J.H. Block, 47–63. New York: Holt, Rinehart and Winston.

Bopp, Judie, M. Bopp, L. Brown, and Phil Lane. 1984. *Sacred tree.* Lethbridge, AB: Four Worlds International Institute.

Boroditsky, Lera. 2011. "How language shapes thought." *Scientific American* (February): 63–65.

Bouvier, Rita. 2001. "Good community schools are sites of educational activism." In Ward and Bouvier, *Resting lightly on Mother Earth,* 49–62.

Bouvier, Rita, and Angela Ward. 2001. "Closing reflections." In Ward and Bouvier, *Resting lightly on Mother Earth,* 169–91.

Breithecker, Dieter. 2011. "Beware of the sitting trap in learning and schooling." http://www.designshare.com/index.php/articles/sitting-trap/.

Brendtro, Larry K., Martin Brokenleg, and Steven Van Bockern. 1990. *Reclaiming youth at risk: Our hope for the future.* Bloomington, IN: National Educational Service.

Bryde, John F. 1971. *Modern Indian psychology.* Rev. ed. Vermillion: University of South Dakota .

Burton, Wilfred, and Anne Patton. 2011. *Call of the fiddle.* Saskatoon: Gabriel Dumont Institute.

Campbell, Maria. 1973. *Half-breed.* Toronto: McClelland and Stewart.

–. 2010. *Stories of the road allowance people.* Saskatoon: Gabriel Dumont Institute.

Canadian Council on Learning. 2009. "The state of Aboriginal learning in Canada: A holistic approach to measuring success." http://www.ccl-cca.ca/pdfs/StateAboriginal Learning/SAL-FINALReport_EN.PDF.

Cardinal, Harold, and Walter Hildebrandt. 2000. *Treaty Elders of Saskatchewan.* Calgary: University of Calgary Press.

Carr-Stewart, Sheila. 2010. "First Nations education: A legal and administrative quagmire." In *Educational leadership today and tomorrow: The law as a friend or foe,* ed. R.C. Flynn, 83–104. Toronto: NR Printing Solutions.

Castagno, Angelina E., and Bryan M.J. Brayboy. 2008. "Culturally responsive schooling for Indigenous youth: A review of the literature." *Review of Educational Research* 78 (4): 941–93. http://dx.doi.org/10.3102/0034654308323036.

Cazden, Courtney B. 1983. "Adult assistance to language development: Scaffolds, models, and direct instruction." In *Developing literacy: Young children's use of language,* ed. R.P. Parker and F.A. Davis, 3–17. Newark, DE: International Reading Association.

Chaput, John. 2005. "Frog Lake Massacre." Encyclopedia of Saskatchewan. Regina: Canadian Plains Research Center.

Chartrand, Rebecca. 2012. "Anishinaabe Pedagogy." *Canadian Journal of Native Education* 35 (1): 144–62.

Chigeza, Philemon, and Hilary Whitehouse. 2011. ""Double Whammy': Where is there space for Indigenous cultural resources in science classrooms?" In *Talking back, talking forward: Journeys in transforming Indigenous educational practice*, ed. G. Williams, 107–16. Darwin, AUS: University of Darwin Press.

Clandinin, D. Jean, and F. Michael Connelly. 1995. *Teachers' professional knowledge landscapes*. New York: Teachers College Press.

Cole, Michael. 1996. *Cultural psychology: A once and future discipline*. Cambridge, MA: Belknap.

Corbin, Juliet, and Anselm Strauss. 2008. *Basics of qualitative research: Techniques and procedures for developing grounded theory*. Los Angeles: Sage.

Coutu, Phillip R., and Lorraine Hoffman-Mercredi. 2002. *Inkonze: The stones of traditional knowledge*. 2nd ed. Edmonton: Thunderwoman Ethnographics.

Coyne, Andrew. 2012. "Get Up, Stand Up – Stand Up for Your Life." *Saskatoon Star Phoenix*, 21 July.

Daschuk, James. 2013. *Clearing the plains: Disease, politics of starvation, and the loss of Aboriginal life*. Regina: University of Regina Press.

Derman-Sparks, Louise, and Carol Brunson Phillips. 1997. *Teaching/learning anti-racism: A developmental approach*. New York: Teachers College Press.

Deyhle, Donna, and Karen Swisher. 1997. "Research in American Indian and Alaska Native education: From assimilation to self-determination." *Review of Research in Education* 22:113–94.

Dion, Susan. 2009. *Braiding histories: Learning from Aboriginal peoples' experiences and perspectives*. Vancouver: UBC Press.

Douaud, Patrick, and Bruce Dawson, eds. 2002. *Plain speaking: Essays on Aboriginal peoples and the prairie*. Regina: Canadian Plains Research Center.

"Elders' roundtable." 2002. In Douaud and Dawson, *Plain speaking*, 101–15.

Elliott, John, Joshua Guilar, and Tye Swallow. 2009. "SNIT … E …: Learning from a traditional place." *Canadian Journal of Native Education* 32 (2): 105–17.

Enzoe, Pete, and Mindy Willett. 2010. *The caribou feed our soul? étthén bet'á dághíddá*. Markham, ON: Fifth House.

Episkenew, Jo-Ann. 2009. *Taking back our spirits: Indigenous literature, public policy, and healing*. Winnipeg: University of Manitoba Press.

Erickson, Frederick, and Gerald Mohatt. 1982. "Cultural organization of participation structures in two classrooms of Indian students." In *Doing the ethnography of schooling*, ed. G. Spindler, 131–74. New York: Holt, Rinehart and Winston.

Ermine, Willie. 1995. "Aboriginal epistemology." In Battiste and Barman, *First Nations education in Canada*, 101–12.

Farrell-Racette, Sherry. 2005. "Sewing for a living: The commodification of Métis women's artistic production." In *Contact zones: Aboriginal and settler women in Canada's colonial past*, ed. K. Pickles and M. Rutherdale, 1–17. Vancouver: UBC Press.

Farrell-Racette, Sherry, Linda Goulet, Joanne Pelletier, and Karon Shmon. 1996. *Aboriginal cultures and perspectives: Making a difference in the classroom*. Diversity in the Classroom series, No. 5. Regina: Saskatchewan Instructional Development and Research Unit.

Fayant, Russell, Linda Goulet, Joanne Pelletier, Calvin Racette, Sarah Longman, Shauneen Pete, and Ken Goodwill. 2010. *Ochapan: Perspectives of Elders and students on the Elders in Residence Program*. Saskatoon: Dr. Stirling McDowell Foundation for Research into Teaching. http://www.mcdowellfoundation.ca/main_mcdowell/projects/research_rep/188_teachers_work_with_elder.pdf.

Federation of Saskatchewan Indian Nations (FSIN). 1997. *Saskatchewan and Aboriginal peoples in the 21st century: Social, economic and political changes and challenges*. Regina: Federation of Saskatchewan Indian Nations.

–. 2002a. Discussion paper for action on K-12 education for Saskatchewan First Nations students. Federation of Saskatchewan Indian Nations, Regina, April.

–. 2002b. A research report on the schooling, workforce and income status of First Nations persons in Saskatchewan. Federation of Saskatchewan Indian Nations, Regina, February.

Feldgus, E.G., and I. Cardonick. 1999. *Kidwriting*. Bothell, WA: Wright Group.

First Nations Pedagogy Online. Talking circles from a First Nations perspective. http://firstnationspedagogy.ca/circletalks.html

Flanagan, Thomas. 2000. *First nations? Second thoughts*. Montreal and Kingston: McGill-Queen's University Press.

Francis, R. Douglas, Richard Jones, and Donald B. Smith. 2004. *Origins: Canadian History to Confederation*. 5th ed. Scarborough, ON: Nelson/Thomson.

Freire, Paulo. 1998. *Teachers as cultural workers: Letters to those who dare teach*. Trans. Donaldo Macedo, D. Koike, and Alexandre Olivira. Boulder, CO: Westview Press.

Friedel, Tracy. 2010. "Finding a place for race at the policy table: Broadening the Indigenous education discourse in Canada." Institute on Governance, Aboriginal Policy Research Series. http://www.iog.ca/.

Friedel, Tracy, Jo-ann Archibald, Ramona Big Head, Georgina Martin, Marissa Muñoz. 2012. "Editorial: Indigenous pedagogies – Resurgence and restoration." *Canadian Journal of Native Education* 35 (1): 1–6.

Fullford, George, with Jackie Moore Daigle, Blair Stevenson, Chuck Tolley, and Tracey Wade. 2007. *Sharing our success: More case studies in Aboriginal schooling*. Kelowna, BC: Society for the Advancement of Excellence in Education.

Gardner, Howard. 1993. *Multiple intelligences: The theory in practice*. New York: Basic Books.

Gillespie, LaVina, and Agnes Grant. 2001. "Children of the Earth High School: An urban model." In *A school on each reserve: Aboriginal education in Manitoba*, ed. L. Gillespie and A. Grant, 163–76. Brandon, MB: Brandon University Northern Teacher Education Program.

Gilliland, Hap, with Jon Reyhner. 1988. *Teaching the Native American*. Dubuque, IA: Kendall/Hunt Publishing.

Glaser, Barney G. 1978. *Theoretical sensitivity: Advances in the methodology of grounded theory*. Mill Valley, CA: Sociology Press.

–. 1992. *Emergence versus forcing: Basics of grounded theory analysis*. Mill Valley, CA: Sociology Press.

–. 1998. *Doing grounded theory: Issues and discussions*. Mill Valley, CA: Sociology Press.

Glaser, Barney G., and Anselm L. Strauss. 1967. *The discovery of grounded theory*. Chicago: Aldine Publishing.

Goulet, Keith. Forthcoming. *Nituskeenan:* Land and the Cumberland Nehinuw (Cree). PhD diss., University of Regina.

Goulet, Linda. 1987. The need for multicultural, anti-racist education in Northern Saskatchewan emphasizing Indigenous cultures. Available from the Northern Lights School Division No. 113.

–. 2001. "Two teachers of Aboriginal students: Effective practice in sociohistorical realities." *Canadian Journal of Native Education* 25 (1): 68–82.

–. 2005. Creating culturally meaningful learning environments: Teacher actions to engage Aboriginal students in learning. PhD diss., University of Regina.

Goulet, Linda, Jo-Ann Episkenew, Warren Linds, and Karen Arnason. 2009. "Rehearsal with reality: Exploring health issues with Aboriginal youth through drama." In *Passion for action in child and family services: Voices from the Prairies*, ed. S. McKay, D. Fuchs, and I. Brown, 99–118. Regina: Canadian Plains Research Center.

Goulet, Linda, Warren Linds, Jo-Ann Episkenew, and Karen Schmidt. 2011. "Creating a space for decolonization: Health through theatre with Indigenous youth." *Native Studies Review* 20 (1): 35–62.

Goulet, Linda, and Yvonne McLeod. 2002. "Connections and reconnections: Affirming cultural identity in Aboriginal teacher education." *McGill Journal of Education* 37 (3): 355–69.

Goulet, Linda, Joanne Pelletier, Shauneen Pete, Calvin Racette, Sarah Longman, Ken Goodwill, and Russell Fayant. 2009. *Asokan (the bridge): Teachers' work with Elders*. Saskatoon: Dr. Stirling McDowell Foundation for Research into Teaching. http://www.mcdowellfoundation.ca/main_mcdowell/projects/research_rep/188_teachers_work_with_elder.pdf.

Grant, Agnes. 1988. *Culture-specific materials: Stories my kokum and mushoom tell*. Brandon, MB: Brandon University.

Graveline, Fyre Jean. 1998. *Circle works: Transforming Eurocentric consciousness*. Halifax, NS: Fernwood.

–. 2002. "Teaching tradition teaches us." *Canadian Journal of Native Education* 26 (1): 11–29.

Greenwood, Margo, and Sarah de Leeuw. 2007. "Teachings from the land: Indigenous people, our health, our land, and our children." *Canadian Journal of Native Education* 30 (1): 48–53.

Haig-Brown, Celia, and Kaaren Dannenmann. 2002. "A pedagogy of the land: Dreams of respectful relations." *McGill Journal of Education* 37 (3): 451–68.

Haig-Brown, Celia, Kathy L. Hodgson-Smith, Robert Regnier, and Jo-ann Archibald. 1997. *Making the spirit dance within: Joe Duquette High School and an Aboriginal community*. Toronto: James Lorimer and Company.

Hampton, Eber. 1995. "Towards a redefinition of Indian education." In Battiste and Barman, *First Nations education in Canada*, 5–46.

Harris, Michael. 1990. *Justice denied: The law versus Donald Marshall*. Toronto: HarperCollins.

Hesch, Rick. 1995. "Teacher education and Aboriginal opposition." In Battiste and Barman, *First Nations education in Canada*, 179–207.

Highway, Tomson. 2001. *Caribou song: Atíhko níkamon*. Toronto: HarperCollins.

Hirschfelder, Arlene B. 1982. *American Indian stereotypes in the world of children: A reader and bibliography*. London: Scarecrow Press.

Howe, Eric. 2011. *Bridging the Aboriginal education gap in Saskatchewan*. Saskatoon: Gabriel Dumont Institute.

Huff, Delores J. 1997. *To live heroically: Institutional racism and American Indian education*. New York: State University of New York Press.

Hull, M. (2002). "Local culture and academic success go together: Place-based education in Russian Mission." *Sharing Our Pathways* (newsletter) 7 (5): 1–3.

Iseke-Barnes, Judy M. 2009. "Grandmothers of the Métis Nation: A living history with Dorothy Chartrand." *Native Studies Review* 18 (2): 69–104.

Jordan-Fenton, Christy, and Margaret Pokiak-Fenton. 2010. *Fatty legs*. Toronto: Annick Press.

Kanu, Yatta. 2005. "Teachers' perceptions of the integration of Aboriginal culture into the high school curriculum." *Alberta Journal of Educational Research* 51 (1): 50–68.

King, Cecil. 1993. "Reflections on the TEPs: Revisiting the purpose." Keynote address at the meeting of Canadian Indian/Inuit Teacher Education Programs, North Bay, Ontario.

Kirkness, Verna J. 1992. *First Nations and schools: Triumphs and struggles*. Toronto: Canadian Education Association.

Kirkness, Verna J., and Ray Barnhardt. 1991. "First Nations and higher education: The four R's – Respect, relevance, reciprocity, responsibility." *Journal of American Indian Education* 30 (3): 1–15.

Kleinfeld, Judith. 1975. "Effective teachers of Eskimo and Indian students." *School Review* 83 (2): 300–44.

Klug, Beverly J., and Patricia T. Whitfield. 2003. *Widening the circle: Culturally relevant pedagogy for American Indian children*. New York: Routledge Falmer.

Kolb, David. 1984. *Experiential learning: Experience as the source of learning and development*. Englewood Cliffs, NJ: Prentice Hall.

Kovach, Margaret. 2009. *Indigenous methodologies: Characteristics, conversations, and contexts*. Toronto: University of Toronto Press.

Kumashiro, Kevin K. 2000. "Toward a theory of anti-oppressive education." *Review of Educational Research* 70 (1): 25–53. http://dx.doi.org/10.3102/00346543070001025.

Ladson-Billings, Gloria. 1990. "Culturally relevant teaching: Effective instruction for Black students." *College Board Review* 155: 20–5.

LaRocque, Emma. 2010. *When the other is me: Native resistance discourse, 1850-1990*. Winnipeg: University of Manitoba Press.

Lee, Tiffany S. 2007. "Connecting academics, Indigenous knowledge, and commitment to community: High school students' perceptions of a community-based education." *Canadian Journal of Native Education* 30 (2): 196–216.

Li, Shu-Chen. 2009. "Brain in macro experiential context: Biocultural co-construction of lifespan neurocognitive development." In *Progress in brain research*. Vol. 178, *Cultural neuroscience: Cultural influences on brain function*, ed. J.Y. Chiao, 17–29. New York: Elsevier.

Lightening, Walter C. 1992. "Compassionate mind: Implications of a text written by Elder Louis Sunchild." *Canadian Journal of Native Education* 19 (2): 215–53.

Lipka, Jerry, with Gerald V. Mohatt and the Ciulistet Group. 1998. *Transforming the culture of schools: Yup'ik Eskimo examples*. Mahwah, NJ: Lawrence Erlbaum Associates.

Macdougall, Brenda. 2010. *One of the family: Metis culture in nineteenth-century northwestern Saskatchewan*. Vancouver: UBC Press.

MacIntosh, Peggy. 1998. "White privilege: Unpacking the invisible knapsack." In *Race, class, and gender in the United States: An integrated study*, ed. P. Rothenberg, 165–69. New York: St. Martin's Press.

Maina, Faith. 1997. "Culturally relevant pedagogy: First Nations education in Canada." *Canadian Journal of Native Studies* 17 (2): 293–314.

Malin, Merridy. 1994. "What is a good teacher? Anglo and Aboriginal Australian views." *Peabody Journal of Education* 69 (2): 94–114. http://dx.doi.org/10.1080/016195694 09538767.

Manitoba Indian Brotherhood. 1977. *The shocking truth about Indians in textbooks*. Winnipeg: Manitoba Indian Cultural Education Centre.

Masse, W. Bruce, Elizabeth Wayland Barber, Luigi Piccardi, and Paul Barber. 2007. "Exploring the nature of myth and its role in science." In *Myth and geology*, ed. L. Piccardi and W.B. Masse, 9–28. London: Geological Society Publishing House.

McKay-Carriere, Lily. 2009. "Learning from Elders." Keynote speech at the Stirling McDowell Foundation "Learning from Practice" annual conference, Saskatoon, Saskatchewan, November 21.

McLeod, Neil. 2002. "*nêhiyâwiwin* and modernity." In Douaud and Dawson, *Plain speaking*, 2002, 35–53.

McNinch, James. 2009. "'I thought Pocahontas was a movie': Using critical discourse analysis to understand race and sex as social constructs." In Schick and McNinch, *"I thought Pocahontas was a movie,"* 151–76.

Memmi, Albert. 1965. *The colonizer and the colonized*. Boston: Beacon Press.

Michell, Herman. 2007. "Nihithewâk Ithiniwak, Nihithewatisîwin and science education: An exploratory narrative study examining Indigenous-based science education in K–12 classrooms from the perspectives of teachers in Woodlands Cree community contexts." PhD diss., University of Regina.

Michell, Herman, Yvonne Vizina, Camie Augustus, and Jason Sawyer. 2008. *Learning Indigenous science from place*. Saskatoon: Aboriginal Education Research Centre, University of Saskatchewan. http://www.ccl-cca.ca/CCL/Research/FundedResearch/200811 LearningIndigenousSciencefromPlace.html.

Miller Cleary, Linda, and Thomas Peacock. 1998. *Collected wisdom: American Indian education*. Toronto: Allyn and Bacon.

Milloy, John S. 1999. *A national crime: The Canadian government and the residential school system, 1879 to 1986*. Winnipeg: University of Manitoba Press.

Mishenene, Rachel A., and Pamela R. Toulouse (advisers). 2011. *Strength and Struggle: Perspectives from First Nations, Inuit, and Métis peoples in Canada*. Whitby, ON: McGraw Hill Ryerson.

Mokakit Education Research Association. 1992. First Nations freedom [kit]: A curriculum of choice (alcohol, drug and substance abuse prevention) kindergarten to grade eight. Winnipeg: Mokakit Education Research Association.

More, Art J. 1987. Native Indian learning styles: A review for researchers and teachers. *Journal of American Indian Education* (October): 17-29.

Mountain Horse, Alvine. (2012). "Canadian Association for the Study of Indigenous Education (CASIE): Responding to the challenge of teaching, learning and researching from Indigenous standpoints." Presentation at the American Education Research Association Annual Meeting, Vancouver, British Colulmbia, April 15.

Mussell, William J. 2008. "Decolonizing education: A building block for reconciliation." In *From truth to reconciliation: Transforming the legacy of residential schools*, ed. M. Brant Castellano, L. Archibald, and M. DeGagné, 323–38. Ottawa: Aboriginal Healing Foundation.

Nadeau, Denise, and Alannah Young. 2006. "Educating bodies for self-determination: A decolonizing strategy." *Canadian Journal of Native Education* 29 (1): 87–148.

National Indian Brotherhood (NIB). 1972. *Indian control of Indian education.* Ottawa: National Indian Brotherhood.

Ng, Roxanna. 1993. "Racism, sexism and nation building in Canada." In *Race, identity and representation in education,* ed. C. McCarthy and W. Crichlow, 50–59. New York: Routledge.

Norris, Mary Jane. 1998. "Canada's Aboriginal languages." *Canadian Social Trends* 51: 9–16.

Office of the Treaty Commissioner. 2002. *Teaching treaties in the classroom: Treaty resource guide.* Saskatoon: Office of the Treaty Commissioner.

–. 2007. *Treaty implementation: Fulfilling the covenant.* Saskatoon: Office of the Treaty Commissioner.

Ogbu, John. 1991. "Immigrant and involuntary minorities in comparative perspective." In *Minority status and schooling: A comparative study of immigrant and involuntary minorities,* ed. M. Gibson and J. Ogbu, 3–33. New York: Garland.

Ormiston, Alice. 2002. "Educating "Indians": Practices of becoming Canadian." *Canadian Journal of Native Studies* 22 (1): 1–22.

Orr, Jeff, John Jerome Paul, and Sharon Paul. 2002. "Decolonizing Mi'kmaw education through cultural practical knowledge." *McGill Journal of Education* 37 (3): 331–54.

Osborne, A. Barry. 1996. "Practice into theory into practice: Culturally relevant pedagogy for students we have marginalized and normalized." *Anthropology and Education Quarterly* 27 (3): 285–314. http://dx.doi.org/10.1525/aeq.1996.27.3.04x0351m.

Otway, Linda. 2002. "Aboriginal women's health and healing on the plains." In Douaud and Dawson, *Plain speaking,* 61–68.

Paradise, Ruth. 1994. "Spontaneous cultural compatibility: Mazahua students and their teacher constructing trusting relations." *Peabody Journal of Education* 69 (2): 60–70. http://dx.doi.org/10.1080/01619569409538765.

Paul, Daniel N. 1993. *We were not the savages: A Micmac perspective on the collision of European and Aboriginal civilization.* Halifax: Nimbus.

Pelletier, Darrell W. 1992. *The Big Storm.* Regina: Gabriel Dumont Institute.

Pelletier, Terrance, Michael Cottrell, and Rosalind Hardie. 2013. *Improving education and employment outcomes for First Nations and Métis people.* Saskatoon: Saskatchewan Educational Leadership Unit, University of Saskatchewan http://www.jointtaskforce.ca/wp-content/uploads/2013/04/Research-Report-for-the-Task-Force-March-26.pdf.

Pewewardy, Cornel. 1999. "Culturally responsive teaching for American Indian students." In *Pathways to success in school: Culturally responsive teaching,* ed. E.R. Hollins and E.I. Oliver, 85–100. Mahwah, NJ: Lawrence Erlbaum Associates.

Philips, Susan U. (1972) 1983. *The invisible culture: Communication in classroom and community on the Warm Springs Indian Reservation.* Reprint, Prospect Heights, IL: Waveland.

Phillips, Susan, and Helen Raham. 2008. "Sharing our success: Promising practices in Aboriginal education; Proceedings of a national conference, Winnipeg, November 23–24, 2007." Society for the Advancement of Excellence in Education, Kelowna, British Columbia.

Pihama, Leonie, Fiona Cram, and Sheila Walker. 2002. "Creating a methodological space: A literature review of Kaupapa Maori research." *Canadian Journal of Native Education* 26 (1): 30–43.

Pratt, David. 2012. "Time to address inadequate First Nations education funding," *Prince Albert Grand Council Tribune* (June).

Preiswerk, Roy. 1981. "Ethnocentric images in history books and their effects on racism." In *The slant of the pen: Racism in children's books*, ed. R. Preiswerk, 131–48. Geneva: World Council of Churches.

Priest, Lisa. 1989. *Conspiracy of silence.* Toronto: McClelland and Stewart.

Rampaul, Winston E., Motie Singh, and John Didyk. 1984. "The relationship between academic achievement and teacher expectations of Native children in a northern community school." *TESL Canada Journal* 2 (1): 27–40.

Renaud, Robert D., Brina E. Lewthwaite, and Barbara McMillan. 2012. "'She can bother me, because she cares': Inuit students' views about teaching and their learning." Paper presented at the American Education Research Association Annual Meeting, Vancouver, British Columbia, April 16.

Reyhner, John, ed. 1988. *Teaching the Indian child: A bilingual/multicultural approach.* 2nd ed. Billings: Eastern Montana College.

Richards, John, and Megan Scott. 2009. "Aboriginal education: Strengthening the foundations." Ottawa: Canadian Policy Research Network Research Report. http://cprn. orgdocuments/51984_EN.pdf.

Rogoff, Barbara. 1990. *Apprenticeship in thinking: Cognitive development in social context.* Toronto: Oxford University Press.

Rohnke, Karl E. 1984. *Silver bullets: A guide to initiative problems, adventure games and trust activities.* Dubuque, IA: Kendall/Hunt Publishing Company.

–. 1995. *Quicksilver: Adventure games, initiative problems, trust activities and a guide to effective leadership.* Dubuque, IA: Kendall/Hunt Publishing Company.

Royal Commission on Aboriginal Peoples (RCAP). 1996. Vol. 3, *Gathering strength.* Ottawa: Canadian Communication Group.

Ryan, James, Katina Pollack, and Fab Antonelli. 2009. "Teacher diversity in Canada: Leaky pipelines, bottlenecks and glass ceilings." *Canadian Journal of Education* 32 (3): 591–617.

Said, Edward W. 1978. *Orientalism.* New York: Random House.

–. *Culture and imperialism.* New York: Alfred A. Knopf.

Sammel, Allison. 2009. "A circle is more than a straight line curved: Mis(sed)understandings about First Nations science." In Schick and McNinch, *"I thought Pocahontas was a movie,"* 49–64.

Sammel, Allison, Warren Linds, and Linda Goulet. 2013. "Dancing together: A conversation about youth and adult relational authority in the context of education." *International Journal of Child, Youth, and Family Studies* 4 (3): 337–56.

Sanders, David. 2012. "Culturally relevant instruction in Indigenous contexts: New sites of meaning." Presentation at the American Education Research Association Annual meeting, Vancouver, British Columbia, April 16.

Sanderson, Steven Keewatin. 2010. *Darkness calls.* Vancouver: Healthy Aboriginal Network.

Saskatchewan Education. 1985. *The flower beadwork people.* Regina: Saskatchewan Education.

Saskatchewan Indian. 1972. *Battleford Hangings* 3, 7: 5.

Saskatchewan Indian Cultural Centre. n.d. *Values of the teepee poles.* [Brochure]. Saskatoon: Saskatchewan Indian Cultural Centre.

Saskatchewan Indian Federated College. 1989. *Annual report*. Regina: Saskatchewan Indian Federated College.

Saskatchewan Learning. 2001. *Aboriginal Elders and community workers in schools: A guide for school divisions and their partners*. Regina: Saskatchewan Learning. http://www.curriculum.gov.sk.ca/

Saul, John Ralston. 2008. *A fair country: Telling truths about Canada*. Toronto: Viking Canada.

Sawyer, R. Keith. 2006. *The Cambridge handbook of the learning sciences*. New York: Cambridge University Press.

Schick, Carol, and James McNinch, eds. 2009. *"I thought Pocahontas was a movie": Perspectives on race/culture binaries in education and service professions*. Regina: Canadian Plains Research Center.

Schick, Carol, and Verna St. Denis. 2003. "What makes anti-racist pedagogy in teacher education difficult? Three popular ideological assumptions." *Alberta Journal of Educational Research* 49 (1): 55–69.

–. 2005. "Troubling nationalist discourses in anti-racist curricular planning." *Canadian Journal of Education* 28 (3): 295–317. http://dx.doi.org/10.2307/4126472.

Schissel, Bernard, and Terry Wotherspoon. 2003. *The legacy of school for Aboriginal people: Education, oppression, and emancipation*. Toronto: Oxford University Press.

Settee, Priscilla. 2011. "Indigenous knowledge: Multiple approaches." In *Indigenous philosophies and critical education: A reader*, ed. G.S. Dei, 434–50. New York: Peter Lang.

Shein, Brian, and Dennis Wheeler. *Potlatch: A strict law bids us dance*. DVD. Directed by Dennis Wheeler. Vancouver: U'mista Cultural Society, 1975.

Silver, Jim, Kathy Mallett, Janice Greene, and Simard Freeman. 2002. *Aboriginal education in Winnipeg inner city high schools*. Winnipeg Inner City Research Alliance. Winnipeg, MB: Canadian Centre for Policy Alternatives. https://www.policyalternatives.ca/publications/reports/aboriginal-education-winnipeg-inner-city-high-schools.

Smith, Graham Hingandaroa. 2000. "Maori education: Revolution and transformative action." *Canadian Journal of Native Education* 24 (1): 57–72.

Smith, Linda Tuhiwai. 1999. *Decolonizing methodologies: Research and Indigenous peoples*. New York: Zed Books.

Sock, Starr, and Sherise Paul-Gould. 2012. *An inquiry into the Mi'kmaq Immersion Program in one community: Student identity, fluency and achievement*. Master's thesis, Saint Francis Xavier University.

Sokoloff, H. 2004. "Education system failing Native pupils," *National Post*, March 17, A4.

St. Denis, Verna. 2002. *Exploring the socio-cultural production of Aboriginal identities: Implications for education*. PhD diss., University of Saskatchewan.

–. 2010. "A study of Aboriginal teachers' professional knowledge and experience in Canadian schools." Ottawa: Canadian Council on Learning/Canadian Teachers Federation. http://www.ctf-fce.ca/Research-Library/Forms/Documents.aspx.

St. Denis, Verna, Rita Bouvier, and Marie Battiste. 1998. *Okiskinahamakewak: Aboriginal teachers in Saskatchewan's publicly funded schools; Responding to the flux*. Regina: Saskatchewan Education.

St. Denis, Verna, and Eber Hampton. 2002. "Literature review on racism and the effects on Aboriginal education: Report prepared for Minister's National Working Group on Education." Ottawa: Indian and Northern Affairs Canada.

Stairs, Arlene. 1996. "Human development as cultural negotiation: Indigenous lessons on becoming a teacher." *Journal of Educational Thought* 30 (3): 219–37.

Sterzuk, Andrea. 2009. "Language as an agent of division in Saskatchewan schools." In Schick and McNinch, *"I thought Pocahontas was a movie,"* 1–14.

Stonechild, Blair. 2002. "Recovering the heritage of Treaty Number Four." In Douaud and Dawson, *Plain speaking,* 1–10.

Strauss, Ansel, and Juliet Corbin. 1990. *Basics of qualitative research: Grounded theory procedures and techniques.* Newbury Park, CA: Sage.

–. 1994. "Grounded theory methodology: An overview." In *Handbook of qualitative research,* ed. N.K. Denzin and Y.S. Lincoln, 275–83. Thousand Oaks, CA: Sage.

Swisher, Karen G., and Donna Deyhle. 1989. "The styles of learning are different, but the teaching is just the same: Suggestions for teachers of American Indian youth." *Journal of American Indian Education,* special issue: 1–14.

Swisher, Karen G., and John W. Tippeconnic III, eds. 1999. *Next steps: Research and practice to advance Indian education.* Charleston, WV: ERIC Clearinghouse on Rural Education and Small Schools.

Taylor, John. 1995. "Non-Native teachers teaching in Native communities." In Battiste and Barman, *First Nations education in Canada,* 224–42.

Tkach, M. 2003, January. *2001 Aboriginal census information: Impact and implications for Saskatchewan.* Regina: Government of Saskatchewan.

Tompkins, Joanne E. 1998. *Teaching in a cold and windy place: Change in an Inuit school.* Toronto: University of Toronto Press.

Tsannie, Rosalie. 2001. "Elts' udi: Preparing teachers to teach in an isolated northern Dene community." Masters project, University of Regina.

Tupper, Jennifer A. 2011. "Disrupting ignorance and settler identities: The challenges of preparing beginning teachers for treaty education." *in education* 17 (3): 38–55.

Vygotsky, Lev. 1986. *Thought and language.* Trans. Alex Kozulin. Cambridge, MA: MIT Press.

Ward, Angela. 2001. "Changing perspectives on intercultural classrooms." In Ward and Bouvier, *Resting Lightly on Mother Earth,* 37–46.

Ward, Angela, and Rita Bouvier, eds. 2001. *Resting lightly on Mother Earth: The Aboriginal experience in urban education settings.* Calgary: Detselig Enterprises.

Watt-Cloutier, Sheila. 2000. "Honouring our past, creating our future: Education in northern and remote communities." In *Aboriginal education: Fulfilling the promise,* ed. M. Brant Castellano, L. Davis, and L. Lahache, 114–28. Vancouver: UBC Press.

Wax, M., R. Wax, and R. Dumont. 1972. "Formal education in an American Indian community." In *The emergent Native Americans: A reader in culture contact,* ed. D.E. Walker, 627–42. Boston: Little, Brown and Company.

Weber-Pillwax, Cora. 2001. "Orality in northern Cree Indigenous worlds." *Canadian Journal of Native Education* 25 (2): 149–65.

Weenie, Angelina. 2009. "Toward an understanding of the ecology of Indigenous education." *First Nations Perspectives* 2 (1): 57–70.

Williams, Lorna. 2012. "Canadian Association for the Study of Indigenous Education (CASIE): Responding to the challenge of teaching, learning and researching from Indigenous standpoints." Presentation at the American Education Research Association Annual Meeting, Vancouver, British Columbia, April 15.

Williams, Lorna, and Michele Tanaka. 2007. "Schalay'nung Sxwey'ga: Emerging cross cultural pedagogy in the academy." *Educational Insights* 11 (3), http://einsights.ogpr.educ. ubc.ca/v11n03/articles/williams/williams.html

Wilson, Peggy. 1991. "Trauma of Sioux Indian high school students." *Anthropology and Education Quarterly* 22 (3): 367–83.

Wilson, Shawn. 2008. *Research is ceremony: Indigenous research methods.* Winnipeg: Fernwood Publishing.

World Commission on Environment and Development. 1987. *Our common future.* Oxford: Oxford University Press.

Wright, Justice D.H. 2004. *Report of the Commission of Inquiry Relating to the Death of Neil Stonechild.* Regina: Department of Saskatchewan Justice.

Yazzie, Tarajean. 1999. "Culturally based curriculum: A research-based rationale." In *Next steps: Research and practice to advance Indian education,* ed. K.G. Swisher and J.W. Tippeconnic III, 83–106. Charleston, WV: ERIC Clearinghouse on Rural Education and Small Schools.

Youngblood Henderson, James [Sákéj]. 2000. "Postcolonial ghost dancing: Diagnosing European colonialism." In *Reclaiming Indigenous voice and vision,* ed. M. Battiste, 57–76. Vancouver: UBC Press.

Index

Note: an "a" indicates an appendix, and bold type indicates a figure.

Absolon, Kathleen, 25
achimowin (storytelling): vs academic writing, 5-6; in the classroom, 50-51, 92-93, 127; and cultural content, 49-55, 150; and interactive learning, 48; value of, 17-18
Acoose, Janice, 38
actions *(iseechigehina)*: of effective teachers, 80-83, 86-94, 206; with impact (creating *kamucwkalha*), 88, 118, 129, 179-80, 206; and life, 203; and relationships, 86-87, 88-94, 105-11; self-determined, 59-60, 60-62, 66-68, 73; and understanding, 216
Adams, Howard, 37, 38
Ah Nee-Benham, Maenette K.P., 23-24
Aikenhead, Glen, 14
Alkashwan, Zahra, **114**
Alphonse, Tina, **7**
Antoine, Eileen, 55
Archibald, Jo-ann, 14, 18
Augustus, Carrie, 14
authority: complexity of, 212-13; contexts of, 6, 75, 89, 130; decolonization of, 45-46, 71-74, 206; imposed, 39, 43-44;

joint, 90-91, 96, 130-31; over oneself, 213-14; responses to, 84, 111; shared, 206; situational, 213. *See also* determination

Ball, Jessica, 13
Banks, James, 19, 42
Barman, Jean, 13
Barnhardt, Ray, 208
Battiste, Marie, 46, 55
belief *(tapuhaugeneetumowin)*: in one's own peoples, 204-5; in self, 93-94, 103, 154-56; in the student, 88-89, 105-6
belonging, sense of, 115-18, 121-23, 134, 192, 202
Bendoni, Rita, **7**
Bennett, Robert, 44
Berryman, Mere, 17
Betty Osborne case, 41
bias: cultural, 44, 115, 176; Eurocentric, 11-12, 42, 139-40, 143; of Western science, 63
Bishop, Russell, 17, 20, 23, 73, 75
Bouvier, Rita, 24, 46, 198-99, 202
Bouvier, Rose, **7**

Brady, Jim, **9**
Brayboy, Bryan, 206-7
Breithecker, Dieter, 203
Brendtro, Larry K., 178-79
Brokenleg, Martin, 178-79
Brundtland Commission, 55
Brunson Phillips, Carol, 37-38
Byrd, Norma Jean, 195

Campbell, Maria, 38, 58
Caron, Angie, **81**, 113-20, **114**
Caron, Stella, **114**
Carriere, Clifford, **49**
case studies: collaborating for bilingual
  language development, 159-65;
  collaborating with local community,
  49-55, 177-81, 191-95; creating learning
  communities, 28-34, 98-104, 113-20,
  134-39, 209; instituting land-based
  learning, 182-89, 204
Castagno, Angelina, 206
Chartrand, Rebecca, 11
Cheechoo, Bev, 43
Chigeza, Philemon, 17
Circle of Courage, 178-79, 181
classroom management, 34, 131, 136, 174
co-determination, 72-73, 74-75, 209-10
cognitive mediators, 47, 94-95, 225n1;
  culturally meaningful, 171-72, 201; the
  land as, 185-89
collectivity, 16, 48-49, 60-62, 90, 113-20,
  190, 202, 205
colonization: effects of, on colonizers, 41;
  and governance, 84-86; legacy of,
  24-28, 38-39, 42-45, 84-85, 184; racist
  ideology of, 36, 37-38; resistance to, 36,
  37, 38-39, 43-44; and teaching, 27-28
community, sense of. See collectivity
Cook, Tracy, **7**
Cree-ative Collaborators, 53-54
cultural genocide, 43-44, 50-52, 86, 99
culture, Indigenous: and anti-racism
  theory, 22-23; contemporary and
  traditional, 142; camps, 153-54;
  decontextualized, 13; and identity,
  51, 52; language and, 51-52; and
  perceptions of teaching, 21 (*see also*

teaching, Nehinuw concepts of);
  respect for, 15-16, 109-10, 121-22,
  155-56; traditional and contemporary,
  45-46, 166
Cumberland House, 5, 8, **9**
curriculum: collaborative development of,
  48-55, 94, 130-31, 145, 160-64, 191-95;
  connecting students to, 94-95, 165-75,
  194, 196, 223a; culturally relevant,
  12-14, 19-20, 25, 51-53, 150, 153-54,
  160-64, 165-67, 177-81, 182-89, 202-3;
  Euro-Canadian bias of, 11-12, 42, 44,
  63, 94, 115, 176

D'Amour, Janelle, **66, 67, 68**
Dannenmann, Kaaren, 190
decolonization: of authority, 45-46, 71-74,
  206; of education, 11, 23, 49-55, 143-
  44, 200-1; Indigenous epistemology
  and, 205-6, 206-7; language and, 50-51,
  143-44; of learning environment, 213;
  of relationships, 205-7, 212-14; of
  thinking, 188. *See also* curriculum;
  Indigenization, of education; model of
  effective teaching; teaching, Nehinuw
  concepts of
Derman-Sparks, Louise, 37
determination: co-, 72-73, 74-75, 209-10;
  framework, 71-75; self-, 61, 72, 73-74,
  110-11, 205, 214; societal or public,
  71-72, 74. *See also* authority
Deyhle, Donna, 22
Dion, Susan, 20
diversity: appreciation for, 137; of dialogue
  rules, 164; of Indigenous communities,
  27-28, 86, 199-200; in learning styles,
  170-71; making a place for, 52, 57; of
  teachers, 80
Donald Marshall case, 40
Dorion, Anne, 28-34, **29**, 35, **66**
Dr. Stirling McDowell Foundation for
  Research into Teaching, 225n3, 226n2

Echodh, Jackie, **7**
education: community involvement in,
  179-80, 209-10; Cree forms of, 65-69
  (*see also* teaching, Nehinuw concepts

of); European vs Indigenous, 78;
hierarchical structure of, 43-44, 139-40;
for hope, 216-17; indigenization of,
13-14, 17, 200-17; inequities in, 198;
institutional racism in, 41-42; role of,
210. *See also* curriculum; Indigenous
education; model of effective teaching
educational theory: anti-racism, 22-23,
142-43; Hawaiian, 214; Lil'wat, 215,
226n2; Māori, 214; Nehinuw (Cree), 5,
207-10, 210-12, 212-14 (*see also* social
relationships, Nehinuw; relational
concepts, Nehinuw; teaching, Nehinuw
concepts of); Western, 8
Effective Teaching Profile, 20
Elders: alliances with, 48-55, 209-10; effect
of, on learning, 195-96; effect of, on
social behaviour, 192-94; as historians,
18; participation in school programming, 166, 174-75; participation in
teaching and learning, 17-19, 49-55,
142, 161, 191-95, 226n3
Ellison, Samantha, 114
Episkenew, Jo-Ann, 38
Ermine, Willie, 205
Eurocentrism, 6-7, 12, 37, 39, 42, 139-40,
143
expectations, 115, 123, 131, 136, 154-55,
185
extracurricular activities, 33, 119

Fayant, Russell, 191, 191-95
feelings (*moosihowin*), 94, 106-8, 125-27
First Nations University of Canada, 73
Freire, Paulo, 210, 212-13
friendship circles, 116-17

Gabriel Dumont Institute (GDI), 10, 73, 99
Gagne, Clement, 114
General Curriculum Model, 13
Germaine, Sherry, 99
Gillespie, LaVina, 24
Glaser, Barney G., 78, 79, 118
Goodwill, Ken, 5, 46, 77-78, 191-95
Goulet, Elzear, 36
Goulet, Keith, 8-10, 9, 49, 56, 71-73, 99,
114, 134, 177, 191

Goulet, Koonu, 49
Goulet, Linda, 6-8, 7, 49, 66, 67, 68, 166,
191, 191-95, 215
Goulet, Monica, 54, 134, 134-39, 211
governance, 37, 39, 71-73, 74-75, 84-86
Grant, Agnes, 24
Graveline, Fyre Jean, 212

Haig-Brown, Celia, 24
Hampton, Eber, 23, 202
Hanohano, Peter, 190
Henderson, James (Sákéj) Youngblood,
37, 55
Herman, Braelyn, 68
Herman, Melva, 158, 159, 159-65, 176,
199, 209, 211
historians, 18, 36-37, 64
history: colonial, 64, 202; European-
Indigenous, 36-39; experiential approach
to, 153, 154; forms of, 18, 62-65, 143,
226n1; importance of knowing, 191;
land and, 190; Métis, 37; Mi'kmaw, 37
Howard Gardner's Multiple Intelligences,
51

identity: cultural, 155-56, 204-5; culture
and, 51, 52, 159; development of, 78,
132, 190-91; language and, 159; and
learning, 116, 155-56; pedagogy and,
17-18; racism and, 44; residential
schools and, 43
ideology: of colonization, 36, 37-38; of
racism, 38, 40, 41-42, 84
Idle No More, 45-46
Indian Act, 40
indigenization, of education, 13-14, 17,
200-17. *See also* curriculum
Indigenous, defined, 224n1
Indigenous education: complexity of, 24-
26, 78, 81; defined, 10-11; Indigenous
control of, 3, 11-12, 73-74, 191, 204;
Indigenous thought and, 5, 47 (*See also*
teaching, Nehinuw concepts of);
intergenerational effects of, 42-43,
44-45, 85, 194, 202; policy/program
initiatives, 14-16, 46; principles of, 78;
as process, 104; sociological issues and,

7, 19-21, 21-24, 197. *See also* curriculum; learning; model of effective teaching

Indigenous epistemology, 205-6, 206-7; Nehinuw, 56, 57-65, 68. *See also* social relationships, Nehinuw; relational concepts, Nehinuw; thinking

Indigenous researchers, 11-12, 36, 38; Nehinuw (Cree), 5-6. *See also* individual Indigenous researchers

Indigenous students: academic achievement of, 154-55, 176; assets of, 85-86, 198-99; in Canadian schools, 3-4, 80; graduation rates of, 4, 102, 103; guardedness of, 189-90; Hawaiian, 15; Inuit, 15; Kainai, 18-19; Lil'wat, 15-16; Māori, 15, 17, 20, 199; Mi'kmaq, 18; Nisga'a, 18; social positions of, 199-200; strengths of, 142-46, 146-47; unique needs of, 4, 24, 81-83, 84-85, 124-27, 145-46, 198; urban, 190-91

individuality, 60-61, 62, 179

interactivity: and co-determination, 72-73, 75; collective, 61-62; of cultural activity, 206; and governance, 75; group skills and, 128; in the learning process, 140, 205-6; and Nehinuw world view, 59, 69-70; of relationships, 87, 90, 207-10, 210-12, 212-14

Ironeagle, James, 197

iseechigehina (actions): of effective teachers, 80-83, 86-94, 206; with impact (creating *kamucwkalha*), 88, 118, 129, 179-80, 206; and life, 203; and relationships, 86-87, 88-94, 105-11; self-determined, 59-60, 60-62, 66-68, 73; and understanding, 216

Javed, Arisha, 114

Jepsen, April, 114

Kaminstigominuhigoskak (Cumberland House), 5, 8, **9**

Kanu, Yatta, 19

King, Cecil, 55, 203

kiskinaumasowin (teaching oneself), 65-67, **67**, 76, 85, 87-88, 91, 93-94, 157, 210-11;

kiskinaumatowin (teaching each other), 68, 71, 76, 85, 87-88, 91, 93, 95, 141, 156-57, 183, 210-12

kiskinaumagehin (teaching oneself), 65-69, **66**, 76, 85, 87, 89, 91, 156, 210-11

Kirkness, Verna, 43, 208

kisewatisihin (respect for Elders), 89, 209

kiskinaumasowin (teaching oneself), 65-68, **67**, 76, 85, 87-88, 91, 93-94, 140, 157

kiskinaumatowin (learning from each other/teaching each other), 65-69, **66**, 71, 76, 85, 87-88, 89, 90-91, 93, 95-96, 140, 141, 156-57, 183

kistenimisowin (respect for self), 208

kistenimitowin (respect): developing, 101, 103, 127, 151; vs domination, 212-13; for each other, 101, 104-5, 110-11, 208; for Elders, 89, 209; and freedom, 212-13; friendship circles and, 116-17; for Indigenous peoples and cultures, 89-91, 109-11, 121-22, 159, 164, 192; for the land, 160; and relationships, 195, 208-9; for self, 208

kituskeenuw (our land), 202, 209, 216

Kleinfeld, Judith, 12

Klug, Beverly, 20-21, 22

knowledge: cultural, 184-85; Euro-Canadian, 65; language and, 51-52; oral narrative forms of, 62-65; shared, 91-92, 141-42, 167-68; traditional, 47-48, 51-52, 55, 57-65; and understanding, 58-59

Kovach, Margaret, 25

La Ronge Region Community College, 10

Ladson-Billings, Gloria, 16

land: all-inclusive nature of, 216; as cognitive mediator, 185-89; connection to, 202-3; and government funding, 198; importance of, 23-24, 209; *kituskeenuw* (our land), 202, 209, 216; as teacher, 190

language: and academic success, 17-18; acquisition, 51; vs communication, 8-9, 12; and decolonization, 50-51, 143-44; Dene, 159; development, 143-44, 159-65, 183; and effective teaching, 15, 17-18; informal, 111; loss, 43-44, 50-52, 86;

structures, 57-59, 225nn4-6; and thought, 48, 56, 57-59, 76; translation (of words vs ideas), 58-59. *See also* Nehinuwehin

Laprise, Breanna, **159**

LaRocque, Emma, 38

Lavallee, Bea, 121, 209

leadership: democratic, 212-13; equitable, 111; shared, 48-49, 71, 91-92, 118, 130-32, 213; situational, 90-91, 130-31, 158; skills, 129; students', 93, 139

learning: cognitive mediators and, 169-72; communities, 113-20; cultural practice and, 47-48; domains of, 94, 106-8, 125-27, 152, 168-69, 195, 201-7; Elders' effect on, 195-96; identity and, 116, 154-56; vs knowing, 215-16; language structure and, 57-58; relationships and, 89-94, 110-11; as risk taking, 80, 112; sense of belonging and, 121-23; sequences, 51, 53-54, 55, 102-3, 160-61, 165, 211; styles, 12; support for *(weechi)*, 92, 95-96; transference of, 115; and understanding, 88; zone of proximal development and, 92

learning, types of: activity-based, 152-53; cognitive mediators and, 169-72; community-based, 93, 153-54, 177-81; connecting to process of, 148-49, 169-70; learning from each other *(kiskinaumatowin)*, 90-91, 95-96; experiential, 152-53, 154, 160-61, 162-63; holistic, 168-69, 180-81, 195; Indigenous vs non-Indigenous, 139-40; interactive, 48-55, 68, 90-91, 95-96, 141-42, 205-7; land-based, 153-54, 182-89, 202-3, **215**; mastery, 92, 149; meaningful, 78, 94, 102-3, 140-41, 147-48, 178-79; multi-level skill development, 144-45; self-determined *(kiskinaumasowin)*, 65-68, 91, 140. *See also* teaching approaches

Lee, Tiffany S., 19

legends, 63-64, 65, 201

Lewthwaite, Brina, 20

life *(pimatsiwin)*, 93, 133, 195, 203, 206; forms, 56

life force system, 56, 59-60

Lightening, Walter, 205

Lipka, Jerry, 15, 23-24

listening, 18, 29, 30, 33, 35

Longman, Sarah, 176, **191**, 191-95

Maina, Faith, 16

Malin, Merridy, 21

Masse, W. Bruce, 63

McCaskill, Don, 13

McKay, Bertha, **49**

McKay-Carriere, Lily, 48, **49**, 49-55, 209

McKenna, Betty, **191**

McKenzie, Leonard, **49**

McMillan, Barbara, 20

Mercredi, Marilyn, **7**

Michell, Herman, 13-14

Miller Cleary, Linda, 16

Misponas, Jaycee, **29**, **215**

model of effective teaching, 87; Category 1 (relationship building), 86, 88-89, 91, 92, 94, 104, 105-11, 121, 221a; Category 2 (working together), 90-91, 93, 95-96, 113, 120-32, 221-22a; Category 3 (connecting to learning process), 91-94, 95, 139-58, 222-23a; Category 4 (connecting to the content), 94-95, 165-75, 194, 196, 223a; contextualizing, 79-80, 80-83, 84-86; cyclical nature of, 95; developing, 77-79; and human development, 204

moosihowin (feelings), 94, 106-8, 125-27

Morin, Cheryl, 182-89, 199, 209, 211

Morrissette, Dylan, **134**

Mountain Horse, Alvine, 19

mumiseetotatowin (trusting reliance), 89

Muskwa, Danny, 63, 225n7

Muskwa, Harriet, 63

myths, 63-64

Nadeau, Denise, 206-7

narratives, oral, 62-65, 201

National Indian Brotherhood, 3, 11, 12, 204

neepuhistumasowin (standing up for oneself), 62, 84, 127, 205, 213-14

Nehinuwehin, 8-10, 224n3; dialects, 182, 218-20a, 224n3; orthography, 219-20a;

relational terms, 225n8, 226n1; structures, 57-59, 225nn4-6; rejuvenation, 15-16, 17-19, 50-51, 121-22, 143-44

nisitootumowin (understanding): interactive learning and, 59, 201; language and, 56, 57-65; learning and, 88, 215-16; and meaning, 216

Ng, Roxanna, 38

Norris, Mary Jane, 50

Ogbu, John, 22

Omeasoo, Dennis, 192

oppression: defined, 80; effects of, 125; resistance to, 45; systems of, 38-39, 40-41, 43-44. *See also* colonization; racism

Orr, Jeff, 16, 24

Osborne, Barry, 16

otootemitowin (interactive openness), 69-70, 89-90, 98, 113, 128, 179-81, 189-90, 193-94, 207-8

Otway, Linda, 38

Paradise, Ruth, 23

Pasqua, Clara, 44, 189, 205

Paul, Daniel, 37

Paul, John Jerome, 16, 24

Paul, Sharon, 16, 24

Paul-Gould, Sherise, 17

Peacock, Thomas, 16, 214

pedagogies, 11, 14-16, 16-20, 23; Nehinuw, 76. *See also* teaching approaches

peer support, 93, 145, 147, 150-51, 155

Peigan, Willie, 197

Pelican Narrows, 182, 226n1

Pelletier, Joanne, 191-95

Pence, Alan, 13

Pete, Shauneen, **191**, 191-95

Peter Ballantyne Cree Nation (PBCN), 182

Pewewardy, Cornel, 16

Philips, Susan, 12

Piapot Nehinuw First Nation, 209

poverty, 4, 24, 37-39, 84, 125, 198; vs *kitimagisihin*, 35

power: of belief, 31, 88-89, 93-94; of including Elders, 54-55; relations of, 21,

22, 23-24, 88, 212-14; students' need for, 118, 179; of trust, 30, 89

programming: anti-racism, 22-23, 38, 142-43; bilingual, 49-55, 54-55; collaborative, 48-55; culturally relevant, 14-16; effective, 16-17; Elders' participation in, 166, 192-95; immersion, 15, 17-19; to students' interests, 167-68

Racette, Calvin, 98-104, **99**, 145, **191**, 191-95, 209, 211

racism: addressing, 22-23, 38, 45, 142-43; and cognitive imperialism, 36, 43; defined, 37-38; in education, 41-45, 193, 198; effects of, 39, 91; forms of, 40-41, 80; ideology of, 36, 37-38, 40, 41-42, 84; and learning environment, 136-37; lived experience of, 82, 83, 84-85; and violence, 135-36

relational concepts, Nehinuw: *kiskinaumagehin* (teaching another), 65-69, **66**, 76, 85, 87, 89, 91, 156; *kiskinaumasowin* (teaching oneself), 65-68, **67**, 76, 85, 87-88, 91, 93-94, 140, 157; *kiskinaumatowin* (teaching each other), 65-69, **66**, 71, 76, 85, 87-88, 89, 90-91, 93, 95-96, 140, 141, 156-57, 183; *neepuhistumasowin* (standing up for oneself), 62, 84, 127, 205, 213-14; *otootemitowin* (interactive openness), 69-70, 89-90, 98, 113, 128, 179-81, 189-90, 193-94, 207-8; *saseepeneetumowin* (perseverance), 205; *tipenimisowin* (moving towards independence), 132, 177-81, 205, 210, 213-14; *weechihisowin* (helping oneself), 60-61, 181-82, 208; *weechihitasowin* (helping/supporting others), 177-81, 208; *weechihitowin* (helping/supporting each other), 60-61, 69-70, 76, 90, 98, 113, 208; *weetutoskemitowin* (working together), 48-49, 61, 113-20, 127-29, 208, 209. *see also* teaching, caring and

relationships: alliances for a common purpose, 48, **49**, 61, 69-71, 74-76, 90, 95, 158, 172-75, 209-10; among students, 90-91, 115-16, 120-32; in classroom and community, 31-33,

94-95, 101; determination framework and, 71-75; and effective teaching, 77, 86-94; with Elders, 174-75, 194; Indigenous-white, 35-45; partnerships, 61, 69-70, 74-76, 90, 95, 158, 172-75, 194, 201, 209; schools' effect on, 85; and student achievement, 111; between students and learning processes, 91-94; between teachers, 100, 136, 158, 173-74, 178; between teachers and students, 31-33, 86-90, 98-104, 111-12, 121, 124-25, 135; between teachers and students' families, 33, 53, 172-73, 178-79. *See also* social relationships, Nehinuw

Renaud, Robert, 20

Renie, Colleen, 7

residential schools, 42-43, 85, 194, 202

respect *(kistenimitowin)*: developing, 101, 103, 127, 151; vs domination, 212-13; for each other, 101, 104-5, 110-11, 208; for Elders *(kisewatisihin)*, 89, 209; and freedom, 212-13; friendship circles and, 116-17; for Indigenous peoples and cultures, 89-91, 109-11, 121-22, 159, 164, 192; for the land, 160; and relationships, 195, 208-9; for self *(kistenimisowin)*, 208; value of, 110

responsibility: and freedom, 213; respect and, 209; and rights, 13, 118; and self-esteem, 155-56; teachers', 184

Richards, John, 3

Richardson, Cath, 17

Riel, Louis, 36

rights: Aboriginal, 40, 202; to belong, 123; democratic, 39; and responsibilities, 13, 118

Roberts, Danielle, 114

Roberts, Henry, 202-3

Robillard, Maggie, 7

Rosteski, Sharise, 49

Royal Commission on Aboriginal Peoples (RCAP), 35-36

safety: for children, 202; emotional, 124-27; physical, 122-23; and sense of belonging, 121-23, 136; social, 123; and student engagement, 147

Sandypoint, Darcy, 7

Sandypoint, Rhonda, 7

Sandypoint, Shirley, 7

saseepeneetumowin (perseverance), 205

Saskatchewan Indian Cultural Centre, 73-74, 131

Saskatchewan Urban Native Teacher Education Program (SUNTEP), 98, 100, 113, 135

Sawyer, Jason, 14

Sayazie, Albertine, 7

Sayazie, Margie, 7

Sayies, Helen, 49

scaffolding, 92, 148

Schick, Carol, 41, 44

schools: band, 183-84; as colonizing institutions, 133; community, 114, 178; Indigenous control of, 73-74; inequitable funding of, 198

Scott, Megan, 3

self, 60-61; belief in, 93-94, 154-56; cultural, 166-67; -esteem, 155-56, 178; personal, 167-68; -respect, 208

self-determination, 61; vs assimilation, 72, 73-74; political and social goal, 214; respect and, 110-11; and working together, 205

settler: societies, 36, 48, 153, 224n2; teachers, 7, 19-20

sexism, 38, 40

Silver, Jim, 45

Smith, Graham, 55, 201

Smith, Linda Tuhiwai, 36, 55, 215

social behaviour, 90-91, 127, 192-94

social relationships, Nehinuw: and decolonization, 205-7; enactment of, 207-10; *wagootowin* (relatives), 69, 70, 76, 225n8; *weechiseechigemitowin* (alliances for a common purpose), 48, 49, 61, 69-71, 74-76, 90, 95, 158, 172-75, 209-10; *weechiyauguneetowin* (partnerships), 61, 69-70, 74-76, 90, 95, 158, 172-75, 194, 201, 209

social skills, Nehinuw. *See* relational concepts, Nehinuw

sociological issues: addiction, 135; attitudes and structures, 21-22; challenges of, 4,

31-32; education and, 210; extreme, 184; poverty, 4, 24, 35, 37-39, 84, 125, 198; power relations, 21, 22, 23-24, 35-45; substance exposure disorders, 31; unemployment, 4, 183. *See also* colonization; racism

Sock, Starr, 17

St. Denis, Verna, 22, 41, 44, 46

standardized tests, 44, 115, 176

stereotypes, 37, 40, 84-85; addressing, 199-200; in curricula, 143; and expectations, 154-55

Stonechild, Neil, 41

stories, Nehinuw: and decolonization, 49-55; Elders', 49-55; as gifts, 188-89; types, 63-65, 201; of (mis)understanding and language, 57-65

storytelling *(achimowin):* vs academic writing, 5-6; in the classroom, 50-51, 92-93, 127; and cultural content, 49-55, 150; and interactive learning, 48; value of, 17-18

Strauss, Anselm L., 78, 79

structures: attitudinal, 21-22; colonial, 71-73; communication, 158, 173; of English, 144; hierarchical, of education, 43-44; language, 57-59; narrative, 63-65

students, Indigenous. *see* Indigenous students

suicide, 31, 125, 193

Swisher, Karen, 22

talking circle: benefits of, 83, 116-17, 125, 139, 195; defined, 23, 225n6; foundational objectives of, 137-38, 151; and learning process, 93, 127-28, 130-31, 133-34, 201; trust and, 138-39

Tanaka, Michele, 206, 215

tapehin (truth), 89

Taylor, John, 19

teacher education: Black Lake Denesuline class, 7; Northern Teachers Education Program (NORTEP), 10; SUNTEP, 98, 100, 113, 135; University of Victoria, 159

teachers: collaboration between, 162, 163-64, 178; and community members, 122;

effective, 4-5, 12, 16-17, 20-21, 78-79, 80-83, 86-94; Euro-Canadian, 8, 19-21, 25, 41, 78-79; Indigenous, 25, 28-34, 49, 78-79, 82, 160, 182-89; role of, 115

teaching: bicultural understanding and, 16-19, 20-21, 21-22, 166-67; caring and, 12, 31, 35, 89, 104, 106-8, 125, 130, 132, 203-4; challenges of, 27-28, 31, 82, 83, 119; Elders' participation in, 17-19, 49-55, 142, 161, 191-95, 226n3; Eurocentric, 6-7, 12, 37, 39, 42, 139-40, 143; Indigenous thought and *(see* teaching, Nehinuw concepts of); land-based, 18-19, 153-54, 160, 164-65, 182-89, 202-4; one-on-one, 93, 145, 147, 150-51; parameters of, 35; personal issues and, 33-34; relationship building and, 100-4 *(see also* relational concepts, Nehinuw); in residential schools, 43; responsive, 140-42; for success, 146-48

teaching, Nehinuw concepts of: enactment of, 210-12; teaching each other *(kiskinaumatowin),* 68, 71, 76, 85, 87-88, 91, 93, 95, 141, 156-57, 183, 210-12; teaching oneself *(kiskinaumasowin),* 65-67, **67**, 76, 85, 87-88, 91, 93-94, 157, 210-11; teaching others *(kiskinaumagehin),* 65-69, **66**, 76, 85, 87, 89, 91, 156, 210-11

teaching approaches: with concrete materials, 149-50, 171; with games, 168-69; with group work, 137, 145, 146-47, 151-52; and learning process, 92, 148-49; with photographs, 160-63, 211; with stories, 50-51; white, 41-42

thinking: decolonization of, 188; emotion and, 203-4; English vs Nehinuw, 48; Indigenous, 5, 47-48, 214-17; individual and collectivist, 62; language and, 48, 56, 57-59, 76

tipenimisowin (independence), 132, 177-81, 205, 210, 213-14

Tompkins, Joanne, 15, 24

Toutsaint, Carrie, 7

Toutsaint, Val, 7

trust, 89, 91, 103-4, 115, 130, 138-39

truth *(tapehin),* 89

understanding *(nisitootumowin)*:
interactive learning and, 59, 201;
language and, 56, 57-65; learning and,
88, 215-16; and meaning, 216

Van Bockern, Steven, 178-79
Vanidour, Natalie, 114
Vaudreuil, Krystal, 183
Vizina, Yvonne, 14
Vygotsky, Lev, 92

wagootowin (relatives), 69, 70, 76, 225n8
weechihisowin (helping oneself), 60-61,
181-82, 208
weechihitasowin (helping/supporting
others), 177-81, 208
weechihitowin (helping/supporting each
other), 60-61, 69-70, 76, 90, 98, 113, 208
weechiseechigemitowin (alliances for a
common purpose), 48, **49**, 61, 69-71,
74-76, 90, 95, 158, 172-75, 209-10
weechiyauguneetowin (partnerships), 61,
69-70, 74-76, 90, 95, 158, 172-75, 194,
201, 209

weetutoskemitowin (working together),
48-49, 61, 113-20, 127-29, 208, 209
Walker, Sheila, 199
Ward, Angela, 23
Waskahat, Peter, 208
Watt-Cloutier, Sheila, 13
Weber-Pillwax, Cora, 17
Werner, Bonnie, **177**, 177-81, 209
white, 41-42, 44, 224n2; privilege, 197
Whitehead, Hailey, **81**, 114
Whitehouse, Hilary, 17
Whitfield, Patricia, 20-21, 22
Williams, Lorna, 15-16, 55, 206, 215,
226n2
Wilson, Shawn, 6, 25
Woodland Cree, 177, 181, 182-89, 184
World Commission on Environment and
Development, 55
writing, 5-6, 163, 225n4; circles, 126, 138,
151; Cree, 218a-20a, 226n1

Yazzie, Tarajean, 13
Young, Alannah, 206